Heroic Disobedience

The Forced Marriage Plot and the British Novel, 1747-1880

Leah Grisham

Series in Literary Studies

Copyright © 2024 Vernon Press, an imprint of Vernon Art and Science Inc, on behalf of the author.

All rights reserved. No part of this publication may be reproduced, stored in a retrieval system, or transmitted in any form or by any means, electronic, mechanical, photocopying, recording, or otherwise, without the prior permission of Vernon Art and Science Inc.
www.vernonpress.com

In the Americas:
Vernon Press
1000 N West Street, Suite 1200,
Wilmington, Delaware 19801
United States

In the rest of the world:
Vernon Press
C/Sancti Espiritu 17,
Malaga, 29006
Spain

Series in Literary Studies

Library of Congress Control Number: 2023941226

ISBN: 978-1-64889-923-2

Also available: 978-1-64889-734-4 [Hardback]; 978-1-64889-781-8 [PDF, E-Book]

Product and company names mentioned in this work are the trademarks of their respective owners. While every care has been taken in preparing this work, neither the authors nor Vernon Art and Science Inc. may be held responsible for any loss or damage caused or alleged to be caused directly or indirectly by the information contained in it.

Every effort has been made to trace all copyright holders, but if any have been inadvertently overlooked the publisher will be pleased to include any necessary credits in any subsequent reprint or edition.

Cover design by Vernon Press.

Cover image: "Can I marry the man I do not love?" Lionel Grimston Fawkes. M. Linton, engraver. 1874. Wood engraving. Illustration for chapter 52, The Way We Live Now by Anthony Trollope. Source: Google Books Library Project and Project Gutenberg's web version. The Victorian Web. https://victorianweb.org/art/illustration/fawkes/22.html

For my own heroically disobedient daughter.

Table of Contents

Acknowledgments — ix

A Note on the Text — xi

Introduction — xiii
The importance of plot — xv
On autonomy — xvii
Forced marriages in eighteenth- and nineteenth-century British society — xix
Money and the novel — xxi
Chapter overview — xxiv

Chapter One
"Such Terms, Such Settlements!": Early capitalism and the family in Samuel Richardson's Clarissa and Charlotte Lennox's The Female Quixote — 1
"A plan that captivates us all": Clarissa Harlowe's forced marriage — 2
The rise of capitalism and the Harlowes — 3
Clarissa's "discovery of female self" — 7
"To comply is impossible": Clarissa's heroic disobedience — 11
Is *Clarissa* a protofeminist novel? — 13
Charlotte Lennox and Heroic Disobedience — 15
Forced marriage and the Clandestine Marriages Act — 18
Arabella's heroic disobedience — 20
Arabella's conversion — 23
Glanville's growth — 29
Conclusion — 31

Chapter Two
"Will there not be virtue in my resistance?": resisting tyranny in Charlotte Smith's "The Story of Henrietta" and Mary Robinson's Angelina; A Novel 33

   The slave trade and wealth accumulation 34
   Smith's "The Story of Henrietta" and the slave economy 35
   Slave owners as Gothic monsters 36
   "The raging multitude": models for resisting the patriarch 40
   "The Story of Henrietta" and colonial unrest 42
   Smith and slavery: a complicated tale 49
   Fighting against the "proud Lords of Traffic": Mary Robinson's *Angelina* 53
   Sir Edward's gothic consumption 56
   Robinson and the slave trade 65
   Conclusion 66

Chapter Three
"Young Ladies that have no Money are to be pitied": Jane Austen and the Forced Marriage Plot 69

   Pride and Prejudice reconsidered: or, why readers should give Mrs. Bennet a break 70
   "The pure and disinterested desire of an establishment": a case study of Charlotte Lucas 77
   Fanny Price's refusal: forced marriage in *Mansfield Park* 79
   Sir Thomas' debts 81
   Mansfield Park's multiple forced marriages 85
   Fanny Price: an unlikely heroine 89
   The *Sanditon* fragment and unfettered capitalism 94
   Conclusion 97

Chapter Four
"Selling a girl": Charles Dickens, Elizabeth Stone, and Post-Industrial Patriarchy 99

   Money, masculinity, and the Victorian family 100
   Speculation and joint stock corporations in Victorian England 102

Ralph Nickleby, "the Capitalist"	103
"Lets…take care of each other": extended kinship networks as anti-patriarchy	109
Dombey and daughter	111
Urania Cottage	114
Dickens' mercenary mothers	116
The Dombey disaster	119
The Cotton Lord's coercion	125
Redemptive friendship	132
Conclusion	136

Chapter Five
"Of course I have to think of myself": Trollope's Non-Conforming Heroines — 137

Dueling ideas of modernity and progress	138
Trollope's take on modernity and progress	141
"Fitting company only for the devils": Trollope's flirtations with forced marriage	143
The Way We Live Now: new money, old patriarchy	147
Trollope's outspoken women	151
"I want to pick and choose": women who stand up for themselves	154
Marie's rebellion	157
The land of the free: Trollope's America	158
Conclusion	167

Coda:
"I do not repent": Heroic Disobedience Beyond 1880 — 169

Bibliography — 175

Index — 187

Acknowledgments

This book would not exist without the many special mentors, colleagues, and friends I made during my doctoral program at The George Washington University, especially Maria Frawley and Tara Wallace, who oversaw my dissertation – the kernel for this book – and provided endless advice and support.

A heartfelt thanks to my editors at Vernon Press for working with me and for your extreme patience. Much of this book was written during the Covid-19 pandemic while I was without childcare. Their understanding each and every time I asked for a deadline extension is what made this finished product possible.

Finally, to Nick and Nora – my husband and daughter – I am so grateful to have your love and support. Though writing this book sometimes felt like a burden, hindsight allows me to see how important it was for me to keep going. Thanks for helping me along the way.

A Note on the Text

This project began its life as my doctoral dissertation at George Washington University, from where my Doctor of Philosophy in English literature was conferred in 2020 in the early months of the Covid-19 pandemic. Restricted physical access to libraries (and the additional fact that many of the primary texts included in this monograph have been out of print for centuries) meant I relied heavily on digitized copies of primary texts. Whenever possible, I have used first editions; when these were not accessible, I have used editions regularly available to the public.

The one key exception is *Clarissa*. Most editions of the novel available from twenty-first-century publishers are derived from the first edition of the novel, which Richardson published in 1748. I, however, used the third edition of the novel (published in 1750). This volume is significantly longer than the first two editions and includes much new material that Richardson added in response to readers' unhappiness with the ending: many readers wanted to see Clarissa marry Lovelace and "reform" him, just as Pamela does to Mr. B in Richardson's earlier novel *Pamela; or, Virtue Rewarded*. In the third edition – which Richardson considered the authoritative version of the novel – Lovelace's villainy is emphasized, as are the novel's critiques of the Harlowe family.

Irregular spelling, capitalization, and italics are profuse in many of these archival materials; I have included the original form as often as possible. All italics in *Heroic Disobedience: The Forced Marriage Plot and the British Novel, 1748-1880*, are original to the texts from which they come.

Introduction

> "[W]e young ladies in the world, when we are exhibiting, ought to have little green tickets pinned on our backs, with 'Sold' written on them; it would prevent trouble and any future haggling, you know. Then at the end of the season the owner would come to carry us home"[1]

In William Thackeray's *The Newcomes*, which was serialized from 1854 to 1855, high-spirited Ethel Newcome compares the Victorian marriage market to an art show in which young women, like paintings, are mere possessions. Ethel later wears one of the little green tickets – essentially a "sold" sign – to dinner, again hinting at the objectification she faces as a young woman of marriageable age. Ethel's stunt is meant to get a reaction from her parents, but it also indicates her sharp – if perhaps darkly humorous – awareness of the state of the marriage market in Victorian England, where women are treated as exchangeable objects. Mimicking Ethel's crass attitude toward this dynamic, the narrator goes on to claim: "as women sell themselves for what you call an establishment every day; to the applause of themselves, their parents, and the world, why on earth should a man ape at originality and pretend to pity them?"[2] Dripping with sarcasm, the narrator continues the analogy raised by Ethel's little green ticket observation, noting how common – and celebrated – it is for women to sell themselves in marriage. Instead of feeling sorry for these women, the narrator suggests, "let us pity Lady Iphigenia's father when that venerable chief is obliged to offer up his darling child…Her ladyship's sacrifice is performed, and the less said about it the better."[3] The narrator extends a semblance of sympathy to a father who must sell – or, in the case of Iphigenia, sacrifice his daughter – but the young women who are exchanged are best ignored. On the surface, the narrator seems to suggest that this is because their sacrifices are expected, but Ethel's bold statement suggests that it is because of the injustice of the marriage system that makes people want to ignore the humanity of women being exchanged for marriage. In wearing a little green ticket, Ethel shines a light on the financial, objectifying underpinnings of marriage.

The socio-economic reality at the heart of Ethel Newcome's sharp insights is at the heart of this project, which examines the ways in which the rise of

---

[1] William Makepeace Thackeray, *The Newcomes*:(London: 1904, 1854), 273.
[2] *Ibid.*, 275.
[3] *Ibid.*, 275.

capitalism in eighteenth- and nineteenth-century British society played a significant role in shifting family dynamics and marriage practices. More specifically, it looks at the ways in which certain novelists from this period understood the socio-economic imperative behind marriage practices and the troubling ways in which this could lead to the commodification of young women. These novelists use what I've termed forced marriage plot novels to explore this dynamic, showing how women are used and abused within this system and – importantly – the ways in which women can work around existing patriarchal power structures to reclaim autonomy.

The forced marriage novels discussed in the following chapters share several key features; the most basic of which is a general plot arc that focuses on a tyrannical father figure who attempts to force his daughter into a marriage that she finds repulsive but would be materially advantageous to the men involved. As I explain in more detail in chapter one, in these forced marriages, the bride-to-be is treated as nothing more than a chattel exchanged between men, who view her as a conduit for wealth transfer. These female characters, who are depicted as the heroines of their respective novels, are dismayed by the contracted marriages and thus reject the union. As will become clear, however, the men involved in the forced marriage do not care whether the heroines consent or not, forcing the intended marriages forward. Despite the prominence of Enlightenment ideas of individual subjectivity, forced marriage plot novels make it clear that their respective socio-economic climates depend on the ability of men to exchange women, a process that – the novels show – strips them of their personhood. "Because man equals self-consciousness, his alienated, objective essence, or *thinghood*, equals *alienated self-consciousness*," writes Karl Marx in his critique of the Hegelian dialectic, "and *thinghood* is thus established though his alienation."[4] That is, a man without self-consciousness, or what we might call a conscious awareness of his individuality as a thinking, feeling, human individual, is nothing more than a mere vessel able to be used and abused by those who exert power over him. Or, as our novelists at hand would point out, over her.

To this end, another important feature shared by forced marriage plot novels is that the heroines, many of whom have been obedient, rule-following daughters up until the point of their forced marriages, come to recognize the social and economic motives spurring their fathers to force them into marriage. Forced marriage plot novels, then, dramatize what Rita Felski has called the

---

[4] Karl Marx and Frederick Engels, *Economic and Philosophic Manuscripts of 1844 and the Communist Manifesto*, trans. Martin Milligan (Prometheus Books, 1988), 152-3. Italics in original.

"discovery of female self," a process in which heroines come to see themselves as thinking, reasoning, individuals who deserve autonomy despite the oppressive, corrupt circumstances in which they live.[5] To borrow Marx's terminology, forced marriage plot novels depict the un-thinghood-ification, if you will, of the female consciousness; their patriarch's capitalistic drive may have alienated women's awareness of their own consciousness, but forced marriage plot novels show women reclaiming their subjective consciousness. The heroines of forced marriage plot novels, then, bring this reclamation to fruition through their heroic disobedience. That is, these novels push beyond exposing the tyrannical, unjust commodification of women and show how these female characters fight against these forces to successfully assert their own autonomy. Samuel Richardson's *Clarissa* (1748), Charlotte Lennnox's *The Female Quixote* (1752), Mary Robinson's *Angelina; A Novel* (1796), Charlotte Smith's *Letters of a Solitary Wanderer* (1800-02), Jane Austen's *Pride and Prejudice* (1813), *Mansfield Park* (1814, 1816), and *Sanditon* (1817 – unfinished at the author's death that year), Charles Dickens' *Nicholas Nickleby* (1838-39) and *Dombey and Son* (1846-48), Elizabeth Stone's *William Langshawe, Cotton Lord* (1842), and Anthony Trollope's *The Way We Live Now* (1874-75) all feature some variation of this plot, aligning fathers with mercenary attitudes toward money and their daughters with both an awareness of the injustice they face and – as this monograph's title indicates – a desire to fight back against it.

The importance of plot

Focusing on the plot, or, in this case, a particular plot type, is a critical lens that has historically been overlooked. As Peter Brooks puts it, "[p]lot is so basic to our experience of reading, and indeed to our very articulation of experience in general, that criticism has often passed it over in silence, as too obvious to bear discussion."[6] Calling on Aristotle's argument that *mythos* is the most important aspect of a narrative, Brooks encourages critics to see the plot as a vehicle for meaning within text. Scholars like Lois Bueler, Katherine Binhammer, and Maia McAleavey have taken up this call; while they each take a slightly different approach to examining the plot, they all agree that focusing on the plot can expand our understanding of the novel as an ideological artifact imbued with specific cultural meanings.[7] Bueler explains that "mature plot structures," plots

---

[5] Rita Felski, *Beyond Feminist Aesthetics: Feminist Literature and Social Change* (Harvard University Press, 1989), 142-3.

[6] Peter Brooks, *Reading for the Plot: Design and Intention in Narrative* (Harvard UP, 1992), xi.

[7] See Maia McAleavey, *The Bigamy Plot: Sensation and Convention in the Victorian Novel* (Cambridge University Press, 2011). McAleavey connects Victorian novels to seemingly disparate genres like ballads, arguing that: "focusing on plot illuminates unexpected

that are repeated across time by different authors, are "intricately patterned from an interlocking, richly motivated, and staggeringly large set of components, [and] they are found in certain cultural habitats and do specific kinds of ideological work."[8] This is, studying a "mature" plot across time reveals useful information about both the individual novels that employ specific plots and about what those plot structures as a whole say about the historical periods out of which they emerged. Over time, certain ideological meanings become attached to a specific plot structure: it takes on an existence of its own that transcends the specificities of each novel in which it appears. For instance, Binhammer analyzes what she calls the "seduction plot" that appears in British novels in the second half of the eighteenth century (in which a relatively innocent young woman is seduced by a man who just wants sex), concluding: "[c]ulture's obsessive retelling of the plot of seduction reflects the search for answers to the questions that became askable for the first time: Who is the female capable of choosing her own desire? How does she speak her will? How does she recognize her heart's truth?"[9] Novels that depict seduction plots, then, can be read within a specific set of historical shifts in British culture that grappling – in some cases advocating for, in other cases reacting against – developing awareness of women's inner desires.

In both Binhammer's and Bueler's analysis of plot types, Samuel Richardson's 1747 *Clarissa; or, the History of a Young Lady* is an important touchstone, just as it is in this project. Binhammer begins her genealogy of the seduction plot with an analysis of *Clarissa*, in which, she claims, rakish Lovelace seduces Clarissa. Though my understanding of *Clarissa* differs from Binhammer's (as chapter one explores), I strongly agree with her view that *Clarissa*, told from the perspective of the feisty young heroine, is an important steppingstone in the development of the novel, especially when it comes to how women are portrayed. According to Binhammer, "[t]he popularity of Richardson's novel and the plurality of responses it invoked reflect how profoundly it spoke to a

---

relationships between canonical and popular texts, allowing us to imagine new literary-historical genealogies" (13). Katherine Binhammer elaborates on this dynamic: "[t]he repetition of a story at a particular moment in time...prompts at least two different interpretations of how history relates to narrative. The same story might be repeatedly told in order to popularize and naturalize a new historical idea, foregrounding a relation of similitude and emphasizing a mimetic or didactic function of narrative" (1).

[8] Lois Bueler, *The Tested Woman Plot: Women's Choices, Men's Judgments, and the Shaping of Stories* (Ohio State UP, 2001), 1.

[9] Katherine Binhammer, *The Seduction Narrative in Britain, 1747-1800* (Cambridge UP, 2009), 9.

cultural awareness of, and interest in, the new inner world of women."[10] Bueler argues along a similar vein, noting: "Richardson is writing a pioneering bildungsroman, and Clarissa is a young person in the process of making her self."[11] Both echo Ian Watt's claims in *The Rise of the Novel* that *Clarissa* is pivotal in the development of the novel as a form of narrative. In *Clarissa*, Watt argues, "Richardson resolved the main formal problems which still confronted the novel by creating a literary structure in which narrative mode, plot, characters, and moral theme are organized into a unified whole."[12] What is even more relevant to my reading of the forced marriage plot is the emphasis that Watt – along with Binhammer, Bueler, and many other critics, such as Nancy Armstrong – places on the novel's detailed, empathetic portrayal of the heroine's inner (intellectual and emotional) complexity. The "primary criterion" of early novels such as *Clarissa* "was truth to individual experience which is always unique," according to Watt, who notes that Richardson gave his characters deep "subjective and inward direction" to a degree that was unprecedented.[13] Individuality and subjectivity – the degree to which Clarissa defines her own will and identity in opposition to those around her – define Clarissa's characterization. Armstrong expands on this idea, describing Richardson's female characters as possessing "a female self who exists outside and prior to the relationships under the male's control."[14] The heroines of Richardson's novels, that is, have "subjective qualities" that render them individual, reasoning, political beings, not just submissive drones.[15]

On autonomy

An emphasis on the heroines' individuality and subjectivity is an important component of the forced marriage plot, helping to ensure readers feel empathy toward the disobedient heroines instead of shock, chagrin, or judgment (these are the reactions, in fact, that some of their peers have within the respective novels: attitudes that are shown to assist the tyrannical fathers). There is an undercurrent of Enlightenment ideology running through forced marriage plot novels, in which an individual's subjectivity is defined along Lockean lines.

---

[10] *Ibid.*, 21.
[11] Beuler, *The Tested Woman Plot*, 172.
[12] Ian Watt, *The Rise of the Novel: Studies in Defoe, Richardson, and Fielding* (University of California Press, 1957), 208.
[13] *Ibid.*, 18, 13.
[14] Nancy Armstrong, *Desire and Domestic Fiction: A Political History of the Novel* (Oxford University Press, 1987), 121.
[15] *Ibid.*, 121.

"Men being, as has been said, by nature all free, equal, and independent, no one can be put out of his estate and subjected to the political power of another without his own consent," according to Locke.[16] These configurations of individual agency and community are rooted in the balance of self-determination and mutually beneficial social structures that allow men the freedom to make decisions about their own lives while living in a prosperous community. The issue that writers like Richardson, Smith, Stone, and Trollope (just to name a few) make clear through their forced marriage plots is that women are not only excluded from enjoying these same freedoms, despite their innate ability to reason just as well as men but that there are specific socio-economic reasons underlying this exclusion that men in positions of power used to their advantage.

Throughout the book, I use terms like "autonomy," "self-determination," and "agency" to describe the outcomes for which forced marriage plot authors and their characters fight. Though it may seem obvious, it is pertinent to note that female autonomy looked different in the eighteenth and nineteenth centuries than it does today, where equality and equity are often defined in terms of having the same socio-economic freedoms, legal rights, and employment opportunities (just to name a few factors) across the gender spectrum. To think that female-identifying people have reached a point of perfect equity with men is laughable (and is even worse for women of color and those in poor or LGBTQ+ communities), but many women today possess the legal right to vote, have better education opportunities than women in previous centuries, can have their own bank accounts and property in their name, and have made some progress in shirking the expectation that mother and home-maker is the only acceptable occupation for women. These were not necessarily the objectives of women's rights advocates in the eighteenth and nineteenth centuries. As will be explored in the following chapters, self-determination, agency, and autonomy meant being recognized as a rational, reasoning, feeling individual – not a commodity – who deserves to have a degree of control over her own path through life. Locke may have claimed that "Men being, as has been said, by nature all free, equal, and independent, no one can be put out of his estate and subjected to the political power of another without his own consent," but the novelists examined in *Heroic Disobedience* understood that such Enlightenment-era understandings of subjectivity and autonomy were only extended to wealthy white men while women were conditioned to acquiesce to patriarchal control.[17] The fact that forced marriage plot heroines

---

[16] John Locke, Second Treatise of Government, 1689, Early Modern Texts Online, ed. Jonathan Bennett (2008), 54.

[17] *Ibid.*, 54.

do not necessarily gain independence or liberation as we understand it according to twenty-first-century metrics does not detract from the radical political stance that these novels take on gender and the socio-economic domain. For characters like Richardson's Clarissa Harlowe and Trollope's Marie Melmotte – the two heroines that serve as the bookends of this project – autonomy means having a semblance of power and control over her life, especially when it comes to a major life event such as marrying. Forced marriage plot novels place the interiority and subjectivity of their heroines at the forefront of the novel, privileging their thoughts, emotions, and decision-making processes in a way that puts readers in the positions of their allies.

Forced marriages in eighteenth- and nineteenth-century British society

The authors of forced marriage novels, it is relevant to note, did not invent the idea of forced marriage for use in their plots but drew from a long history of real women being used as pawns for the socio-economic ambitions of men. Claude Levi-Strauss famously observed this dynamic in what he – problematically – terms primitive cultures, concluding in *The Elementary Structures of Kinship*: "it is exchange, always exchange, that emerges as the fundamental and common basis for all modalities of the institution of marriage…Exchange…has in itself a social value. It provides the means of binding men together."[18] That is, marriage is not about the connection between the two partners involved in the marriage but about exchanging a woman – a daughter or sister – for the benefit of the men who control her. Economic in nature, the marriage exchange encompasses many possible advantages, "such as power, influence, sympathy, status, and emotion; and the skillful game of exchange," which "consists in a complex totality of conscious or unconscious maneuvers in order to gain security and to guard oneself against the risks brought about by alliances and rivalries."[19] Marriage is simply a tool for men to navigate their own place within their societies.

One can't help but wonder if eighteenth- and nineteenth-century British novelists would be surprised that Levi-Strauss finds these marriage practices only among "primitive" cultures, as he condescendingly terms the indigenous communities he observed, given the profuse evidence that forced marriage for patriarchal gain was commonplace within post-Enlightenment Western society. While my argument in *Heroic Disobedience* is less focused on the forced marriage plot as a representative (or proof) of real-life forced marriage – the authors at hand are more invested in using forced marriage as a fictional device

---

[18] Claude Lévi-Strauss, *The Elementary Structures of Kinship* (Beacon Press, 1969), 479-80.
[19] *Ibid.*, 54.

that represents the gendered, mercenary repression of their contemporary socio-economic climates – it is important to remember that marriage as an economic tool was absolutely a manifestation of the power structures the novelists write against. In a 1710 *Tatler* article, for instance, Richard Steele commented: "the best of our peers have often joined themselves to the daughters of very ordinary tradesmen," because of "valuable considerations."[20] Similarly, Lawrence Stone and Jeanne C. Fawtier Stone quote "an indignant pamphleteer" who in 1733 "complained bitterly about the rise of 'a set of brocaded tradesmen, clothed in purple and fine linen, and faring sumptuously every day, raising themselves to immense wealth, so as to marry their daughters to the first rank, and leave their sons such estates as to enable them to live to the same degree.'"[21] James Nelson's 1763 *An essay on the government of children* claims: "[t]he Man of Trade marries the Daughter of the Gentleman; the Gentleman the Tradesman's Daughter: and again, the Gentleman makes his Son (the younger at least) a Man of Trade."[22] As late as 1884, Friedrich Engels characterized all bourgeois marriages as to some degree coerced by parents for financial or social capital, since "[i]n the countries with English law, where parental consent to a marriage is not legally required, the parents on their side have full freedom in the testamentary disposal of their property and can disinherit their children at their pleasure," which leads to coerced and forced marriages: "in spite and precisely because of this fact, freedom of marriage among the classes with something to inherit is in reality not a whit greater in England and America than it is in France and Germany."[23] Examples such as these cause Stone and Stone to declare that "judicious marriages with heiresses" were a common mechanism for socio-economic elevation.[24]

Steele, Engels, Stone and Stone, and Levi-Strauss recognize the economic role women were forced into, but what is missing from their texts is any sort of in-depth acknowledgment of the trauma this caused women or even any empathy with young brides exchanged for wealth and status. In the passages from *The*

---

[20] Richard Steele, *The Tatler and the Guardian, complete in one volume* (Edinburgh, 1880), 410.

[21] Lawrence Stone and Jeanne C. Fawtier Stone, *An Open Elite? England, 1540-1880* (Clarendon Press, 1984), 19.

[22] James Nelson, *An Essay on the Government of Children* (London, 1763), 317.

[23] Friedrich Engels, *The Origin of the Family, Private Property and the State* (1884; Chicago, 1902), 88; See also Pierre Bourdieu, "The Forms of Capital," in Handbook of Theory and Research for the Sociology of Education, ed. J. Richardson (Greenwood Press, 1986), 241-258. Bourdieu makes a similar claim about modern society: that parents use indirect, coercive means to dictate their children's marriages by controlling who their children meet.

[24] Stone and Stone, *An Open Elite?*, 10.

Newcomes quoted at the beginning of this Introduction, in fact, the narrator cheekily urges readers to ignore women exchanged for a lucrative marriage settlement and just pity the fathers who arranged the marriages. While it is obvious that the narrator says this sarcastically, it is my contention that forced marriage plot authors give voice to the women in those economic transactions. This monograph, then, shows how the novel – specifically the forced marriage plot novel – is the ideal conduit for exploring the costs women pay when living in societies that see them as exchangeable commodities and not autonomous beings. Richardson, Lennox, Smith, Robinson, Austen, Stone, Dickins, Stone, and Trollope narrativize this conflict, privileging the perspectives of the women victimized by these economic practices; empathizing with their struggles against being defined by their exchangeability and celebrating the heroines' rebellion against the role prescribed by their respective societies.

Money and the novel

Before turning to my analysis of the novels, a brief overview of the intersections between the novel and finance will be useful in differentiating my argument from existing perspectives. Reading novels alongside economic contexts is not a new line of inquiry; as Patrick Brantlinger puts it, "from Defoe forward, realistic fiction, at least, is always in some sense about money."[25] This is a nutshell version of Franco Moretti's argument in *The Bourgeois: Between History and Literature*, in which he claims the rise of the novel is inseparable from the emergence of the bourgeoisie, reading "aesthetic forms as structured responses to social contradictions."[26] In another vein, "A Friend to Mammon: Speculation in Victorian Literature," by John Reed, is one of the first essays to posit that British novelists used the figure of the speculator as "a topos for what many English people feared as the chief economic disease of their time," a theme more recently and extensively taken up by Tamara Wagner in *Financial Speculation in Victorian Fiction: Plotting Money and the Novel Genre, 1815–1901*, where she traces manifestations of a character type she calls the "stock market villain" – a figure I'll address in more detail in chapter five.[27] Francis O'Gorman focuses specifically on Trollope's and Dickens' critiques of capitalism in his essay "Financial Markets and the Banking System" and his Introduction to Penguin's 2016 edition of *The Way We Live Now*. Many of these

---

[25] Patrick Brantlinger, *Fictions of State: Culture and Credit in Britain, 1694-1994* (Cornell University Press, 1996), 144.

[26] Franco Moretti, *The Bourgeois: Between History and Literature* (Verso, 2013), 14.

[27] Reed, "A Friend to Mammon,"; Tamara Wagner, *Financial Speculation in Victorian Fiction: Plotting Money and the Novel Genre, 1815-1901* (Ohio State University Press, 2010), 165.

scholars argue in the vein of Jonathan Rose's claim that "[l]iterary criticism apparently cannot help but read capitalism suspiciously," in large part, as this project will show, due to the critical ways in which eighteenth- and nineteenth-century novelists depicted the insidious capitalist ethos.[28]

Studying literature through its intersections with capitalism, however, often loses sight of the specific ways in which capitalism impacted women – a critical gap this project undertakes to fulfill. There are, of course, some notable exceptions to the void. For example, Lana L. Dalley and Jill Rappoport's *Economic Women: Essays on Desire and Dispossession in Nineteenth-Century British Culture* is a collection of essays that explores instances in which "Economic Man" was, in fact, "Economic Woman," showing that women found ways to engage with capitalist markets within the prescribed limitations.[29] Mona Scheuermann's *Her Bread to Earn: Women, Money, and Society from Defoe to Austen*, which zooms in on novels that depict women as active financial agents, has been especially helpful to my own project. "This emphasis on money [in eighteenth-century novels] suggests an orientation in the novels that place women in the real world, functioning within and dealing with practical daily problems," she writes.[30] Her project, like mine, traces connections between fictional worlds and the contemporary moments in which they were created, making the case that authors like Samuel Richardson meant for *Clarissa* in particular – and the novel more broadly – to be in conversation with his original readers' own lives.

Women and money, or, more specifically, women with money, are the subject of Elsie B. Michie's *The Vulgar Question of Money: Heiresses, Materialism, and the Novel of Manners From Jane Austen to Henry James*, in which she argues that heiresses "posed a social problem. If those rich women were exchanged outside of the group to which they belonged, the group's property would go with

---

[28] Jonathan Rose, "Was Capitalism Good for Victorian Literature?" *Victorian Studies* 46, no. 3 (2004): 490.

[29] *Economic Women*, Lana A. Dalley and Jill Rappoport, eds., *Economic Women: Essays on Desire and Dispossession in Nineteenth-Century British Culture* (Ohio State UP, 2013), 1. Historian Amy M. Froide discusses similar examples in *Silent Partners: Women as Public Investors During Britain's Financial Revolution*, 1690-1750, as do Davidoff and Hall in *Family Fortunes: Men and Women of the English Middle Class, 1780-1850*. While these examples include some discussions of literature, they are more accurately categorized as historical or cultural studies, which suggests to me that literary scholars are behind historians in addressing women and capitalism in the British novel.

[30] Mona Scheuermann, *Her Bread to Earn: Women, Money, and Society from Defoe to Austen* (University Press of Kentucky, 1993), 30.

them."[31] She quotes Engels, who wrote in *The Origins of the Family, Private Property, and the State*: "the girl was not only permitted but ordered to marry within the gens, in order that her property [be] retained for the gens."[32] Though Engels is discussing the ancient Greek family system, the characteristics of their culture that lead to forced marriages – a shift from material power to paternal authority and accumulation of wealth – apply to the eighteenth and nineteenth centuries, as well. Michie and I examine a similar subject matter, the marriages of wealthy women, but our conclusions diverge. In the nineteenth-century marriage plot, according to Michie, the "hero is positioned between a rich and a poor woman and his choice of the poor woman is represented as enabling him to prove himself free from the crassness, vulgarity, and improper pride that taint the novel's wealthy women."[33] Echoing the configuration of anti-aristocratic femininity that Nancy Armstrong discusses in *Desire and Domestic Fiction: A Political History of the Novel*, Michie posits that in Victorian novels the heiress is "[o]ften older and potentially infertile, she is engrossed by and identified with her wealth," and that it is in Trollope's novels that "for the first time, the rich woman is a character that is not only appealing but that represents what the novelist represents as positive values."[34] According to Armstrong and Michie, eighteenth- and nineteenth-century British novels portrayed wealth-possessing women negatively: the converse of ideal domesticity.

This project, however, resists such categorizations, focusing instead on the extent to which masculine desire for wealth victimized women across socio-economic boundaries through overt (threats, violence, legal restrictions) and covert methods (coercion, social norms) that actively denied women basic rights over their own lives. The women portrayed here are, with a few exceptions, the inheritors of immense wealth; rather than villainizing them for this wealth, novelists like Samuel Richardson, Charlotte Lennox, Charlotte Smith, Mary Robinson, Jane Austen, Charles Dickens, Elizabeth Stone, and Anthony Trollope depict the problems this wealth causes. For instance, in Anthony Trollope's novel *Sir Harry Hotspur of Humblethwaite* (discussed in chapter five), Emily Hotspur balks at her father's demand that she marry dull Lord Alfred instead of her second cousin George (whom she passionately loves), and "suffered under a terrible feeling of ill-usage. Why was she, because she was a girl and an heiress, to be debarred from her own happiness?"[35] A

---

[31] Elsie B. Michie, *The Vulgar Question of Money: Heiresses, Materialism, and the Novel of Manners From Jane Austen to Henry James* (Johns Hopkins University Press, 2011), 10.

[32] Engels, Quoted in *The Vulgar Question*, 10.

[33] Michie, *The Vulgar Question*, 4.

[34] *Ibid.*, 16, 103.

[35] Anthony Trollope, *Sir Harry Hotspur of Humblethwaite* (1870; London, 1882), 205.

simple question but a resoundingly profound one asked by nearly all the heroically disobedient characters in the following chapters. Recognizing the socio-economic factors that are impacting her life – restricting her ability to determine her own path in life – Emily Hotspur concludes:

> [h]er father would fain treat her like a beast of burden kept in the stables for a purpose; or like a dog whose obedience and affections might be transferred from one master to another for a price...She would be dutiful and obedient as a daughter, according to her idea of duty and of principle; but she would let them know that she had an identity of her own, and that she was not to be moulded like a piece of clay.[36]

Fully awake to the injustice of her situation, Emily resolves to live by her own code. Recognizing her father's authority as *paterfamilias*, the narrator emphasizes that Emily will live "according to her idea of duty and principle" – her own system of values rooted in her independent formation of an "identity of her own," rather than blindly accepting the submissive role her father expects. This is a pattern that is repeated throughout forced marriage plot novels of the eighteenth and nineteenth centuries: the heroic disobedience of these characters recognizes the injustices they face and their moral right to stand up for themselves. In each of these examples, the forced marriage plot tells of a woman's fight for and triumph in autonomy.

Chapter overview

As I examine in detail in chapter one, Clarissa was certainly not the first narrative to contain a father who sees his daughter's marriage as a *quid pro quo* economic exchange, but Richardson used this plotline, reminiscent of Euripides' tragedy *Iphigenia in Aulis* and Aphra Behn's play *The Forc'd Marriage, or, the Jealous Bridegroom* (1670), to reveal insights into his own specific historical moment when large-scale wealth acquisition and upward mobility were obtainable to a larger class of people. Clarissa Harlowe's character dramatizes these changes in terms reaching allegory; the empathy with which she is portrayed, the sound reason she possesses, and adherence to her own set of moral values (that contradict the mercenary ones of her family) obviously align Clarissa with good, while her greedy father, cruel brother, and despicable suitor, Solmes, are clearly bad. Clarissa's steadfastness in refusing her forced marriage marks her as disobedient by the moral code of her society, but this disobedience is framed as morally superior to the mercenary attitudes of her family.

---

[36] *Ibid.*, 205-6.

Chapter one also includes a discussion of Charlotte Lennox's novel *The Female Quixote*, from which this book's title is taken. While *Clarissa* obviously endorses its heroine's right to refuse the forced marriage with Solmes, her death at the end of the novel seems to indicate that her society makes it impossible for her to thrive and live by her own personal moral system. However, *The Female Quixote* contains its own forced marriage plot that, though obviously connected to *Clarissa*, diverges from it in a few key aspects. Most important is the fact that Lennox's heroine, Arabella, boldly rejects marrying her cousin Glanville simply on the basis that it is forced. My understanding of Arabella diverges from the standard critical interpretation – that she is a silly, irrational girl who needs patriarchal figures to take away her silly French romance novels and mold her into a proper lady. Instead, I look at the ways in which the strong female characters in those novels inspire what she calls her "heroic disobedience" to her father's demands.

Chapter two examines two turn-of-the-century novels that situate the forced marriage plot and heroic disobedience in another specific economy: the transatlantic slave trade. Mary Robinson's *Angelina; A Novel* and Charlotte Smith's novella "The Story of Henrietta" combine the despotic, marriage-forcing fathers with the figure of the slave owner, exposing material connections between the plights of the enslaved and white British women. These novels go beyond the metaphorical link between slavery and women's oppression Susan Meyer writes of in *Imperialism at Home: Race and Victorian Women's Fiction*, instead illuminating the cause-and-effect relationship between the two through the all-encompassing power money provides to the slave owner.[37] Aligning the rebellion of enslaved people with the heroic disobedience of women, these radical novels go so far as to suggest retributive violence against the patriarch is the solution to tyranny.

Chapter three, which focuses on forced marriage in Jane Austen's later novels *Pride and Prejudice*, *Mansfield Park*, and (briefly) *Sanditon*, follows roughly the same pattern as Smith and Robinson's forced marriage plots (in fact, an earlier version of this project included *Mansfield Park* in the same chapter as *Angelina;*

---

[37] See Susan Meyer, *Imperialism at Home: Race and Victorian Women's Fiction* (Cornell University Press, 1996). She argues: "The yoking of the two terms of the recurrent metaphor, the 'white woman' and 'dark race,' produces some suggestion in the text of the exploited or vulnerable situation of the people in the race invoked" (142). That is, when white European authors described the circumstances of white women as "slavery" they inherently acknowledge the plight of enslaved Africans and suggest a kindred connection between the two groups. As I discuss more fully in chapter two, this is a fallacy that fails to acknowledge the differences between oppressed white women and actual chattel slavery.

A Novel and "The Story of Henrietta"), with an emphasis on the complex ways in which the slave trade impacted the commodification of women in the metropole. Austen's Regency England was teetering on the edge of industrialization; as capitalist practices ramped up, class structure in England became ever more shifting and complex, which is in turn reflected in Austen's forced marriage plots, especially as they depict the struggles faced by financially insecure women in this period. Austen's forced marriage plots show that rich heiresses were not the only women impacted by the capitalist fracture of the British family, but this was a very pressing issue for women like Charlotte Lucas and Fanny Price, who lacked the means to support themselves.

Novels by Charles Dickens (*Nicholas Nickleby* and *Dombey and Son*) and the little-studied Elizabeth Stone (*William Langshawe, the Cotton Lord*) move chapter four into post-industrial England amidst the rise of stock-market speculation and precarious social attitudes about the morality of capitalism. Specifically, both Dickens and Stone are invested in exploring the impacts of this economy on women, who are depicted within the novels as largely excluded from the male-dominated world of finance and left with limited opportunities. Chapter four includes a discussion of the ways in which working-class and poor women, like Kate Nickleby and Edith Granger, are also forced into marriages, as youth and beauty are shown to be commodifiable qualities upon which women with few other options can rely. The writings of Dickens' and Stone's contemporary Karl Marx help provide the framework for this chapter, especially in terms of the extreme sexualization of women under capitalism: marriage, in these novels, is shown to be little more than sex work.

The fifth and final chapter extends the dissertation's discussion of speculative finance into the later Victorian period via Anthony Trollope's *The Way We Live Now* with brief forays into *The Three Clerks* (1857), *Sir Harry Hotspur of Humblethwaite* (1870), *The Prime Minister* (1876), and *The Duke's Children* (1880), which variously attend to the deep impact social and economic capital retained over marriage practices. Trollope is an author who utilized the forced-marriage plot often throughout his *oeuvre* and who – uncoincidentally – also had sharp words for Richardson and his late-Victorian publisher Eneas Sweetland Dallas, whose 1868 abridged edition of *Clarissa* claimed that Victorian women enjoyed more autonomy than eighteenth-century women. Trollope's novels, which closely engage with contemporary financial habits, prove this claim categorically untrue as they reveal the many ways in which, despite the period's self-styled progress, women faced the same oppression Clarissa Harlowe did in the 1740s.

These novels are certainly not the only forced marriage plot novels written in the eighteenth and nineteenth centuries. For instance, Miss Melvyn of Sarah Scott's *A Description of Millenium Hall* [sic] (1762) faces a forced marriage, as does Jane West's heroine Sophia in *The Infidel Father* (1802). Mary Wollstonecraft wrote a forced marriage novella, *Mary: A Fiction* (1788), the advertisement to which states that the heroine "is neither a Clarissa, a Lady G –, nor a Sophie," distinctly invoking Richardson's heroines.[38] Laura Fairlie in Wilkie Collins' *The Woman in White* (1859) is told by her father on his deathbed that he wants her to marry Percival Glyde, which Laura takes as a binding command, forcing her to marry Glyde. The marriage between John Harmon and Bella Wilfer in *Our Mutual Friend* (1864-5) is forced, given that Old Harmon stipulates his son must marry Bella or lose his fortune. Additionally, in *Daniel Deronda* (1876), both Gwendolyn Harleth and Princess Halm-Eberstein are forced into unwanted marriages.

While, of course, some level of culling for the sake of brevity is necessary for any book, the novels I decided to include share several through-lines that make them especially productive for analysis. First, the novels included for discussion follow the basic structure of the forced marriage plot as written by Richardson and Lennox. These include a father figure who seeks to use his daughter's marriage as a *quid pro quo* business exchange wherein he will gain capital, strategic alliance, and/or security for his own fortune; a clear disrespect of his daughter's rejection of the marriage (and not seeking her consent before contracting the betrothal); an active scheme – whether through force or gentler measures of coercion – to force the daughter into this marriage; a clear and persistent rejection of both the forced marriage and the larger mercenary values it represents; and, a brave act of heroic disobedience that signals the heroine's commitment to reclaiming a sense of identity and autonomy. The plots of these novels are fundamentally concerned with raising awareness of the diverse ways in which the socio-economic climate of capitalism did not just cause but was predicated on keeping women powerless, both within their homes and in the *polis*. There are, of course, some variations from text to text (mothers, for instance, play important roles in some of the forced marriage novels discussed in chapters three and four), but as I will explain, these are all strategically done to expand understandings of capitalist-based oppression of women and the specific ways in which its agents actively prevented women from gaining the same personal freedoms and financial opportunities available to white British men.

The second most important factor in selecting the novels I have is simply that the forced marriage is a major component of each novel's plot in a way that centers the action around the perspective of the young woman faced with the forced marriage. In *Clarissa*, for instance, Clarissa's interiority – her thoughts,

---

[38] Mary Wollstonecraft, *Mary and The Wrongs of Women* (1798), ed. Gary Kelley (Oxford World Classics, 2007), 3.

feelings, stream-of-consciousness, et cetera – are provided in the first-person by Clarissa Harlowe herself, which centers the entire novel on her subjectivity and lets readers see the actions of the novel through the eyes of the heroine. All the subsequent forced marriage plot novels discussed in this project share this same feature. That is, the forced marriage plot is a – if not the most – important plot line in the novel and is told in a way that lets readers into the mind of the heroine. This grants the disobedient heroine a complex subjectivity while also encouraging readers to view her and the difficult, sometimes taboo, decisions she must make with empathy and understanding. Like Ethel Newcome in *The Newcomes*, these authors want readers to see and understand the sacrifices that were expected from women in their contemporary moments. Unable to look away, readers are made to confront these injustices and see the heroism in fighting against them.

Chapter One
"Such Terms, Such Settlements!": Early capitalism and the family in Samuel Richardson's Clarissa and Charlotte Lennox's The Female Quixote

In the first volume of Samuel Richardson's *Clarissa*, James Harlowe, Clarissa's cruel, self-obsessed brother, flippantly tells his sister that: "a man who has sons brings up chickens for his own table...whereas daughters are chickens brought up for the tables of other men."[1] That is, James believes that daughters – like his sister Clarissa – only have value when they can be bartered away in a marriage that will benefit her *paterfamilias*. As will be discussed at length, James' callous comment represents a core belief of eighteenth- and nineteenth-century socio-economic discourse that primarily saw women as exchangeable objects with the potential to enrich the men who possessed them – a belief system that necessarily stripped women of autonomy over important life decisions. Writing at a time when capitalist ideologies and practices were on the rise in England (slowly replacing the mercantilist economy that dominated the earlier centuries), authors like Samuel Richardson and Charlotte Lennox witnessed their society's recognition that – since upward mobility was becoming possible for a wider group of people – women were a useful means of exchanging wealth and status. Though the novel as we know it today was still in its infancy, Richardson and Lennox recognized early on its use as a mirror for their own society; their novels *Clarissa* and *The Female Quixote* explore the challenges that women faced under their changing social order.

The protagonists of *Clarissa* and *The Female Quixote*, Clarissa and Arabella, are both treated as chattels: exchangeable commodities which are only as valuable as what they can be exchanged for via marriage. However, these characters do more than just expose the oppression women faced because of these practices, but they both evidence with Arabella calls "heroic disobedience" when they stand up for themselves by refusing their respective forced

---

[1] Samuel Richardson, *Clarissa: Or, the History of a Young Lady: Comprehending the most Important Concerns of Private Life*, third edition (London, 1751), 1:73.

marriages. In *Clarissa* and *The Female Quixote*, which I consider the prototypes of the forced marriage plot, readers are made to empathize with the perspective of the heroically disobedient characters, who believe they possess a fundamental right to marry on their own terms. Both Clarissa and Arabella, readers are told, were raised with typical eighteenth-century ideas that daughters owed obedience to their parents, but throughout the course of their forced marriage plots, Clarissa and Arabella realize that such standards of acceptable femininity only serve to subordinate women. Both heroines learn that there are consequences for standing up to their patriarchs but trusting their own reason and morals despite the pressure to capitulate. While Clarissa struggles to escape from under her father's tyrannical thumb, Arabella joyfully refuses to marry under terms other than her own, becoming a triumphant – if a bit unusual – heroine along the way.

"A plan that captivates us all": Clarissa Harlowe's forced marriage

The injustice of the Harlowes forcing their daughter Clarissa to marry their wealthy neighbor Roger Solmes is, according to Richardson himself, one of the primary points of the novel. In the Preface to *Clarissa*, Richardson writes that one of his aims is: "To caution Parents against undue exercise of their natural authority over their Children in the great article of Marriage."[2] Drawing on narratives like the Iphigenia myth and Aphra Behn's play *The Forc'd Marriage*, in which fathers sacrifice their daughters, Richardson creates what I consider the first forced marriage plot novel. There are a few key features of the forced marriage plot, as it exists throughout the eighteenth and nineteenth centuries, that are first seen together in *Clarissa*, which can be broadly summarized by the following movements.

First, the novel establishes that the father figure, often described as a tyrant, primarily values his daughter as an exchangeable commodity, not as an individual with basic rights; she is a means for him to achieve his own end. Inevitably, this is where the specter of capitalism looms over these narratives. As will be made clear below, from its earliest beginnings in British society, capitalism – often depicted as a drive for personal wealth to the detriment of others – is predicated on men's ability to use women as a means of transferring wealth, signaling (much like Marx will argue in the Victorian period) – a dissolution of the family unit.

A second standard feature of forced marriage plot novels seen in *Clarissa* is that the heroines, as Rita Felski puts it, experience a "discovery of female self" that is "grounded in a moral and aesthetic revulsion against the very nature of

---

[2] *Ibid.*, 1:5.

contemporary social reality, which is perceived as alienating and debased."[3] That is, the heroine of a forced marriage plot novel recognizes her victimhood: in most cases, articulating her insightful understanding that the socio-economic systems operating in the novel purposefully mold young women into compliant drones who are willing to blindly follow the orders of their patriarchs. The heroine comes to understand that this treatment is inherently unjust, recognizing that she is a rational, moral individual who deserves to have a say in determining her own future instead of being forced into an unwanted marriage for the benefit of the men with whom she is exchanged.

Third, the heroines of forced marriage plot novels enact what Arabella calls "heroic disobedience"; a moment – or moments – in which she takes action to prevent the forced marriage. In most of the novels included in this project, there is a direct line that can be drawn from the heroine's moment/s of heroic disobedience to her happy ending. While these individual endings vary, they all show the heroines choosing their own paths through life, free from the tyranny of their fathers and valued for more than their economic exchange value, frequently in a way that de-centers romance and finding a husband from the main plot, focusing instead on the heroine's fight for independence.

The rise of capitalism and the Harlowes

The origins of the forced marriage plot novel have roots in a specific historical moment in which the British economy was transforming from mercantilism to capitalism. While it has been a tradition to pinpoint the nineteenth-century Industrial Revolution as the beginning of capitalism in Great Britain, there are a handful of scholars who trace its origin to earlier centuries. Nicholas Hudson, for example, argues that the Glorious Revolution in 1688 instituted "a nation ruled by the old elite but increasingly dominated by commerce."[4] Immanuel Wallerstein makes a similar claim, arguing that the Industrial Revolution did not bring capitalism to Great Britain but was its result.[5] According to Wallerstein, capitalism was more than an economic system, but a social one, as well, in which one's "primary objective or intent [was] self-expansion," making conditions

---

[3] Felski, *Beyond Feminist Aesthetics*, 142-3.

[4] Nicholas Hudson, "Literature and Social Class in the Eighteenth Century," in *Oxford Handbooks Online*, (Oxford: Oxford UP, 2015), 1.

[5] See Immanuel Wallerstein, *Historical Capitalism* (Verso Books, 2014). He writes: "The political structures in general were getting weaker and their preoccupation with the internecine struggles of the politically powerful meant that little time was left for repressing the growing strength of the masses of the population," claiming that by 1650, "the basic structures of historical capitalism as a viable social system had been established and consolidated (69-70, 71).

right for fierce competition and greed.[6] As Adam Smith explains in *The Wealth of Nations*, "[i]t is not from the benevolence of the butcher, the brewer, or the baker, that we expect our dinner, but from their regard to their own interest. We address ourselves, not to their humanity but to their self-love."[7] The eighteenth century, as Daniel P. Gunn puts it, was characterized by "a small but predatory class of people" who are in competition for "substantial land, substantial capital, or both."[8] Or, as Lawrence Stone and Jennifer Fawtier Stone explain in *An Open Elite?*, there were a number of eighteenth-century social climbers who "amassed so much wealth that they were able within one generation to acquire very extensive estates, build or enlarge a 'prodigy' house, and establish one of England's great aristocratic families."[9] The door to upward mobility was opened, and families like the Harlowes clamored to reach the upper limits of their society.

What is at the heart of *Clarissa* is the way in which this obsession with upward mobility, as displayed by families like the Harlowes and Solmeses, negatively impacted the British family unit, particularly in terms of the submissive roles that women were expected to play within the shifting social order. As Clarissa writes to Anna Howe:

> I have more than once mentioned to you the darling view some of us have long had of *raising a family*...a view too frequently, it seems, entertained by families which having great substance, cannot be satisfied without rank and title. My uncles had once extended this view to each of us three children, urging as they themselves intended not to marry, we each of us might be so portioned, and so advantageously matched, as that our posterity if not ourselves might make a first figure in our country.[10]

The Harlowes are a newly-monied family whose fortunes have been made through trade ("new-found mines," an unexpected inheritance, and "East-India traffick," according to Clarissa), and they are eager to amass more wealth to increase their political standing.[11] When Clarissa mentions her uncles' goal

---

[6] *Ibid.*, 6.

[7] Adam Smith, *An Inquiry into the Nature and Causes of the Wealth of Nations* (1776; Dublin, 1801), 1:19.

[8] Daniel P. Gunn, "Is Clarissa Bourgeois Art?," in *Passion and Virtue: Essays on the Novels of Samuel Richardson*, ed. David Blewett (University of Toronto Press, 2001), 143. Gunn argues that the Harlowes epitomize this behavior.

[9] Stone and Stone, *An Open Elite*, 10.

[10] Richardson, *Clarissa*, 1:77. Italics in original.

[11] *Ibid.*, 1:28.

of "raising a family," they are not referring to having children but rather to elevating their social and political rank: a subtle but significant difference in thinking about family life. As Clarissa also notes, her uncles have stayed single and childless to help the Harlowe family reach their desired socio-economic status, which – again – redefines family as an economic unit, and they try to instill the same understanding of family and marriage to the next generation. The husband they intend for Clarissa, Solmes, is, in fact, a product of a scheme such as the Harlowes hope to carry out. "[N]ot born to the immense riches he is possessed of," Clarissa explains, "Riches left by one niggard to another, in injury to the next heir, because that other is a niggard," Solmes plans to "rob" the rest of his family of their rightful share of the family money to negotiate a sizable marriage settlement for Clarissa.[12] Clarissa is surrounded by people who only see personal relationships in terms of their economic value and who assume that she will willingly comply to be a means to their ends.

Richardson makes it clear in *Clarissa* that all the Harlowes care about is money; with an offer as lucrative as the one Solmes offers in exchange for obtaining Clarissa as his wife, the Harlowe family – particularly her father – cease to see Clarissa as anything other than an object, and they are willing to use any means necessary to force her into the marriage that she so desperately wants to avoid. Clarissa's consent – or lack thereof – does not concern them. As with many forced marriage plot novels, the heroine's father transforms into the novel's clear villain through the tyrannical way he treats his daughter's wishes. For Mr. Harlow, this tyranny is translated through his rage and his unwavering belief that Clarissa must obey him simply because she is his daughter. "No protestations, girl! No words! I will not be prated to! I will be obeyed!" he screams, "I have no child, I *will* have no child, but an obedient one... No expostulations! No *but's*, girl! No qualifyings! I will be obeyed, I tell you; and cheerfully too! – or you are no child of mine!"[13] He expects total compliance from Clarissa, constantly silencing her attempts at a rational discussion of the unwanted marriage. In fact, as this outburst makes clear, he wants more than just obedience: he demands unquestioning submission to his authority – and for her to put on a happy face about it.

Mr. Harlowe's tyrannical attitude toward forcing Clarissa into a marriage against her will identify him as a central villain within the world of the novel. To be sure, James Jr.'s greed and Lovelace's profligacy certainly put them in the running for the novel's most evil man (Solmes is certainly in the competition, too), but the novel represents Mr. Harlowe's failure to protect and nurture his

---

[12] *Ibid.*, 1:80-1.
[13] *Ibid.*, 1:49-50.

daughter as the root cause of Clarissa's problems: the buck, so to speak, stops with him. Mr. Harlowe deviates from model parents, who are, as Locke defines them: "by the law of nature, under an obligation to preserve, nourish, and educate the children they had begotten; not as their own workmanship, but the workmanship of their own maker, the Almighty, to whom they were to be accountable for them."[14] In Locke's formulation of parent/child relationships, it is the parents who owe a debt of duty to their children – not the other way around, as Harlowe demands – to nurture and care for them as gifts from God, who is the being to whom parents must eventually answer. "God hath woven into the principles of human nature such a tenderness for their offspring," Locke continues, "that there is little fear that parents should use their power with too much rigour; the excess is seldom on the severe side, the strong bias of nature drawing the other way."[15] This nurturing version of fatherhood is echoed in Daniel Defoe's *The Family Instructor*, which was originally published in 1715 but reprinted by Richardson himself in 1732. Defoe encourages men to foster emotional connections with their children. Realizing that he has been lax in his son's religious instruction, a father in one of the guide's vignettes exclaims: "Dear Child! You ought to have been told who God is before now; indeed I have neglected to instruct thee as I ought to have done, but I'll tell thee now, my Dear."[16] The father is loving and affectionate, bestowing gentle endearments on his son and inculcating a strong sense of Christian morality in him, similar to Locke's ideal.

Mr. Harlowe rejects these nurturing models of fatherhood, instead seeming to follow the teachings of Sir Robert Filmer, who argued in his 1680 treatise *Patriarcha* that fathers possess "Royal Authority over their Children...by the Ordination of God himself," a notion that compared a king's divine right to rule over his kingdom with a father's right over his family.[17] By extension, fathers are inherently owed unquestioned authority over their subordinates. Mrs. Harlowe, who is bullied into supporting the forced marriage, warns Clarissa against "stand[ing] in defiance of a jealous Father, needlessly jealous, I will venture to say, of the prerogatives of his Sex...and still ten times more jealous of the authority of a Father; ---. That is now the point with us. You know your father has made it a point; and did he ever give up one he thought he had a right to carry?'"[18] That is, Mr. Harlowe possesses a firm belief that he, both as a man

---

[14] Locke, *Second Treatise*, 33.
[15] *Ibid.*, 39.
[16] Daniel Defoe, *The Family Instructor*, 16th ed. (London, 1766), 22.
[17] Robert Filmer, *Patriarcha: or, The Natural Power of Kings* (London: 1680), 12.
[18] Richardson, *Clarissa*, 1:109.

and a father, believes in the primacy of his word, and his pride has been wounded by Clarissa's rejecting the marriage with Solmes. The more she resists, the greater his determination becomes, especially since "My Father, you know, my dear, has not (any more than my Brother) a kind opinion of our Sex."[19] That is, he cannot handle the fact that it is his daughter – a woman – who resists his authority. According to Lois Bueler, Mr. Harlowe believes that "sons inherit their fathers' positions and become superiors themselves, but daughters never do, being given instead into the possession of other men."[20] When Clarissa resists this plan, her father responds with increasing force, isolating her to a single room in her home, denying visits with her friends and mother, prohibiting her from writing, and – to her dismay – moving forward with wedding plans and settlements without her consent. As far as Mr. Harlowe is concerned, her consent is irrelevant: his will is all that matters.

Clarissa's "discovery of female self"

Clarissa's dismay at her family's plan to marry her off in exchange for Solmes' land and money is apparent from the start; their refusal to empathize with her own desires more fully awakens her sense of authority over her own life that dovetails with contemporary Enlightenment ideas of individual free will. Earlier, I mentioned Rita Felski's description of novels of feminist awakening; novels that, as she describes them, depict heroines who realize the unjust, immoral nature of their society and – importantly – the realization that their own values, feelings, and desires are valid, even though they deviate from those espoused by their social circle. While Felski refers to a specific genre of novels, her dynamic is useful in understanding what is at stake in *Clarissa*. That is, *Clarissa* was published during a period in which Enlightenment ideologies proliferated. If the financial world was seeing a gradual end to royally chartered monopolies dominating trade, the philosophical world was also shifting away from a Hobbsian view of society, in which royal authority was the sole locus of power and authority, to one that emphasized individual free will. "Enlightenment," Kant famously defines, "is man's emergence from his self-imposed nonage...Dare to know! 'Have the courage to use your own understanding' is, therefore, the motto of the enlightenment."[21] Education, rational thought, reason, and – above all else – using these as tools to help individuals think for themselves is, to Kant, the basis of enlightenment. Locke makes a similar claim when he

---

[19] *Ibid.*, 1:49.
[20] Bueler, *The Tested Woman Plot*, 27.
[21] Immanuel Kant, *Toward a Perpetual Peace and Other Writings on Politics, Peace, and History*, ed. Pauline Kleingeld, trans. David Colclasure (Yale University Press, 2006), 17.

defines freedom as a man's "liberty to dispose and order freely as he lists his person, actions, possessions, and his whole property within the allowance of those laws under which he is, and therein not to be subject to the arbitrary will of another, but freely follow his own [will]."[22] Cultivating an individual's capacity to reason, according to Locke, is the key to living a life of personal freedom versus one defined by tyranny.

Adopting Enlightenment-type manifestations of individualism and applying them to her own life is a process that happens gradually over the first volume of *Clarissa*, which allows readers to watch the process by which her feminine self is awakened and her heroic disobedience enacted. In earlier letters to Anna, Clarissa describes her feelings toward the forced marriage as akin to anxiety and worry. In the novel's opening chapter, for instance, she expresses a wish that she had died during her last illness rather than cause trouble within her family.[23] When it comes to the pressure her family puts on her to accept Solmes' suit, she frequently insists that she is not strong enough to withstand their pressure. "They have begun so cruelly with me that I have not spirit enough to assert my own Negative," she tells Anna, adding: "How difficult it is, my dear, to give a negative where both duty and inclination join to make one wish to oblige."[24] Though she knows for certain that she wants no association with Solmes – let alone a marriage – she initially feels unable to subvert her role of dutiful, meek daughter and voice her opinion. Toward the second half of the first volume, however, a shift occurs, and her tone is one of justified self-righteousness as she becomes increasingly repulsed by – and frustrated with – the ways in which her family fails her. Adopting ideology similar to Locke's and Kant's configuration of free will, she begins to articulate her dawning awareness that she, as a reasoning individual, deserves to be the designer of her own future. She writes to Anna: "I never can be, that I never *ought* to be, Mrs. Solmes.—I repeat, that I *ought* not: for surely, my dear, I should not give up to my Brother's ambition the happiness of my future life…for the sake of further aggrandizing a family (altho' *that* I am of) which already lives in great affluence and splendour."[25] Fully cognizant of the motives behind the match into which her family is forcing her, Clarissa rejects the premise of being traded away like a commodity against her will. Instead of feeling powerless amidst this dynamic, she allows herself to feel angry and acknowledges that she deserves better. Quite simply, Clarissa hates Solmes (the man, "Madame," she tells her mother,

---

[22] Locke, *Second Treatise*, 34.
[23] Richardson, *Clarissa*, 1:5.
[24] *Ibid.*, 1:44.
[25] *Ibid.*, 1:127. Italics in original.

"person and mind, is a monster in my eye"), and the novel depicts her burgeoning awareness that she is entitled to be happy.[26]

Of course, just because Clarissa comes to understand her life through an Enlightened lens does not necessarily mean her social circle agreed that she was entitled to live out those principles: Locke's "mankind" is not gender-neutral. As Catherine Besley explains, "[t]he Enlightenment commitment to truth and reason, we can now recognise, has meant historically a single truth and a single rationality, which have conspired in practice to legitimate the subordination of black people, the non-Western world, women."[27] In other words: European white men were the creators, and primary beneficiaries of Enlightenment thought. However, as critics like Janet Todd and Barbara Taylor point out, that prominent enlightenment thinkers largely excluded women does not mean women were not involved with or impacted by these ideas.[28]

Richardson's depiction of the Harlowes and Solmes as greedy, villainous monsters makes it clear that, within the world of the novel at least, Clarissa is the heroine who deserves to have her decisions respected: there is an obvious good and evil dynamic at play within forced marriage plot novels that makes the gender politics clear. It is important to note, though, that the fact that Clarissa must become awakened to her sense of self – her own desires and wishes that are separate from her family's – provides a glimpse into the ways in which even intelligent, reasoning women like Clarissa were subjected to discourse that taught them to think of themselves primarily as subordinates. As many scholars have expressed, conduct guides were an important conduit for disseminating idealized performances of femininity.[29] For example, Richard Allestree's *The Ladies Calling* (1673; regularly in print for the next century) cites Biblical precedent alongside Classical philosophers like Aristotle to argue that women are inherently inferior to men and thus must be controlled by them to

---

[26] *Ibid.*, 1:127.

[27] Catherine Besley, "A Future for Materialist Feminist Criticism?," in *The Color of Equality: Race and Common Humanity in Enlightenment Thought*, ed. Devin J. Vartija (Philadelphia: University of Pennsylvania Press, 2021), 262.

[28] See Janet Todd, *The Sign of Angellica: Women, Writing and Fiction, 1660-1800* (Columbia University Press, 1989), in which she discusses how some women, like Mary Astell intervened in this debate. Taylor makes a similar claim in her essay "Enlightenment and the Uses of Woman."

[29] As Nancy Armstrong explains in *Desire and Domestic Fiction: A Political History of the Novel*: "So popular did these books become that by the second half of the eighteenth century virtually everyone knew the ideal of womanhood they proposed" (61).

ensure salvation: standard gender-based directives for the genre.[30] What is much less discussed are the ways in which eighteenth-century conduct guides actively worked to turn women into docile products amenable to their patriarch's will. For instance, James Fordyce's *Sermons to Young Women*, first published in 1766 and in print for the next century and a half, is an excellent synthesis of eighteenth-century conducts guides' directives to young women. "It is natural to me to wish well to my own sex, and therefore you will not wonder if I be solicitous for your possessing every quality that can render you agreeable companions" Fordyce claims, framing his advice as instructions for making women ideal companions for men.[31] Women, in Fordyce's guide, exist only in terms of how well they can please their patriarch. "Ah! my young friends, what pleasure can be compared to that of conferring felicity? What honour can be enjoyed by your sex, equal to that of showing yourself every way worthy of a virtuous tenderness from ours?"[32] To make oneself amenable to men is the single-minded goal of Fordyce's ideal woman. Interestingly, Fordyce also addresses the material ways in which a dutiful wife will impact a family. "I please myself with the prospect of seeing you," he writes:

> my honoured auditress, surrounded with a family of your own, dividing with the partner of your heart the anxious, yet delightful labour, of training your common offspring to virtue and society, to religion and immortality; while, by thus dividing it, you leave him more at leisure to plan and provide for you all, a task, which he prosecutes with tenfold alacrity, when he reflects on the beloved objects of it, and finds all his toils both soothed and rewarded by the wisdom and sweetness of your deportment to him and to his children.[33]

Drawing on gender norms that dictated a woman's place was within the home and a man's out in the world, the reason women must learn to keep house efficiently is to allow their husbands the freedom to focus on making money, going so far as to claim that an effectively run home will allow the *paterfamilias* to make money with "tenfold alacrity." While Fordyce does not completely abandon the moral and religious imperatives of earlier conduct guides like Allestree's, he is clear that for young women like Clarissa Harlowe, contributing to the economic prosperity of their family is of central importance to acceptable

---

[30] Richard Allestree, *The Ladies Calling*, 8th ed. (Oxford, 1705), Early English Books Online (EEBO).

[31] James Fordyce, *Sermons for Young Women*, 14th ed. (London: Printed by T. Bensley for T. Cadell and W. Davies, 1814), 25.

[32] *Ibid.*, 26.

[33] *Ibid.*, 26-7.

femininity; implying, of course, that a woman's primary desire must be the advancement of the husband – certainly not addressing her own desires and needs.

"To comply is impossible": Clarissa's heroic disobedience

Of all the characteristics of forced marriage plot novels, the one that most closely exemplifies the novels' radical arguments about the rights women inherently deserve is connected to what I term the heroines' heroic disobedience. As outlined in the Introduction, heroic disobedience – a term borrowed from *The Female Quixote*'s Arabella – refers to the action that each novel's heroine takes in order to make her desire for autonomy a reality. As the term suggests, the heroines are disobeying the norms and expectations placed on young women by their patriarchal societies (and specifically, their fathers), but this disobedience is depicted in a manner that makes it clear to readers that the heroines are morally justified in the actions they take to save themselves.

For Clarissa Harlowe and subsequent heroically disobedient heroines, the dawning recognition that her family sees her as a chattel ignites a streak of rebellion that guides her self-preservation. That is, she knows she must act to save herself. Speaking of her family in a letter to Anna, Clarissa notes: "they have all an absolute dependence upon what they suppose to be meekness in my temper. But in this they may be mistaken; for I verily think, upon a strict examination of myself, that I have almost as much in me of my Father's as of my Mother's family."[34] Though she does not specifically name the qualities of the Harlowe line to which she's referring, the context of her letter suggests she is referencing their stubbornness and high spirit, indicating that she will not meekly or submissively consent to their plan. "My aunt advises me to submit for the present to the interdicts they have laid me under; indeed to encourage Mr. Solmes's address," she goes on, "I have absolutely refused the latter, let what will (as I have told her) be the consequence."[35] She continues to refuse Solmes' addresses and even devises a sneaky plan to send Anna letters after her parents forbid her from corresponding with her friend. As the situation escalates – and her family structure continues to deteriorate – Clarissa remains steadfast in her resolve even as her father's threats worsen. In response to a letter from him telling her that she will be forcibly removed to her Uncle's home and married to Solmes with or without her consent, she tells Anna: "If this resolution be adhered to, then will my Father never see me more!—For I will never be the Wife

---

[34] Richardson, *Clarissa*, 1:150-1.
[35] *Ibid.*, 1:51.

of that Solmes—I will die first—!"³⁶ Within the narrative, Clarissa – as a heroically disobedient character – firmly and repeatedly declares her intentions to avoid the detested marriage through any means necessary: her dignity and free will as a human are more important to her than blind obedience, and she knows she will have to make hard choices to obtain her goal. "Yet I must oppose [their will] (to comply is impossible)," she states, "and *must* without delay *declare* my opposition or my difficulties will increase; since, as I am just now informed, a lawyer has been this very day consulted (Would you have believed it?) in relation to settlements."³⁷ Though she has been raised to be obedient, her family forces her to take dramatic steps.

Clarissa's heroic disobedience takes several forms. She attempts to use reason to cajole her family members (both immediate and extended) into calling off the wedding; she defies her father's order that she stop writing letters, going around his back to confer clandestinely with Anna and Lovelace; and she even confronts Solmes directly, bluntly relating her feelings toward him. "[W]ould a prudent man wish to marry one who has not a heart to give? Who cannot esteem him? Who therefore must prove a bad Wife!—And how cruel would it be to make a poor creature a bad Wife, whose pride it would be to make a good one!"³⁸ There is no ladylike pretense of politeness or meekness in her attitude, just blunt honesty.

Unfortunately for Clarissa, though, the longer she refuses the marriage, the more drastic are the measures her family adopts to try and force her to the altar, which lays Clarissa vulnerable to the machinations of Lovelace and his offer to extricate her from her home, freeing her from her family's plot. As Clarissa puts it, "For my own part, I am very uneasy to think how I have been *drawn* on one hand, and *driven* on the other, into a clandestine, in short, into a mere loverlike correspondence, which my heart condemns," noting "It is easy to see, if I do not break it off, that Mr. Lovelace's advantages, by reason of my unhappy situation, will every day increase, and I shall be more and more entangled."³⁹ Though she has reservations about Lovelace's character, he is also a conduit to the outside world; as a man (unlike Anna), he also has connections, power, and resources that could be useful to Clarissa in escaping the forced marriage hanging over her head. While it is important to note that Lovelace abducts her – ultimately, she waivers regarding if she should let Lovelace save her from her parent's home – none of the six and a half subsequent volumes would exist

---

³⁶ *Ibid.*, 1:285-6.

³⁷ *Ibid.*, 1:183-4. Italics in original.

³⁸ *Ibid.*, 1:227.

³⁹ *Ibid.*, 1:149. Italics in original.

without the extreme measures that her family led by her father, forced her to take. Desperate times, to fall back on a cliché, call for desperate measures.

Is *Clarissa* a protofeminist novel?

Whether or not *Clarissa* ultimately supports or overturns oppressive patriarchal ideologies is an issue that has caused debate among Richardson scholars for generations. For instance, Nancy Armstrong argues: "simply by introducing the figure of the female with a capacity to say 'no' and then providing a basis on which she could find such refusal advantageous, Richardson overthrew the longstanding tradition of thinking about courtship and kinship relations."[40] That is, Armstrong believes Richardson's endowing *Clarissa* with such a strong sense of self – despite the socio-economic strictures she faces – is evidence of the author's genuine belief in women as individual, reasoning beings who possessed at least some right to determine their own path through life. Other critics, however, dissent from this reading of the novel. Terry Eagleton argues that Richardson "is not, as we shall see, quite the ardent feminist [his portrayal of female characters] makes him sound," but admits "his writing is nevertheless part of a deep-seeded 'feminization' of values throughout the eighteenth century which is closely allied with the emergence of the bourgeoisie."[41] In his introduction to *Selected Letters of Samuel Richardson*, John Carroll goes even further, arguing that Richardson's writing "betrays his quite conventional assumption of male superiority" and that the author "did not trust women to act independently."[42] Others find more of a middle ground; Catherine Binhammer, for instance, claims Richardson's goal was for *Clarissa* to spark open discussion about women's obligations to their *paterfamilias*, while Tom Keymer asserts that Richardson was "caught between equal and potentially opposite allegiances to patriarchal authority and individual liberty," and saw no clear-cut answers to the questions his novel poses.[43]

---

[40] Armstrong, *Desire*, 123.

[41] Terry Eagleton, *The Rape of Clarissa: Writing, Sexuality, and Class Struggle in Samuel Richardson* (University of Minnesota Press, 1982), 14.

[42] John Carroll, ed., *The Selected Letters of Samuel Richardson* (Clarendon Press, 1964), 22-3.

[43] Binhammer, *The Seduction Narrative in Britain, 1747-1800*, 122. According to Binhammer, "…Clarissa has had a spectacularly rich dialogic history since its publication, soliciting a multiplicity of interpretations that Richardson, himself, invited. The popularity of Richardson's novel and the plurality of responses it invoked reflect how profoundly it spoke to a cultural awareness of, and interest in, the new inner world of women. [Yet]…its code for understanding the inner affective life of its heroine remains sublimely confounding" (21); Thomas Keymer, *Richardson's Clarissa and the Eighteenth-Century Reader* (Cambridge University Press, 1992), 122.

Debates on the novel's – or Richardson's personal – proto-feminist stance, I argue, are not a useful matrix for analyzing the novel, given the degree to which it requires anachronizing twenty-first-century understandings of women's rights. Toni Bowers provides a useful reminder of this point when she writes: "[r]eaders have debated for centuries the degree to which Richardson's work achieves credible balance between the impulse to defend patriarchal family governance despite its potential for abuse and impulse to revise the structure itself. Today, most readers tend to consider these impulses mutually exclusive, but they need not be looked at that way during the eighteenth century."[44] This is an important caveat for understanding both *Clarissa* and the function of the forced marriage plot throughout time: that Richardson dramatized the oppressive nature of socio-economic practices via the devastating impact these have on a young woman is a radical political move in its own right.

When literary scholarship began a concentrated turn to the history of the novel, critics like Ian Watt and Nancy Armstrong were quick to point out the significance that Richardson's novels are told from the perspective of a young woman had profound significance on what the novel would become in the eighteenth century and on the political message it imparts. Watt argues that the "primary criterion" of early novels such as *Clarissa* "was truth to individual experience which is always unique" claiming that Richardson gave his characters deep "subjective and inward direction" to a degree that was unprecedented.[45] Noting that Clarissa Harlowe and Pamela Andrews both refuse the sexual advances of powerful men, Armstrong asks: "[w]hen in the history of writing before *Pamela*, we might ask ourselves, did a female, let alone a female servant, have the authority to define herself so? To understand the power Richardson embodies in the non-aristocratic woman, one need only observe how he endows her with subjective qualities."[46] Richardson's female heroines are rational thinkers who are victimized by the male-dominated, materialist culture in which they live; as Watt's and Armstrong's analyses point out, the fact that readers are positioned within Clarissa's consciousness – meant to feel her challenges and trauma alongside her – is a radical move itself, since it necessitates acknowledging the undeniable harm that their society's dominant power structures did to women. Reading the last letters Clarissa wrote them before her death:

---

[44] Toni Bowers, "Family." in *Samuel Richardson in Context*, ed. Peter Sabor and Betty Schellenberg (Cambridge University Press, 2017), 240.

[45] Watt, *The Rise of the Novel*, 13, 18.

[46] Armstrong, *Desire*, 121.

> The unhappy Parents and Uncles, from the perusal of these Extracts, too evidently for their peace, saw, That it was entirely owing to the avarice, the ambition, the envy of her Brother and Sister, and to the senseless confederacy entered into by the whole family, to compel her to give her hand to a man she must despise, or had she not been a CLARISSA, and to their consequent persecutions of her, that she ever thought of leaving her father's house.[47]

This conclusion written by Mr. Belford, first included as part of the expanded third edition, is unequivocal in its condemnation of the Harlowe family's attempt to force Clarissa's marriage with Solmes and the subsequent ways in which this rendered her susceptible to Lovelace's trickery. While it is understandable that twenty-first-century readers may take issue with the fact that Clarissa had to die for her family to learn their lesson, it is important to note that the Harlowes not only repent of their actions but also pay heavy prices for their sins. James Jr. and Arabella live out their days in the misery of their own making, while Mr. and Mrs. Harlowe are so distressed that both die shortly after Clarissa. The message is clear: the changing economic tides that lead to the rise of the bourgeoise empowered men like Mr. Harlowe and Solmes to care about money – and the power it provides – above all else, a trend that Richardson obviously viewed with alarm. Crafting a forced marriage plot in which the father is a greedy villain who persecutes his loving, intelligent daughter creates an ideal plot arc for dramatizing the horrible consequences the capitalist ethos has on women in particular and the family dynamic more broadly. That is, *Clarissa* is ultimately a tragedy – with a heavy dose of cautionary tale for parents who overstep their authority over their children. Though authors like Charlotte Lennox (discussed below) will ultimately revise this component of the forced marriage plot, the point that readers cannot miss is that Clarissa Harlowe would never have been vulnerable to Lovelace if her father valued her reason and free will over her exchange value and his need to be obeyed.

Charlotte Lennox and Heroic Disobedience

The connections between *Clarissa* and *The Female Quixote* – and their authors – are numerous and complex. In fact, Susan Carlile begins her critical biography of Lennox by conjuring an image of young Charlotte standing at Richardson's front door. "[T]o Charlotte," Carlile explains, "his influence could make the difference between paying the rent in the space she shared with her unreliable husband…or having to slip away again in the night because they

---

[47] Richardson, *Clarissa*, 8:252.

could not pay their bills."[48] This meeting, obtained with the help of Lennox's friend Samuel Johnson, was one that Lennox hoped would propel her career forward:

> Her clothes were worn, even threadbare, and she may have worried he would only see her as a charity case…Making an impression on him was essential, but she wouldn't do it in the usual way that women impressed men at this time. Her mind was the commodity he would assess, and he had a draft of the early part of her second novel, *The Female Quixote*. She was desperate for him to see her literary talent…Richardson's help could be the difference between a few more years of stability or a return to the transience that had dominated her young life.[49]

In Carlile's telling, Lennox's career – and economic stability – hinged on this meeting with Richardson, configuring him as a crucial player in her literary success. Similarly, Margaret Doody articulates: "Richardson was to act as her agent and advisor in the preparation of *The Female Quixote* for the press."[50] "[A]s a novelist," Duncan Isles adds, "he gave her literary advice; as a printer, he printed the first edition of *The Female Quixote*; as one of London's most prominent men of letters, he used his influence in the literary world on her behalf."[51] Lennox is commonly seen as an acolyte of Richardson's, to whom credit for Lennox's professional career is often given.

While it can, indeed, be productive to read Lennox and Richardson together – especially *The Female Quixote* and *Clarissa*, which share many plot points and themes – the remainder of this chapter makes the case that they should be considered on equal footing. That is, Richardson undoubtedly had an impact on *The Female Quixote*, but not necessarily in the ways that critics like those above argue. *The Female Quixote*'s heroine, Arabella, faces the same barriers to

---

[48] Susan Carlile, *Charlotte Lennox: An Independent Mind* (University of Toronto Press, 2018), 3.

[49] Carlile, *Charlotte Lennox*, 3.

[50] Charlotte Lennox, *The Female Quixote*, 1752, ed. Margaret Anne Doody (Oxford World Classics, 2008), xiii. Hereafter *FQ*.

[51] Lennox, *FQ*, 419; Isles contends Richardson's feedback on *The Female Quixote* was fairly superficial, though she did follow his advice that she shorten the intended-three volume novel to two volumes (422). Additionally, as archival discoveries have shown – see O. M. Brack and Susan Carlile, "Samuel Johnson's Contributions to Charlotte Lennox's 'The Female Quixote,'" *The Yale University Library Gazette* 77, no. 3/4 (2003) – Lennox became very frustrated with Richardson during the printing process of the novel, as there were serious delays in its printing. Lennox seems to have retained at least a little resentment toward Richardson for this for some time, and the second volume of *The Female Quixote* was printed by a different printer.

her sense of autonomy as Clarissa Harlowe, but she pushes back against these in an even stronger manner than Clarissa does. *Clarissa* is the prototype for forced marriage plotlines, but it is Lennox who introduces radically pro-woman ideas into the plot that other authors will replicate for generations.

Understanding *The Female Quixote* as a forced marriage plot, which most existing scholarship fails to do, opens new avenues for understanding the gender politics Lennox analyzes within the novel. Deborah Ross is one of a few scholars to address the forced nature of Arabella's betrothal to her cousin Glanville but argues that Arabella's resistance to the marriage "is made to seem especially foolish because her father is less overtly bullying than Juliet Capulet's or Clarissa Harlowe's. He simply expresses the wish that his daughter marries the man of his choice and hopes that her filial affection will incline her to accept."[52] While she is correct that the Marquis does not resort to the same overt cruelty that Clarissa's father does, an analysis of their father/daughter relationship reveals that he has every intention of forcing her into the marriage with her cousin Glanville. That is, the Marquis embodies the struggle present in mid-eighteenth-century culture when it comes to treating young women as rational beings who, like their male counterparts, deserve the right to make decisions about their own lives. While in some respects a caring, affectionate father to Arabella, the Marquis transforms into a tyrant when it comes to Arabella's marriage. Making a show of telling Glanville, his nephew and intended son-in-law, that he must "bring me her consent," before their engagement is official, the Marquis is, at the same time, "perfectly assured of her Consent whenever he demanded it."[53] Between Arabella's subordinate status as his daughter, prevailing social norms that dictated filial obedience, and her previously obliging relationship with her father, the Marquis assumes that Arabella will always consent to his wishes. Her refusal to provide this consent, however, dissolves the façade that she ever had a choice in the matter. The Marquis quickly changes his tone, demanding to Arabella that she "must consent to marry" Glanville; he only cares about forcing verbal consent out of her, not about her actual opinion on the match.[54]

The Marquis' intention to use Arabella as a socio-economic object is an under-discussed but crucial component of the novel that situates *The Female Quixote* firmly within eighteenth-century debates around women's economic role, especially within the family unit. Since the Marquis has no sons, his

---

[52] Deborah Ross, "Betsy Thoughtless & Harriot Stuart: Unacknowledged Sisters," in *The Excellence of Falsehood: Romance, Realism, and Women's Contribution to the Novel*, edited by Deborah Kaplan (University Press of Kentucky, 1991), 99.

[53] Lennox, *FQ*, 31, 28.

[54] *Ibid.*, 54.

nephew Glanville, whose father is only a Baronet, will inherit the Marquis' title, while Arabella will inherit her father's money. According to contemporary property law, ownership of a woman's property was transferred to her husband upon marriage. Glanville, then, represents an endogamous marriage that allows the family estate and title to remain within their clan, cementing the Marquis' legacy in future generations while securing the prestige of the Glanville line. As in *Clarissa*, readers are presented with a father who sees his daughter as the vehicle for actualizing this process of inheritance. He insists: "you must not think it strange, if I insist upon directing your Choice in the most important Business of your Life."[55] Despite the level-headed tone he takes with his daughter, the Marquis unwaveringly demands that Arabella's choice of husband is his to make and, tellingly, describes it in economic terms: he sees marriage as a business decision to be made by the *paterfamilias*. Already at an advanced age when Arabella is born, he knows that her future husband will become the caretaker of his estate, to which the Marquis has a deep emotional connection and wants it managed accordingly. It is likely that, in addition to his personal hubris, class pride is also a factor in the Marquis' attitude. From as early as the seventeenth century, Stone and Fawtier Stone explain, there was concern among the aristocracy about the infiltration of their ranks by "self-made newcomers" who would lead to the "decline of the gentry" by "men from outside the country and of dubious background."[56] There was an impulse among those who held these fears that prestige (land, titles) must be kept among those whose birth – not new money – qualified them for it. The Marquis trusts Glanville and believes a marriage between his nephew and Arabella will secure the future of his estate.

Forced marriage and the Clandestine Marriages Act

The Marquis's obsession with estate preservation was shared by real-life lawmakers who wanted to preserve their ancestral lines from upwardly mobile merchants (like the Harlowes and Solmeses). Marriage, they realized, could be a convenient tool for upward mobility, which inspired those who were already in high social, economic, and political situations to try and close ranks among themselves. From 1736-1753 Parliament held dozens of debates on how to best use marriage laws to fit their elitist purposes. For instance, before 1736, the only prerequisites for marrying in the Church of England were the mutual consent of the couple and the absence of other living spouses. In 1736, however, Viscount Thomas Gage argued that "many Persons under age [sic], who are

---

[55] *Ibid.*, 42.
[56] Stone and Stone, *An Open Elite?*, 17.

entitled to considerable Fortunes, are frequently married without the Consent of their Parents and Guardians, to the great Prejudice and Ruin of many Families" and that fathers needed to have better legal control over whom their adult children marry.[57] Although Gage's proposal fizzled, the cause was taken up again in 1753 in Lord Hardwicke's Act for the Better Prevention of Clandestine Marriages. Clandestine marriages were, according to Keith A. Francis, not necessarily secret marriages (as the name would suggest) but marriages that were not conducted in strict adherence to canon law: a fairly quotidian occurrence at the time.[58] The Clandestine Marriages Act mandated that Anglican clergymen must officiate weddings; banns must be read three times in the parish where the marriage was to take place or a special license could be granted by the bishop; and – following Grange's lead – the written consent of fathers was required for marriages of individuals under 21 years of age.[59]

According to Cobbett's *Parliamentary History*, the bill's supporters celebrated policing marriage as a method of consolidating wealth among the already affluent. Member of Parliament A. G. Ryder exclaimed in 1753: "How often have we known the heir of a good family seduced, and engaged in a clandestine marriage, perhaps with a common strumpet? How often have we known a rich heiress carried off by a man of low birth, or perhaps by an infamous sharper?"[60] The suitability of a spouse was primarily measured by their economic potential; both heirs and heiresses were considered vulnerable and in need of legal protection. Fathers, then, would have the authority to prevent imprudent marriages in the name of protecting – and augmenting – family wealth. Critics of the Act called out its self-interested nature; M.P. Robert Nugent, for example, rebutted his aristocratic colleagues, claiming "should the Bill be passed into a

---

[57] Quoted in Probert, *Marriage Law and Practice in the Long Eighteenth Century: A Reassessment* (Cambridge University Press, 2009), 215.

[58] Keith A. Francis, "Canon Law Meets Unintended Consequences: The Church of England and the Clandestine Marriage Act of 1753," *Anglican and Episcopal History* 72, no. 4 (2003): 156-7.

[59] A father's approval or disapproval of a child's marriage always over-ruled the mother's if they disagreed. Additionally, a father could appoint a guardian or trustee to provide dis/approval in case of his death. This guardian or trustee's dis/approval took precedence over the mother's, as well. If the father was dead and had not appointed a trustee, only then would power of legally approving or disapproving of her child's marriage go to the mother. However, as Probert points out, if the mother remarried then her new husband, not her, would get the power of approval. Additionally, mothers could be deemed insane or unfit to provide written approval, but fathers or male guardians could not (226).

[60] William Cobbett, *Cobbett's Parliamentary History of England*, vol. 15 (London, 1813), 3.

law, they will thereby gain a very considerable and a very particular advantage; for they will in a great measure secure all the rich heiresses in the kingdom to those of their own body."[61] By the mid-eighteenth century, even lawmakers saw marriage not as a religious sacrament or about the companionship between two individuals but as a method of consolidating wealth and power; the Clandestine Marriages Act augmented the power that fathers had to engineer advantageous matches.

Arabella's heroic disobedience

The forced marriage plot was an ideal vehicle for exploring the ways in which these legal developments impacted the family unit, showing how the authority of fathers was applied unevenly to sons and daughters, often hindering young women from having the same rights to autonomy as their male peers. As discussed above, even liberal configurations of family dynamics, such as those espoused by Locke, were – at the very least – ambiguous about whether daughters deserve to be treated as rational beings in the same way as sons. Leslie Richardson explains: "[a]lthough Locke had no notion of extending this 'freedom' or equality to women, skeptics like Mary Astell were quick to note the fundamental contradiction of contract theory, which, speaking of *mankind*, refers to *men*."[62] *The Female Quixote*, then, both challenges and mocks the patriarchal structure that undergirds even the more progressive-seeming theory of nurturing fatherhood, showing how, ultimately, when the socio-economic gain is possible, the women's subjectivities are disregarded in the name of the estate.

According to the narrator, the Marquis has "always designed to marry *Arabella* to this Youth," and is surprised at her spirited reaction to hearing this news for the first time.[63] In a long passage worth quoting in its entirety, the narrator explains:

> *Arabella*, whose Delicacy was extremely shocked at this abrupt Declaration of her Father, could hardly hide her Chagrin; for, tho' she always intended to marry at some time or other, as all the Heroines had done, yet she thought such an Event out to be brought about with in infinite deal of Trouble; and that it was necessary she should pass to this State thro' a great Number of Cares, Disappointments, and Distresses of various Kinds, like them; that her Lover should purchase her with his

---

[61] *Ibid.*, 14.
[62] Leslie Richardson, "Leaving Her Father's House: Astell, Locke, and Clarissa's Body Politic," *Studies in Eighteenth-Century Culture* 34 (2005): 154. Italics Richardson's.
[63] Lennox, *FQ*, 26. Italics in original.

"Such Terms, Such Settlements!" 21

> Sword from a Croud [sic] of Rivals; and arrive to the Possession of her Heart by many Years of Services and Fidelities. The Impropriety of receiving a Lover of a Father's recommending appeared in its strongest light."[64]

Critics often point to this passage as an example of Arabella's lack of reason, arguing that since she has read too many novels, Arabella has unrealistic, fantasy-based expectations of courtship. However, when boiled down to its simplest terms, her reaction is very reasonable: she wants a say in whom she will marry and is angry that her father would presume otherwise. This is a declaration of her heroic disobedience: Arabella wants a husband who "arrive[s] to the Possession of her Heart by many Years of Services and Fidelities," not one whom her father has selected for his own selfish reasons. Though couched in the rhetoric of romance novels, what she wants is simply a man of her own choosing who has proven himself to be loyal and loving. She wants trust, not forced marriage. As the narrator will later explain, Arabella does not have any particular grudge against Glanville *per se* – in fact, she finds him physically attractive – but the anger she feels toward her father for making this demand sends her down a path of resistance. She tells the Marquis, "she would always obey him in all just and reasonable Things; and, being persuaded that he would never attempt to lay any Force upon her Inclinations, she would endeavor to make them comfortable to his, and receive her Cousin with that Civility and Friendship due to so near a Relation."[65] Taking a measured tone, Arabella attempts to reason with her father while making her own boundaries clear. She will be polite to her cousin and nothing more and underscores that she expects him, as her father, to never "Force upon her Inclinations." The Marquis will go on to dig in his heels on the matter, an attitude that is passed on to Glanville and his father after the Marquis' untimely death, but Arabella clings to her personal beliefs. "What Lady in Romance ever married the Man that was chosen for her?" Arabella wonders, "In those Cases the Remonstrances of a Parent are called Persecutions; obstinate Resistance, Constancy, and Courage," are, she believes, the characteristics upon which she must call upon to maintain control of her own future. [66] Looking to her favorite romance heroines helps Arabella "strength[en] her own Resolutions by those Examples of heroic Disobedience" she so admires in her novels.[67] To Arabella, "heroic Disobedience" represents a promise to herself that she will not give in to the marriage with Glanville just because it is what her father wants, and only for

---

[64] *Ibid.*, 27.
[65] *Ibid.*, 27.
[66] *Ibid.*, 27.
[67] *Ibid.*, 27.

socio-economic reasons, at that. This moment – her moment of heroic disobedience, when she states her intention to disobey the patriarchal power structures undergirding her father's views of marriage – is Arabella's rallying cry: her manifesto. Her declaration that she believes her life has value beyond that of a socio-economic pawn in her father's coffers and is the driving force that will carry her through the remainder of the novel.

In *The Female Quixote*, novels serve as a complex symbol of Arabella's subordination and her rebellion by providing models of femininity that provide a guide for Arabella's heroic disobedience. The novels, it is salient to note, came to Arabella from her deceased mother, for whom romances were the only escape from the monotony of life with the Marquis: she wanted them "to soften a Solitude which she found very disagreeable."[68] Margaret Doody has remarked that these novels "represent the only inheritance from her mother," which "prove[s] a trap as well as a bond."[69] Though Doody's interpretation presents romance novels as a negative influence on Arabella, she helpfully points out that the late Marchioness's life was unhappy thanks to her marriage; Arabella is the inheritor of her mother's unhappy fate.[70] The Marquis loves his daughter (and loved his late wife), but control is a prominent component of his love. For example, when Arabella turns four, he "took her from under the Direction of the Nurses and Women appointed to attend her, and permitted her to receive no Part of her Education from another."[71] This is a double-edged sword in the sense that, on the one hand, it follows Locke's edict that parents should be involved in their children's education – and perhaps even applauds the care with which the Marquis gives to educating a daughter – but there is also a level of possessiveness to his actions: the Marquis has total control over what his daughter learns and isolates her from other women. As she grows, the Marquis further restricts her interactions with the outside world. "[S]ometimes" being allowed to ride her horse, for instance, is "the only Diversion she was allowed, or ever experienced."[72] Like her mother before her, the Marquis possessively hides his daughter away, permitting her little to no interaction with the world outside of his estate. Romance novels, then, are a logical distraction for a bored, micro-managed girl to exercise her mind and escape her monotonous existence.

---

[68] *Ibid.*, 7.

[69] Margaret Anne Doody, "Shakespeare's Novels: Charlotte Lennox Illustrated," *Studies in the Novel* 19, no. 3 (1987): 299.

[70] Doody also claims of the conversion scene: "But a truth had to be faced: that women's tradition, their lore and language, are all considered false and must be given up," a reading from which I diverge ("Shakespeare's Novels," 300).

[71] Lennox, *FQ*, 6.

[72] *Ibid.*, 19.

Beyond functioning as a symbol of the isolation her father imposes on her, the romance novels introduce Arabella to heroines who model alternative forms of femininity that embody strength, resilience, and independence, inspiring Arabella's heroic disobedience. For instance, Arabella admires the Amazonian character Thalestris for her physical strength and bravery: "tho' the most stout and courageous of her Sex, [Thalestris] was, nevertheless, a perfect Beauty; and had much Harmony and Softness in her Looks and Person, as she had Courage in her Heart, and Strength in her Blows."[73] While Arabella's cousin Charlotte teases Arabella for admiring Thalestris, since Charlotte believes physical strength, bravery, and beauty are incompatible in a woman, Arabella understands that strength (physical and emotional), bravery, and beauty are complimentary aspects of femininity and strives to emulate these aspects of her role models. At one point in the novel, Arabella becomes enthralled with the story of Princess Melisintha, who, when faced with a forced marriage, "set Fire to the Palace, in order to avoid the Embraces of a King who forc'd her to marry him," a situation that has an obvious relevancy to her own life.[74] She admires Melisintha's "Fortitude and Patience" and the way in which "when taken Captive with the King her Father, [she] bore her Imprisonment and Chains with a marvellous [sic] Constancy; and who, when she had enslaved her Conqueror, and given Fetters to the Prince who held her Father and herself in Bonds...devoted herself to Destruction, in order to punish the Enemy of her House."[75] Not only does Melisintha serve as a protector to her father's rule, but she goes further outside the bounds of demure femininity by enacting vengeance against her father's enemy in his name: she is a violent warrior for justice who stands up for herself and those she loves, even though traditionally her father (also a king) would have been expected to fulfill those roles.

Arabella's conversion

Further evidence of Arabella's rationality and intellect is found in the somewhat-infamous penultimate chapter of the novel, which is subtitled "Being in the Author's Opinion, the Best Chapter in this History." This chapter, in which a patriarchal figure variously called "The Doctor" and "The Divine" sits Arabella down to convince her to give up romance novels and marry Glanville, has been the source of much discussion – and contention – among Lennox scholars. Part of this has to do with the persistent, though the now-debunked, myth that Samuel Johnson wrote this chapter; a theory that goes

---

[73] *Ibid.*, 125.
[74] *Ibid.*, 282.
[75] *Ibid.*, 282.

back to an article by literary critic John Mitford that appeared in an 1843 issue of *Gentleman's Magazine* in which Mitford claims the style of the chapter is Johnson's writing style. Though he produces no evidence for this theory, Mitford nevertheless instituted a serious misreading of *The Female Quixote* that persisted for over a century and a half before being debunked by twenty-first-century scholars like O. M. Brack Jr. and Susan Carlile's collaboration in "Samuel Johnson's Contributions to Charlotte Lennox's *The Female Quixote*" and Norbert Schurer in his *Charlotte Lennox: Correspondence and Miscellaneous Documents*.[76]

While Johnson did not write this chapter, he – and Samuel Richardson – both figure prominently in it – not, I argue, in an adulatory way, but in a way that satirizes and criticizes their connections to patriarchal power structures.[77] In fact, Lennox provides several avenues of attack against the patriarchal wisdom the Doctor/Divine is trying to impart. First, there is simply the fact that Arabella makes something of a fool of him – her reasoning against his arguments is so airtight, the narrator explains, that she renders him "completely embarrass'd," his words become "entangled," and his manner "submissive."[78] The Doctor finds himself "not so well prepar'd [to instruct her] as he imagin'd," and is "at a Loss for some leading Principle, by which he might introduce his Reasonings."[79] He expects to lecture her, not engage in an intellectual sparring match with one whose intelligence challenges his own. Despite the frequency with which her family constantly underestimates her mental capacity and mocks her thought process, this exchange shows her mastery of reason. "It rests upon you to shew

---

[76] Among the most convincing evidence that these scholars point to in their respective arguments is found in letters sent between Lennox, Johnson, and Richardson. Of particular interest is a letter that Lennox sent to Johnson with a copy of her book fresh from the first printing that indicates Johnson had yet to read the final chapters of the novel. Brack and Carlile also examine the publication history of the novel to show how the stylistic differences that occur in the penultimate chapter can be attributed to Lennox's need to write a longer chapter than she had planned and variances in the typeset that the printer made to avoid wasting paper. See Norbert Schurer, ed., *Charlotte Lennox: Correspondence and Miscellaneous Documents* (Bucknell UP, 2012); John Mitford, "Dr. Johnson's Literary Intercourse with Mrs. Lennox," *The Gentleman's Magazine*, vol. XX, 1843, pp. 132.

[77] The traditional reading of this chapter can be found in Betsey Schellenberg's claim that: "Lennox chose to write an ending, in short, which does nothing to dismantle the hierarchies of gender and reading upon which her plot is constructed." See Betsy Schellenberg, *The Professionalization of Women Writers in Eighteenth-Century Britain* (Cambridge University Press, 2005), 10.

[78] Lennox, *FQ*, 370, 374.

[79] *Ibid.*, 368.

[sic]," Arabella tells him, "That in giving Way to my Fears, even supposing them groundless, I departed from the Character of a reasonable Person."[80] She sets the ground rules for their debate, reminding him that the burden of proof rests with him. Instead of proving his point – that Arabella's behavior is irrational, her mind muddled from the drama of her romance novels – the interaction with the Doctor heightens the ways in which Arabella's way of seeing the world is, in fact, a fairly accurate depiction of the threats women face in a patriarchal society.

Interestingly, much of their debate hinges on a discussion of *Clarissa*; which, according to the Doctor, is an example of a novel that – unlike bad translations of French romances – can provide practical instructions to young women. "An admirable Writer of our own Time," the Doctor claims, "has found the Way to convey the most solid Instructions, the noblest Sentiments, and the most exalted Piety, in the pleasing Dress of a Novel, and to use the Words of the greatest Genius in the present Age, 'Has taught the Passions to move at the command of Virtue.'"[81] There is a lot to unpack in this loaded passage. To begin, the inset quote ("has taught…virtue") is, in fact, a direct quote from Samuel Johnson, the very person upon whom the Doctor character is based (according to Lennox's own letters), meaning that the Doctor here is quoting himself while referring to himself as "the greatest genius of the present age" – perhaps a dig at Johnson's inflated sense of self. More importantly, however, bringing up *Clarissa* betrays the fallacy of the Doctor's argument that romance plots are absurd distortions of life unfit for young women. "Has it ever been known that a Lady of your Rank was attack'd with such Intentions, in a Place so publik [sic], without any Preparations made by the Violator for Defence or Escape? Can it be imagin'd that any Man would so rashly expose himself to Infamy by Failure, and to the Gibbet by Success? Does there in the Records of the World appear a single Instance of such hopeless Villainy?" he asks her, hoping to highlight the disparity between her novels and reality.[82] However, the situations he describes could apply equally to *Clarissa* – the novel he cites as the antidote to romances – as it does to romances. Clarissa is unfairly persecuted by her parents, abducted and raped by Lovelace, and introduced to a variety of lowlifes who cause her no end to suffering.

It is not just romances that introduce young women to the dangers inherent in courtship, but – ironically – even highbrow, moralistic novels like *Clarissa*. In fact, as Doody points out in her Introduction to the Oxford University Press

---

[80] *Ibid.*, 371.
[81] *Ibid.*, 377.
[82] *Ibid.*, 372.

edition of *The Female Quixote*, "it is nonsense to tell a young woman that rape and abduction are only in fictions," especially given "the high value placed on virginity in well-born marriageable girls."[83] To Doody, "the novel itself has presented such dangers as distinctly possible in contemporary real life."[84] That is, the lessons the Doctor tries to teach Arabella do not align with the realities that women (fictional and real) faced in the mid-eighteenth century but parallel the conduct book ideology that sought to shape women into submissive agents of their own oppression. In addition to poking fun at the Doctor's self-importance, this exchange also highlights how disconnected men like him are from the experiences of women, especially when trying to force them into the role of dutiful, submissive wives.

The Doctor's mention of a novelist who "'Has taught the Passions to move at the command of Virtue,'" refers to an essay Samuel Richardson wrote for the *Rambler* in February 1751, which brings Richardson into their debate on gender performance. In his *Rambler* article, Richardson chastises British youths for their alleged lack of domestic joy. Young women have "generally given up to negligence of domestick [sic] business, to idle amusements, and to wicked rackets, without any settled view at all but of squandering time," he alleges.[85] Young men are guilty of shifting social customs given their affinity for gambling, drinking, and sex workers; grave enough on their own, these sins are compounded by the debt they cause, which leads young men to seek expedient marriages.[86] Money, both spending it frivolously in the public sphere and the issues that needing more of it cause, is depicted as a major barrier to happy marriages. Richardson writes:

> Two thousand pounds in the last age, with a domestik [sic] wife, would go farther than ten thousand in this. Yet settlements are expected, that often, to a mercantile man especially, a fortune into uselessness; and pin-money is stipulated for, which makes a wife independent, and destroys love, by putting it out of a man's power to lay any obligation upon her, that might engage gratitude, and kindle affection: when to all this the card tables are added, how can a prudent man think of marrying?[87]

---

[83] Doody, "Introduction" to *FQ*, xxx-xxxi.

[84] *Ibid.*, xxx.

[85] Samuel Richardson, "Rambler No. 97," in *The Rambler*, ed. Samuel Johnson (London, 1751), 241.

[86] *Ibid.*, 249.

[87] *Ibid.*, 249.

"Such Terms, Such Settlements!"   27

While, on the one hand, the attitude of young people, in general, is blamed for the decline of marriage, on the other hand, there is a particular emphasis on women who shirk domestic duties as the underlying problem. Though Lennox found professional allies among men like Johnson and Richardson, patriarchal hegemony was so entrenched that even these allies were susceptible to internalizing and enforcing discourse that supported their own social primacy. In *Rambler no. 97*, Richardson advocates for companionate marriage entered willingly by both parties, but in his diatribe against the monetization of marriage, he falls back on patriarchal understandings of feminine financial submissiveness that suggest a woman who has access to her own money is a dangerous force.[88] As a woman, Lennox no doubt saw gender roles differently: she was a professional writer and wife to a spendthrift in a time when married women had no legal rights to the money they earned, no doubt enabling her to see the gender-based contradictions present in Richardson's work.

An example that highlights this disconnect between Lennox's viewpoint and Richardson's is found in their other writings, as well. In Richardson's sequel to *Pamela*, for instance, there arises a conflict between now-married Pamela and Mr. B over whether she will breastfeed their child when he is born. Though wetnurses were still common, the mid-eighteenth century saw an increasing awareness of the health benefits of nursing one's own baby: views Pamela shares. "Where there is good Health, free Spirits, and plentiful Nourishment; I think [nursing] an indispensable Duty. For this was the Custom, of old, of all the good Wives we read of in Scripture. Then the Nourishment of the Mother must be most natural to the Child," she reasons.[89] Mr. B, however, is adamant that Pamela will not breastfeed their child for purely selfish reasons, fearing that breastfeeding will somehow diminish Pamela's beauty, that spending time around a nursing baby will be bothersome to him, and that nursing will keep Pamela from engaging in sex with him. The narrative makes it clear that Pamela is in the right – she has eighteenth-century science and biblical precedent on her side – but Mr. B's word is law in their household. Pamela writes to Miss Darnford: "could you ever have thought, Miss, that Husbands have a Dispensing Power over their Wives, which Kings are not allowed over the Laws?... Can you believe, that if a Wife thinks a Thing her Duty to do, and her

---

[88] In trying to understand Richardson's motive in *Rambler no. 97*, it's also worth pointing out that he was known to be intentionally provocative in his private writings and essays, playing, one might say, devil's advocate in order to get a reaction out of his readers.

[89] Samuel Richardson, *Pamela: Or, Virtue Rewarded, In a Series of Familiar Letters from a Beautiful Young Damsel to Her Parents: and Afterwards, in Her Exalted Condition, Between Her, and Persons of Figure and Quality, Upon the Most Important and Entertaining Subjects, in Genteel Life*, fourth edition (London, 1742), 4:10.

Husband does not approve of her doing it, he can dispense with her performing it, and no Sin shall lie at her Door?"[90] Mobilizing political discourse, she explains that within their society, a husband's power over his wife is more exhaustive than the power a King has over his subjects, rendering her compliance compulsory. A husband's opinion thus takes precedence over a woman's own wishes, even if his opinion is deeply flawed and selfish. What is most important to their society – more important than following one's own conscious – is obeying the patriarch. Bonnie Latimer argues that Pamela's ability to use reason to come to her own conclusion on the issue signals "the fictionality of submissive femininity" since she develops her own opinions on the issue rather than blindly following the demand of her husband; "[h]er judgement and action are separate – but both morally validating, because she understands the requirements of motherhood but also the regrettable necessity for wifely submission."[91] In Richardson's novels, women are endowed with reason and have their own desires: that they are unable to live the lives they want for themselves is unjust.

Lennox's novels, while also highlighting the tyranny of men who only see women as exchangeable objects, empower women to act against these unjust forces. In her 1750 novel *Harriot Stuart*, for example, the titular heroine goes to great lengths to fight against men who try to impose their tyranny over her – in one scene, she actually stabs a man who tries to rape her. According to Susan K. Howard, "[w]hile Lennox uses and transforms many of Richardson's plot actions (the abduction from the garden, for instance, or the penknife scene), her emphasis is on an active and realistic heroism...[Harriot] adapts to the threatening world in which she finds herself."[92] Harriot embodies empowered female agency, taking it upon herself to act against oppression instead of just recognizing it.

The heroines of Arabella's romances model a type of non-submissive, non-normative femininity that teach Arabella heroic disobedience; uncoincidentally, their depiction of femininity is exactly why the Doctor disapproves of them:

> [T]hey teach women to exact vengeance, and men to execute it; teach women to expect not only worship, but the dreadful worship of human sacrifices. Every page of these volumes is filled with such extravagance of praise, and expressions of obedience, as one human being ought not

---

[90] *Ibid.*, 3:370.

[91] Bonnie Latimer, *Making Gender, Culture, and the Self in the Fiction of Samuel Richardson: The Novel Individual* (Ashgate, 2013), 83.

[92] Susan K. Howard, "Identifying the Criminal in Charlotte Lennox's The Life of Harriot Stuart," *Eighteenth-Century Fiction* 5, no. 2 (1993): 151.

to hear from another; or with accounts of battles, in which thousands are slaughtered for no other purpose than to gain a smile from the haughty beauty, who sits a calm spectatress of the ruin and desolation, bloodshed and misery, incited by herself…Love, madam, is, you know, the business, the sole business of ladies in romances.[93]

Ultimately, the doctor's primary complaint about romances is that they depict women who reject the patriarchal, submissive ideal of femininity. In Arabella's beloved romances, femininity is not just one thing: women are leaders, they are passionate, they are powerful, and they are, in a nutshell, free to enact femininity however they please – a notion that is, of course, antithetical to eighteenth-century submissive femininity. It is especially telling that the Doctor concludes his tirade against romance heroines by concluding that "love" is the "sole business of ladies in romances," since a woman motivated by love, instead of duty or obedience, is likely to prioritize her own desires over those of the patriarchs in the lives.

Kant describes enlightenment as rebelling against "the guardians of the great masses," who instruct mankind "do not argue!" with outdated, corrupt systems of power.[94] These "independent thinkers" are the harbingers of an enlightened age "who will spread the spirit of rational appreciation of one's own worth and the calling of every human being to think for himself."[95] The catch with Kant's directive, of course, is that he is not speaking about women: only white European men. In this exchange between Arabella and the Doctor, the latter functions as the voice of the "great masses" through his repeated attempts to strip her of her unique way of seeing the world since it encourages her to argue with prescribed notions of acceptable gender performances. She is an independent thinker, which is a great threat to the power hierarchy represented through the Doctor, her father, and her uncle. His message: do not argue. Arabella, however, does argue. She effectively argues her case while calling attention to the fallacies inherent in the Doctor's perspective. Setting her own standards for selecting a husband is a right Arabella firmly believes she possesses. All she wants is a husband who will see her as a partner, not a possession.

Glanville's growth

The Female Quixote appears to have a conventional ending in which the heroine learns the error of her ways, but there is much more to this story.

---

[93] Lennox, *FQ*, 380.
[94] Kant, "What is Enlightenment," 17.
[95] *Ibid.*, 17.

Despite Ros Ballister's assessment that "Arabella's concessions to the doctor, and her conversion to domestic ideology, and her agreement to marry Glanville, mark however the book's closure and containment, indeed, silencing its heroine…Arabella's verbal power comes to an end," there is a strong case to be made that it is Glanville, not Arabella, who changes throughout the narrative, growing into the dependable partner Arabella expects in a husband.[96] From the moment he first hears the Marquis' plan for Arabella to marry him, Glanville is pleased. While he is certainly charmed by his cousin, the novel is explicit about the financial arrangement behind their marriage in a way that implies this is also a possible motivating factor in his courting Arabella. Through marrying his cousin, Glanville secures ownership of the Marquis' entire estate; if they do not marry, however, Glanville will only inherit one-third of the estate. Despite his admiration of her beauty, it is obvious that Glanville does not initially understand her habits, interests, or motivations: there is a disconnect between the two he is slow to broach. For instance, believing her affront at his romantic advances to be in jest, Glanville jokes that he will "be revenged" and make Arabella "repent the Tricks" she plays on him – which she takes as a serious threat, causing her to (mistakenly) identify him as a threat.[97] Later, Glanville promises to read some of her favorite novels but only pretends to do so. Easily seeing through his dishonesty, Arabella further doubts Glanville's sincerity. As their story unfolds, it at times seems that Glanville's inability – and unwillingness – to understand Arabella dooms any chance of a happy future together.

However, over the course of the novel, Glanville comes to better understand Arabella's view of the world and respect her intellect. For instance, early on in their courtship, he muses: "her Character was so ridiculous, that he could propose nothing to himself but eternal Shame and Disquiet, in the possession of a Woman, for whom he must always blush," and feels embarrassed at the prospect of introducing her to London society.[98] In the same train of thought, however, he also admits "[h]e admired the Strength of her Understanding; her lively Wit; the Sweetness of her Temper; and a Thousand aimable Qualities which distinguished her from the rest of her Sex…he feared it was impossible to stop loving her."[99] Notably, it is the very characteristics that make her different from women who embodied eighteenth-century ideal femininity that he admires in her, especially her intelligence and wit. Initially balking at her

---

[96] Ros Ballaster, *Seductive Forms: Women's Amatory Fiction from 1684 to 1740* (Oxford University Press, 1998), 208.

[97] Lennox, *FQ*, 34.

[98] *Ibid.*, 116.

[99] *Ibid.*, 116-17.

tendency to embarrass herself (and, by extension, him) in public with her unusual manners, dress, and tendency to mistake fictional characters for historical figures, over time, Glanville comes to see that, though her belief system is different from that of mainstream society, it is still valid. Different does not mean inferior, and he even grows to admire her different belief system. "He dreaded to see her exposed to Ridicule by her fantastical Behaviour, and become the Jest of Persons who were not possessed of half her Understanding," the narrator explains.[100] There is a perceptible shift in his thinking: society – not Arabella – is flawed. He no longer blames her for social *faux pas*, but blames everyone around her for their failure to comprehend her genius. Later in the novel, when his sister Charlotte is mocking Arabella, Glanville stands up for Arabella, chiding: "I would advise you, *Charlotte*, said Mr. *Glanville*, not to aim at repeating your Cousin's Words, til you know how to pronounce them properly...she is superior to you in many Things; as much so in the Goodness of her Heart, as in the Beauty of her Person --."[101] His insult highlights that it is Charlotte whose intelligence (and kindness and beauty) are lacking – not Arabella's. "Then turning the Discourse on his beloved *Arabella*," the narrator explains, he "pronounc'd a Panegyrick [*sic*] on her Virtues and Accomplishments an Hour-long; which, if it did not absolutely persuade his Sister to change her Opinion, it certainly convinc'd his Father, that his Niece was not only perfectly well in her Understanding, but even better than most others of her Sex."[102] Glanville comes to value her for the woman that she is, even if this is not a typical representation of femininity. Over the course of the novel, the narrator periodically inhabits his consciousness in a way that reveals his devotion and honest appreciation of her character; by the end of the novel, Glanville has proven himself a constant, loyal lover – which is all Arabella ever really wanted – and she happily consents to marry, not a forced husband, but a lover who has proven himself to be true after a series of trials.

Conclusion

The novel, as utilized by Richardson and Lennox, became a vehicle for exposing and (especially in *The Female Quixote*) subverting male dominance. In creating novels that portray fathers who force their daughters into marriages that the young women resist, Richardson and Lennox distill the socio-economic and philosophical debates of their period into a simple plot structure that effectively portrays the nuanced, systemic gender issues working against

---

[100] *Ibid.*, 117.

[101] *Ibid.*, 309. Italics in original.

[102] *Ibid.*, 309.

women. In each novel, the *paterfamilias* abuses his role as a father, commodifying his daughter into an object of exchange for his own use, a process that necessarily strips women of control over their own lives. In *Clarissa*, Richardson portrays the ways in which emergent capitalism infected British life at the level of the family unit. The greed of Harlowe and his brothers blinds them to all other considerations: they want to elevate the Harlowe family name at any cost and see young, beautiful, marriageable Clarissa as an object they can give to Solmes in exchange for land, money, and power. Disobeying her father goes against everything which Clarissa believes, but she recognizes that she has the right to control over her life and that participating in her father's economic scheme would betray her own value system. Although she never gets to enjoy the fruits of her resistance, Clarissa Harlowe ultimately dies a heroic, righteous death: a martyr whose belief in her own values is a cause for celebration. Lennox adopts and adapts Richardson's version of the forced marriage plot via Arabella's "heroic disobedience," elevating non-traditional enactments of femininity that empower Arabella to marry only on her own terms, not simply to fulfill her father's wishes for his estate. As the title of this book suggests, the idea of heroic disobedience will become a distinguishing characteristic of the forced marriage plot for the next century and a half. The heroically disobedient heroines of these novels recognize the mercenary nature of their societies and, shirking the pressure to acquiesce, fight for their right to live by their own system of values – one in which their desires are respected. To Clarissa and Arabella, a woman's value is far more than the market value men assign to her.

Chapter Two
"Will there not be virtue in my resistance?": resisting tyranny in Charlotte Smith's "The Story of Henrietta" and Mary Robinson's Angelina; A Novel

The previous chapter examined novels by Samuel Richardson and Charlotte Lennox, *Clarissa: or, the History of a Young Lady* and *The Female Quixote*, that dramatize the socio-economic changes taking place in Great Britain during the mid-eighteenth century. During this period, mercantilism gave way to a new system of wealth accumulation that afforded individuals the ability to amass personal wealth through commerce, causing some men – like Richardson's Mr. Harlowe – to gain money and influence previously only open to the landed gentry. This burgeoning capitalist ethos inspires men like Harlowe and the Marquis to use their own daughters as economic pawns, forcing them into marriages that are economically beneficial to the men but repugnant to the young women. This chapter considers how late-eighteenth-century authors further adapted the forced marriage plot as a tool for exploring the mercenary economic practices of their period, which, in this case, was defined by the slave trade and violence. Charlotte Smith's "The Story of Henrietta" (1800-02) and Mary Robinson's *Angelina; A Novel* (1796) introduce readers to heroines who, like Clarissa Harlowe and Arabella, are threatened with forced marriages. Interacting with their historical moment, the forced marriage plots in these novels show the specific ways in which British subordination of women (especially via marriage) is inextricably linked to the slave trade.

While it is true that towards the end of the eighteenth century, slavery became a popular analogy for the oppression of white British women – a practice Susan Meyer analyzes in *Imperialism at Home: Race and Victorian Women's Fiction* – Smith and Robinson invoke slavery as more than a metaphor.[1] They work to

---

[1] In fact, writers from opposite ends of the socio-political spectrum commonly applied "slave" to white women. For example, the socially-conservative Hannah More does so in

reveal the complex symbiotic socioeconomic relationship between the trade of enslaved people and the patriarchal power system in place within the British Empire. In these novels, the status of British women is not simply *like* that of the enslaved, but both enslaved people and women are oppressed because of the way the slave trade allowed wealth to accumulate. Such extreme wealth created a system in which the slave owner was viewed as all-powerful; his abuse of women and the enslaved was tolerated because of the importance society put on wealth. Rather than creating heroines whose virtue emanates from mercy, humility, or desire to sacrifice themselves for the good of their patriarchs, Smith and Robinson create strong female characters whose virtue lies in their resistance.

The slave trade and wealth accumulation

Because the long arc of this project examines the specific impact that the rise of capitalism had on women's rights, it is worth reflecting on the relationship between the transatlantic slave trade and capitalism since, as Edward Baptist articulates, "[s]tories about industrialization emphasize white immigrants and clever inventors, but they leave out cotton fields and slave labor."[2] That is, there is a tendency to configure slavery and the sugar industry as separate from modern capitalism: a dark, pre-modern economy eliminated by the Industrial Revolution. However, this false narrative ignores slavery's significant role in the emergence of capitalism. Karl Marx, for instance, explains in *The Poverty of Philosophy*: "[w]ithout slavery you have no cotton, without cotton you cannot have modern industry. It is slavery which has given their value to the colonies, it is the colonies which have created the commerce of the world, it is the commerce of the world which is the essential condition of the great industry."[3]

---

her 1805 (semi-satirical) essay "Hints towards forming a Bill for the Abolition of the White Slave Trade, in the Cities of London and Westminster," in which she describes young women as slaves of fashionable, immoral culture, as does the more radical Mary Hays in her essay "An Appeal to the Men of Great Britain in Behalf of Women" (1798), in which she describes the customs that have made women "slaves of man" (see Mary Hays, *An Appeal to the Men of Great Britain in Behalf of Women* [London, 1798], ii). In fact, Samuel Richardson, Mary Astell, Mary Wollstonecraft, Charles Dickens, and Anthony Trollope all, at various points in their texts that are under consideration in this project, call on slavery as an analogy for the oppression of white women.

[2] Edward E. Baptist, *The Half Has Never Been Told: Slavery and the Making of American Capitalism* (Hachette Book Group, 2016) 17; Baptist examines American slavery, but many scholars, such as Williams (1944), Mintz (1985), Tomich (1991), Beckles (1997), Carrington (2003), Harvey (2019) (just to name a few) argue, the same dynamic applies to the British West Indian context as well.

[3] Karl Marx, *The Poverty of Philosophy*, ed. Harry Quelch, et al. (United States, 1910), 121.

Eric Williams is even more explicit, arguing in *Capitalism and Slavery* that the plantation economy "combined the vices of feudalism and capitalism with the virtues of neither"; he goes on to call sugar planters "the biggest capitalists of the mercantilist epoch."[4] This observation is especially pertinent to the role that Smith's and Robinson's plantation owners play in their narratives. While sugar planters benefitted tremendously from the mercantilist conditions present in the late seventeenth and early eighteenth centuries, the gradual shift to capitalism enriched those men who were able to buy into the slave trade, which in turn strengthened the drive for self-enrichment. As the following discussion shows, profits and personal influence were, according to Smith and Robinson, the driving factor among plantation owners, much to the detriment of those they commodified.

Smith's "The Story of Henrietta" and the slave economy

Letters of a Solitary Wanderer is a five-volume epistolary novel that is, at its core, a novel about the socio-economic struggles women faced in Smith's period. United under this theme, each of the five volumes is a stand-alone story about a different female character as told to a main narrator who weaves the tales together. The first volume is the tale of Edourarda and her cruel father, Sir Mordaunt Falconberg, whose decision to marry a young woman against her will causes a ripple effect that tears apart generations of his family. The second volume, "The Story of Henrietta," is about Henrietta Denbigh, wife of the narrator's adopted brother, who escapes from her cruel slave-owning father during a Maroon uprising in Jamaica to avoid a forced marriage. In the third volume, readers are taken back to sixteenth-century war-torn France, where a young woman named Corisande is forced out into the dangerous world unprotected. Volumes four and five relate the narrator's adventures in helping a Hungarian man and his Irish sister-in-law, who are both unfairly persecuted by their families, the former by his greedy older brother and the latter by her wastrel husband. The unfair social and familial persecution of women pervades the novel as a whole, especially in terms of oppression by fathers and husbands. In total, there are six separate forced marriage storylines. This chapter focuses on the second volume of the novel, "The Story of Henrietta," as it depicts the most extreme example of female persecution within the novel coupled with a unique take on the slave trade, leaving readers with the radical wisdom that that retributive violence is the only method of combatting tyranny.

---

[4] Eric Williams, *Capitalism and Slavery*, 3rd edition (University of North Carolina Press, 1994), 13, 85.

Slave owners as Gothic monsters

"The Story of Henrietta" showcases the evils of the plantation owner on a micro-level; how its effects permeated the family unit, showing a causal, cyclical relationship between owning enslaved persons, believing one's own authority is absolute, and using violence to assert that authority. Maynard is a tyrannic plantation owner whose reputation for cruelty precedes him. Sent to England as a young child while her father remained in the West Indies, Henrietta is anxious to learn what her father is like. When a mutual acquaintance responds to her inquiry by speaking of the "luxury of the table at [her] father's house; of the number of slaves kept solely for domestic purposes; of the quantity of wine consumed at his table, and of his consequence in the island," she is disheartened and left to wonder: "[b]ut why do I hear nothing of his benevolence; of his private friends; of his kindness to his people, and of his being beloved as well as feared?"[5] Upon acquaintance with her estranged father, Henrietta's misgivings are proven valid. Maynard is a tyrant distinguished by his immense wealth and power, which he uses to unleash unspeakable suffering on the enslaved people forced to work for him – and, Henrietta finds – everyone else he deems his subordinate. Within the narrative, there is a causal relationship between the power of slave owners – due to their enormous wealth and lack of moral scruples – and the mistreatment of women in British society. For instance, later in the narrative, Henrietta's Uncle George explains that Maynard's lust for power and violence developed during childhood as a direct result of his family's proximity to the slave trade. He "had been used to exercise the caprices of a very bad temper on half a dozen African boys and girls," and, drunk with that power, often turned to violently beating George, as well.[6] After leaving school at the age of ten, Maynard vows never to return to England, having "conceived such an aversion from a place where he had been on the footing of equality with other boys."[7] Though a seemingly small episode, these childhood remembrances concretize the link between the socio-economic privilege of the slave owner and violence. That is, young Maynard's freedom to beat enslaved children translates, in his mind, to a power over everyone he encounters. His need to feel superior is so pronounced, according to George, that it compels young Maynard to leave England, where he is around men presumed to be his equal, in exchange for Jamaica, where he can be the king of his plantation. This attitude extends to Henrietta, who learns upon arriving in

---

[5] Charlotte Smith, *The Story of Henrietta*, ed. Janina Nordius (Richmond: Valencourt Books, 2021), 44.

[6] *Ibid.*, 150.

[7] *Ibid.*, 8.

Jamaica that her father intends to force her into a marriage with one of his lackeys to ensure that the future of his plantation rests in the hands he trusts.

Though his kingdom is a Caribbean plantation, rather than a crumbling gothic castle, Maynard fits the role of a gothic villain, a stylistic move that underscores his role as the source of evil within the narrative despite contemporary Caribbean gothic novels that set the locus of evil within the racialized other. "By the 1790s," Lisbeth Paravisini-Gerbert explains, "Gothic writers were quick to realize that Britain's growing empire could prove a vast source of frightening 'others' who would, as replacements for the villainous Italian antiheroes in Walpole or Radcliffe, bring freshness and variety to the genre. With the inclusion of the colonial, a new sort of darkness – of race, landscape, erotic desire, and despair – enters the Gothic genre."[8] In Smith's telling, however, the terror comes from the plantation owner's unfettered power. "From being a despot on his own estate," Henrietta says, "he imagined he might exercise unbounded authority over every being that belonged to him."[9] David Turley explains that this type of authority is related to the historical role that plantation owners played in British history. "For 200 years in British colonial territories and what became the United States, the slave trade and slavery underpinned an economic, social, and racial order that projected the power of slaveholders into the centre of their respective political systems."[10] The British plantation system brought vast amounts of wealth and goods into the British economy that, as Turley explains, put those who owned slaves and plantations into influential positions of power. Identifying this abuse of power, authors often used the gothic genre to explore Britain's hegemonic rule in the colonies.

Sexual villainy is a key source of terror in gothic novels: for instance, Horace Walpole's *The Castle of Otranto* (1764), often viewed as the first British gothic novel, features Manfred's persecution of Isabella; threatening sexuality is ubiquitous among the villains of Matthew Gregory Lewis' *The Monk: A Romance* (1796); and Ann Radcliffe's Emily St. Aubert, the heroine of her popular *The Mysteries of Udolpho* (1794), is under constant sexual persecution by her stepfather Montoni, just to name a few of the genre's most popular

---

[8] Lisbeth Paravisini-Gerbert, "Colonial and Post-Colonial Gothic: The Caribbean," in *The Cambridge Companion to Gothic Fiction*, ed. Jerrold E. Hogle (Cambridge University Press, 2002), 229.

[9] Smith, *Henrietta*, 102.

[10] David Turley, "Complicating the Story: Religion and Gender in Historical Writing on British and American Anti-Slavery," in *Women, Dissent, and Anti-Slavery in Britain and America, 1790-1865*, edited by Elizabeth J. Clapp and Julie Roy Jeffrey, (Oxford University Press, 2011), 20.

examples. Smith draws on the tradition of creating gothic villains who exhibit sexually predatory behaviors. Smith is less explicit in naming Maynard's perverse sexual violence, but it is clear from Henrietta's experience meeting "the daughters of my father by his black and mulatto slaves" – who have then forced into bondage themselves – that he has raped and engaged with coercive sex with many of the enslaved women on his plantation.[11] He fits the description of the villainous West Indian planter in Thomas Thelwall's 1801 novel *The Daughter of Adoption; A Tale of Modern Times*: "the habits of the order, or *disorder*, of society [in the West Indies] established, had seized, with irrepressible violence, on [his] mind…He had his amours, his intrigues, his sensual revelries; he had also his avaricious projects, his rapacious pursuits, and usurious speculations."[12] As with Maynard, violence is the hallmark of Montfort's character, drawing a direct line between the socio-economic power of the planter, his lack of any recognizable morals, and the sadistic violence he inflicts on others.

Maynard's violent self-interest extends to his treatment of his daughter; while he does not seek an incestuous sexual relationship with her, as other famous gothic fathers do, he does want to trade her – as a marriageable, sexual object – to another man. Shortly after arriving at their Jamaican plantation from England, Amponah, one of the many men enslaved on the plantation, asks unceremoniously: "'Master not tell you, Miss? dat man [Sawkins] is one day n'other to be our master…master give him you, Miss, and all this great rich estates, and pens and all.'"[13] Like the novels discussed in the previous chapter, Maynard's greed compels him to arrange a forced marriage for his daughter Henrietta; as his only child, her marriage presents his best hope of maintaining his vast plantations after his death. He possesses a "strange resolution to *raise* a dependent to the rank of his son-in-law; to make the fortune of a man in humble life wholly dependent on, and owing every thing [sic] to him."[14] This description parallels James Harlowe's dream of "*raising a family*" to financial and political prominence.[15] While the Harlowes attempt to concentrate their

---

[11] Smith, *Henrietta*, 56.

[12] John Thelwall, *The Daughter of Adoption: A Tale of Modern Times*, ed. Michael Scrivener, Yasmin Solomonescu, and Judith Thompson (Broadview Press, 2021), 72. Italics in original.

[13] Smith, *Henrietta*, 117; In this period "pen" could refer to either to a West-Indian estate and its grounds (more frequently spelled "penns,") or the specific locations in which the enslaved were quartered on the plantations; I suspect that Amponah is referring to the former here.

[14] Smith, *Henrietta*, 116. Italics in original.

[15] Richardson, *Clarissa*, 1:77. Italics in original.

family's wealth into James, here Smith indicates that Maynard wants to raise Sawkins out of poverty, creating a debt of gratitude and molding Sawkins into the ideal subordinate. Since Maynard's only son is dead, he wants to ensure that someone whom he approves will take over his plantation. As Michael Craton explains, sugar plantations were the most lucrative West Indian plantations; Jamaica was its own "mini-empire."[16] Historically, those who ruled over this "mini-empire" relied on "dynastic marriages" to make beneficial alliances between plantocratic families.[17] This meant that young women were often treated as pawns in the family business; marriage infused capital into a plantation or joined two abutting plantations, for example.

In a passage that mirrors the language Marx used in the mid-nineteenth century, Henrietta explains that her father is "always accustomed to command, and to look on those about him rather as machines which were to move only at his nod, than as beings who had wills and inclinations of their own, a man of equal or even of affluent or independent fortune would not on these terms become a part of his family."[18] Maynard sees people as "machines": tools for his own enrichment rather than autonomous beings. Exchanging his daughter in marriage to an heir whom he has handpicked, Maynard postulates, will provide his mini-empire with security, just like Lennox's Marquis does in *The Female Quixote*. As Amponah succinctly describes him, Sawkins "is poor man, bad man, cruel man" who possesses the building blocks of an ideal plantation owner.[19] When Henrietta attempts an open dialogue with her father about the impending marriage, she "was forbidden all reply; and ordered not to remonstrate, but to prepare to obey"; Maynard even threatens her life, warning: "any opposition will be fatal to yourself." So obsessed with his own sense of power, Maynard actually threatens to kill his daughter if she does not obey him.[20] The extreme wealth that the slave trade gives Maynard – and its concomitant power – provides ultimate authority over the life and death of everyone in his path.

---

[16] Bernard Crayton, "Strangers within the Realm: The Pomeroon People and the Atlantic World," in *Strangers within the Realm: Cultural Margins of the First British Empire*, ed. B. Bailyn & P. D. Morgan, 241-270 (University of North Carolina Press, 1991), 320.

[17] *Ibid.*, 380.

[18] Smith, *Henrietta*, 118.

[19] *Ibid.*, 117.

[20] *Ibid.*, 118-119.

"The raging multitude": models for resisting the patriarch

In addition to echoing the financially motivated forced marriage that sets off the plot of *Clarissa*, Charlotte Smith adopts and innovates another aspect of Samuel Richardson's novel through her depiction of a previously obedient young woman who gains an awareness of the hegemonic power structures behind her culture's configuration of ideal femininity. As I discussed in chapter one of this book, critics have long noted that *Clarissa* is especially remarkable within the history of the novel for its in-depth depiction of a female consciousness; raised to unquestionably accept the conduct-guide version of submissive femininity taught to her, Clarissa's forced marriage awakens her to the fact that prescribed femininity was intended to keep her from questioning her father's authority – an aspect of the forced marriage plot Smith expands upon to ensure that Henrietta's eventual awakening is clear. For example, when her eventual husband, Denbigh, first meets Henrietta, he is torn between his affection for her and the frustration he feels toward her enactment of submissive femininity. "You must often," Denbigh writes to a friend, "have seen and lamented the occasional weakness of the strongest minds when either from habit or prejudice, they put their understandings into the guidance of others and are either too indolent or too timid to dare to think for themselves."[21] He sees her unquestioning obedience to authority as a character flaw rather than ideal femininity, implying that even intelligent women can fall prey to predatory patriarchal standards. What is better, he implies, is women who use reason and logic to question their circumstances instead of accepting the *status quo* than those who have "feeble mind[s]."[22] For instance, Henrietta is docile and dutiful at the beginning of her narrative, accepting the advice of her chaperone Mrs. Apthorp that "a young woman should have no will of her own."[23] At this early point in the narrative, Henrietta models the cycle that her Uncle George describes later in the novel: "[w]e set out with saying that women must do so and so, and think so and so, as their grandmother and mothers thought before them. If any of them venture even to look as if they had any will of their own or supposed themselves capable of reasoning, how immediately are they marked as some-thing monstrous, absurd, and out of the course of nature."[24] Women, according to late eighteenth-century society, are meant to do as they are told, not develop their own consciousnesses.

---

[21] *Ibid.*, 26.
[22] *Ibid.*, 31.
[23] *Ibid.*, 45.
[24] *Ibid.*, 213-4.

The forced marriage she faces in Jamaica, however, provides Henrietta with a crash course, so to speak, in the patriarchal power structures behind idealized submissive femininity, awakening her to her own desires and the courage necessary to take matters into her own hands, running away from her father's home to save herself from the repulsive marriage. Henrietta's transformation from meek obedience to empowerment is played out more blatantly than in Lennox's and Richardson's forced marriage novels; the narrative explicitly pinpoints the moment in which Henrietta experiences the discovery of her female self to borrow Felski's terminology.[25] "[I]n that moment," Henrietta writes to Denbigh of the moment she discovered her rising sense of self, "I solemnly repeated a vow to Heaven, that never should my hand be given in marriage but to you. Having thus called upon all that is held sacred to witness my unalterable resolution, I felt my courage renewed."[26] Repulsed by the marriage her father tries to force upon her, Henrietta recognizes that she has rights over her own life – and understands that she must act in opposition to socially-acceptable femininity to save herself from the degrading marriage. "I acted on those principles of duty towards my father, and of reverence for the opinion of the world, which every body [sic] around me had taught me," she admits but realizes it is better "that a woman should acquire fixed principles, and upon them act with decision; and that there is nothing else that can prevent that wavering imbecility which makes us the sport of every accident, and often ridiculous as well as wretched."[27] Acquiescing to the culture of feminine submission turns women into victims, according to Henrietta; she understands that "those principles of duty" she was taught were meant to prevent her from developing her own desires or sense of agency – to turn her into a product for her father's disposal.

As she sees it, confronting Sawkins and taking measures to physically escape from her father's home are necessary actions she must take to fight the prescribed "imbecility" and gain some semblance of authority over her future. "My father might take away my life," she tells Sawkins, referring to Maynard's death threats, "but never should compel me to plight at the altar my faith to a man of whom I knew little, and towards whom that little had only served to excite my dislike, nay, even my contempt."[28] Her moment of feminist awakening shatters her previous understanding of femininity and reorients her own performance of femininity to one based on her own autonomy. Like other forced marriage plot heroines, her resistance is rooted in action; Henrietta

---

[25] Felski, *Aesthetics*, 142.
[26] Smith, *Henrietta*, 68-9.
[27] *Ibid.*, 73-4.
[28] *Ibid.*, 69.

confronts her father and Sawkins on multiple occasions, and when her repeated refusals are ignored, Henrietta takes matters into her own hands and runs away from the gothic plantation, which her father has isolated her from any allies. Though, like Clarissa Harlowe, her escape is aided by a man who has sexual ulterior motives (more on that below), Henrietta makes a conscious, strategic decision to take the only escape route available. When Amponah, an enslaved man formerly forced to work for Henrietta's late brother, provides intel that Maynard, Sawkins, and the minister hired to perform the forced marriage will arrive at the residence where Henrietta has been isolated, she sees no other option than to follow his advice and escape, physically removing herself from the situation. "The scheme was plausible," she writes to Denbigh, "my situation was desperate, and to deliberate was, I thought, to hazard irrevocable misery."[29] Though she does not fully trust Amponah – much like Clarissa does not trust Lovelace – Maynard has purposefully created a scenario in which Henrietta has no other option than to follow his orders. Or so he thinks. Like her fellow heroically disobedient heroines, Henrietta is a woman of action for whom even the risk of warring Maroons and their enslaved brethren is not as bad as the degradation of a forced marriage.

"The Story of Henrietta" and colonial unrest

Violence permeates every aspect of "The Story of Henrietta"; from the death threats Maynard lofts at his daughter to his prodigious violence against the enslaved and Maroons – including his prolific sexual violence against enslaved women – it all emanates from the planter, whose sense of superiority is fueled by the legal power his society affords him over his subordinates. He is a perfect example of a Filmerian father figure who sees himself as the monarch, or, in this case, perhaps the despot, of his world, believing that his authority must go unquestioned, a configuration of fatherhood that defies Locke's enlightened understanding of fatherhood, which "puts no scepter into the father's hand, no sovereign power of commanding."[30] While Locke believed that a father "has no dominion over his son's property or actions; nor any right, that his will should prescribe to his son's in all things," Smith's version of the forced marriage plot shows that this imperative applies to women too.[31] That is, Henrietta comes to understand that her father's tyranny over her life is groundless, and it is necessary for her to act on her convictions to save herself from a life of submission. Her rebellion against her father's rule, running away from his

---

[29] *Ibid.*, 140.
[30] Locke, *Second Treatise*, 40.
[31] *Ibid.*, 40.

"Will there not be virtue in my resistance?" 43

home on the eve of her wedding, coincides with a rebellion by the Marooned and enslaved black people on the island, a move that gestures toward the political nature of Henrietta's actions. These dual rebellions – Henrietta's and the black Jamaicans' – create a link between the two groups that underscores the shared source of their oppression. That is, there is no way for either women or the enslaved to move forward if the slave trade – here represented with Maynard as a figurehead – exists.

Gesturing beyond her fictional world to her historical moment, Smith shows that legislation and social movements were not making sufficient progress. So disaffected with British society after his failed attempts at emancipating his family's enslaved workers, George Maynard, for example, believes, "where will he who ventures to dissent from established prejudices, and to controvert the maxims of policy which the tyranny of custom has established, that the strong may trample on the weak — where, I say, will he who dares do this, go and not find enemies?"[32] According to "The Story of Henrietta," the only way to defeat what George calls "the tyranny of custom" and move toward a society in which both black people and women are liberated is to dethrone the tyrants who uphold their connected oppression.

Published in the aftermath of several historical West Indian uprisings, including the Second Maroon War (Jamaica, 1795-6) and the Haitian Revolution (Saint Domingue, 1791-1804), "The Story of Henrietta" provides commentary on historical rebellions that took place in the Caribbean world. During the 1730s and again in the 1790s, British colonizers fought highly publicized battles against Jamaican Maroons over issues including the Maroons' land rights, political autonomy, and their role in aiding escaped slaves. "The Second Maroon War was both a colonial war fought in the cockpit country of Jamaica, and a war of words fought out across the Atlantic geography of Britain's empire...a paper war," according to Miles Ogborn.[33] Many popular books on the subject were printed in this period, including Bryan Edward's influential *The History, Civil and Commercial, of the British Colonies in the West Indies* (1793), which went through five successive editions and was translated into Spanish, French, German, and Dutch. This text spawned a huge flurry of responses, including Robert Charles Dallas' popular *The History of the Maroons* (1803). Additionally, most local newspapers regularly featured articles by special West Indian correspondents or picked up stories from the colonial papers. These became especially popular during the Second Maroon War as

---

[32] Smith, *Henrietta*, 287-88.

[33] Miles Ogborn, "A war of words: speech, print, and script in the Maroon War of 1795-6," *Journal of Historical Geography* 37 (2011): 204.

local magistrates in Jamaica and their supporters in Parliament tried to justify the war by vilifying the free and escaped black persons on the island. Borrowing from the lexicon of gothic literature, one July 1796 story claimed the Maroons were "banditti who had entered into a most dangerous and ungrateful rebellion."[34] Those who supported the slave trade and British commercial interests in the West Indies were eager to suppress the Maroons as quickly and with as much force as possible to maintain sugar production on the island.

The connection between the literature of the 1790s and the violence of the revolutions that took place in the West Indies (not to mention other uprisings in France, Ireland, America, and Gordon Riots in London) is an important one, and one that can help decode Smith's stance toward enslavement in "The Story of Henrietta." While many British accounts of these uprisings emphasized the perceived barbarity of the black rebels – thus justifying the need for British control – there existed those who believed the opposite: that violence is the only way to overthrow tyranny. As Ottobah Cugoano puts it in his *Thoughts and Sentiments on the Evil of Slavery*, first published in 1791:

> For we may be assured that God will certainly avenge himself of such heinous transgressors of his law, and of all those planters and merchants, and of all others, who are the authors of the Africans graves, severities, and cruel punishments, and no plea of any absolute necessity can possibly excuse them…It is therefore necessary that the inhabitants of the British nation should seriously consider [emancipation] for their own good and safety, as well as for our benefit and deliverance, and that they may be sensible of their own error and danger, lest they provoke the vengeance of the Almighty against them.[35]

Speaking in the first person from the perspective of a formerly-enslaved person, Cugoano warns that all Britons – not just those directly involved in the slave trade – are committing such a heinous sin in allowing the trade to persist that they are risking vengeance from their God. Published, like "The Story of Henrietta," amidst a spate of revolutions (including several in the West Indies, the context to which Cugoano refers), it is easy to see that he is implying that the Almighty's vengeance may very well come from the uprising of the enslaved. Noting they must be fearful of their safety and are in danger, he brings

---

[34] "The Maroon War," *Times* (London), 8 July 1796, The Times Digital Archive, accessed 24 Jan. 2018.

[35] Ottobah Cugoano, *Thoughts and Sentiments on the Evil of Slavery* (Penguin Classics, 1999), 84.

urgency to the situation, making it clear that white oppressors will face retribution for their sins.

Thomas Thelwall makes a similar case in *The Daughter of Adoption*, in which two British men, one a kindly, benevolent slave owner and the other a member of *Amis des Noirs*, argue whether those enslaved on the Island of Saint Domingue are justified in their uprising.[36] Parkinson, who possesses two enslaved men but paradoxically claims to believe in emancipation, claims, "I wish for their emancipation as eagerly as you can. I would die to emancipate them; but I cannot wish for their revolt."[37] Obvious hypocrisy aside, Parkinson believes that emancipation must be done through English political and legal channels, claiming that violence against white planters will inevitably turn public favor against emancipation and set progress back. Edmunds, however, urges: "If you were a poor negro, Sir, and had been stolen away from your parents, your friends, and your country, if you had been dragged in chains and fetters across the ocean, in a vile floating charnel house, been sold to stripes and bondage by a vile man stealer…you, sir, would have done, what I am sure I should, and what these poor nergoes [sic] have."[38] He explains that the island's enslaved population is not just justified in their violence but that they have no other choice. Thelwall's Edmunds, like Cugoano, makes it clear that white men will not save the oppressed – the oppressed must try and seize autonomy for themselves.

The necessity of meeting violence with violence is on display in "The Story of Henrietta," as well, where characters trapped by Maynard's greed and power are left with no other options. For instance, Henrietta notes that the Maroon community "is frequently increased by fugitive negroes, and is lately become so formidable, that means have been devised wholly to extirpate and destroy them; which is, perhaps, very politic, but I can hardly think it just."[39] That is, the planters are so threatened by the Maroons that they plan to eradicate the population, hoping to both eliminate the threat they pose and discourage their own enslaved workers from trying to escape bondage. Given the context and contemporary usages of the word "politic," Henrietta is saying that, though violence against slaves was legal, such bloody antagonism is unfair.[40] A driving

---

[36] A French anti-slavery society founded in the late eighteenth century.

[37] Thelwall, *Daughter*, 160.

[38] *Ibid.*, 160.

[39] Smith, *Henrietta*, 92.

[40] The Oxford English Dictionary notes that "politic" can mean: "Of an action or thing: judicious, expedient, sensible; skillfully contrived," though an archaic use of the world (that also fits Henrietta's meaning) is: "Of or relating to a constitutional state, as opposed

force behind this extermination, Maynard is known "to be particularly obnoxious to them."[41] He "had indulged his vindictive temper in great and unjustifiable severities towards the people upon all his estates; severities which served only to irritate the minds even of those who had till then most faithfully adhered to him."[42] It is Maynard's violent cruelty against the enslaved people imprisoned on his plantations that turns them against him – he brings their violence upon himself. These are not African "savages" revolting against their kindly white overseers out of spite or greed, as plantocrats commonly framed the conflict, but unfairly enslaved people rejecting the arbitrary violence inflicted upon them.

That's not to say, however, that "The Story of Henrietta" is void of racism: in fact, the text is rife with racist depictions of enslaved people and Maroons. The drama of Henrietta's escape from her father's home is heightened by a score of violent black men who are obvious sexual threats to Henrietta and jealous, violent, lascivious black women. The racism of these stereotypes will be addressed in more detail below, but it is pertinent to note that these black Maroons are more complex than they appear at first glance. For instance, it is relevant that the Maroon soldiers who frighten Henrietta so much are bedecked in an uncanny hodgepodge of British apparel and accessories, a visual reminder of how the British have caused this situation. As Denbigh describes them, they are passionate "savages…in whom the fierce inclination for European women was now likely to be exalted by the desire of revenge on a man so detested as the father of my unhappy Henrietta!"[43] That is, their presumably innate desire for white women (a common racist trope discussed in more detail below) is exacerbated by the tyranny of white men: these Maroons want revenge on Maynard for his unspeakable violence against them, which Denbigh speculates may manifest as sexual violence against Henrietta. It is also pertinent to note that though they are alarmed by the behavior of the Maroons, neither Denbigh nor Henrietta would have survived the violence of the uprising without their help; the Maroons save Henrietta from Amponah's attempted rape and save Denbigh from bleeding to death in the forest after he is shot in the scuffle of the uprising. In fact, they make it clear that they do not see Denbigh as a threat (he is a Jacobean and anti-slavery advocate) – only the planters and their supporters are. There is a sort of code of conduct to which

---

to a despotic one; constitutional. See: "politic, adj. and n.," *OED Online*, Oxford University Press, December 2019, accessed January 31, 2020.

[41] Smith, *Henrietta*, 92.
[42] *Ibid.*, 148.
[43] *Ibid.*, 114.

they adhere: they kill Maynard in retribution for his violence against them and their enslaved brethren but have nothing against Denbigh, so they help him. The Maroons follow the code of Thelwall's character Mozambo, an enslaved man who explains: "me love poor negro man, whom cruel white man whip to die. Me love poor negro man, who hab no bed to lie in but dirt; who groan, and sweat, and toil...Me murder him who murder.'"[44] There are many racist elements to Mozambo's characterization, including his uneducated dialect, but what is radical about Mozambo is Thelwall's portrayal of his deep emotional connection to his people and the justice in his own acts of violence. While Smith's black characters do not display the same emotional depth and were not, perhaps, as likable to eighteenth-century readers as Mozambo, there is nonetheless an element of subversion in her portrayal of them; their character flaws can almost always be related back to their experiences as victims of white oppression. As Henrietta's Uncle George states, "[m]isery...is, indeed, the certain concomitant of slavery. It follows with undeviating step the tyrant who imposes and the slave who endures the fetters."[45] That is, the slave trade causes a ripple effect of misery, corrupting everything that falls under its influence, including the lives of the enslaved and the lives of women.

Violence as a justified form of retributive justice against tyrants and the misery they cause is a theme that appears elsewhere in Smith's *oeuvre*, indicating Smith's sustained belief in the idea. For instance, in her 1793 poem *The Emigrants* (1793) the speaker warns:

...if oppress'd too long,
The raging multitude, to madness stung,
Will turn on their oppressors; and, no more
By sounding titles and parading forms
Bound like tame victims, will redress themselves![46]

The speaker explains that most of the French population – urban and rural poor – were pushed to a breaking point by their "oppressors," wealthy aristocrats and the Catholic Church, who disenfranchised the poor and took advantage of their labor. In other words, they brought the violence of revolution on themselves. Implicit in this argument is the possibility that the same pattern of violence against the ruling class might repeat itself in England. As Kerri Andrews paraphrases the poem: "Britain must either reform or find itself embroiled in a

---

[44] Thelwall, *Daughter*, 162-3.
[45] Smith, *Henrietta*, 138.
[46] Charlotte Smith, "The Emigrants," in *Major Poetical Works*, ed. Knowles and Horrocks (Broadview Press, 2017), lines 1.333-7.

bloody chaos."[47] This violence, however, is not necessarily bad. Andrews puts forth that "war, the poem concludes, has a cleansing effect which, though violent, is nevertheless of benefit."[48] Readers are left with the notion that revolution and insurrection are necessary reactions to tyranny. When applied to "The Story of Henrietta," this allows readers to see that, as Henrietta is morally justified in disobeying her father and taking open action against him by running away, so too are the Maroons and slaves justified in rebelling against their oppressive master. Furthermore, the fact that the unjust ruler in both cases is the same person highlights the intricate ways in which the institution of slavery and the oppressive ways in which marriages were contracted for young women, both driven by economic, selfish greed, are connected to and enable each other.

Smith's fiction and poetry enact Mary Wollstonecraft's call to "root out those deleterious plants, which poison the better half of human happiness," as she argues in her 1794 *Historical and Moral View of the Origin and Progress of the French Revolution*.[49] Like Smith, Wollstonecraft defends the French Revolution long after most of her initially enthusiastic peers tempered their support in the wake of the September massacres of 1792. Without specifically condoning the Terror, she makes a clear argument that violence is a sometimes-necessary tool:

> If the degeneracy of the higher orders of society be such, that no remedy less fraught with horrour [sic] can effect a radical cure; and if enjoying the fruits of usurpation, they domineer over the weak, and check by all the means in their power every humane effort, to draw man out of the state of degradation, into which the inequality of fortune has sunk him; the people are justified in having recourse to coercion, to repel coercion.[50]

White, wealthy, politically powerful men created a world in which the lower classes have no legal or democratic methods by which to contest the unfair treatment they suffer. In these cases, according to Wollstonecraft, violent uprisings are the only available option. She goes on to state that "[f]or civilization hitherto, by producing the inequality of conditions, which makes wealth more desirable than either talents or virtue, has so weakened all the organs of the body-politic…The rich have for ages tyrannized over the poor…

---

[47] Kerri Andrews, "'Herself… Fills The Foreground': Negotiating Autobiography in the Elegiac Sonnets and the Emigrants," in *Charlotte Smith in British Romanticism*, ed. Jacqueline M. Labbe and Mark Parker (Routledge, 2008), 22.

[48] Andrews, "Negotiating," 23.

[49] Mary Wollstonecraft, *Historical and Moral View of the Origin and Progress of the French Revolution and the Effect it Has Produced in Europe* (London, 1794), 71.

[50] *Ibid.*, 70.

How, in fact, can we expect to see men live together like brothers when we only see master and servant in society?"[51] The inequalities underlying the French Revolution, Wollstonecraft explains, exist in England, as well, resulting in a distinct threat of justified violence against the oppressive classes.

Smith and slavery: a complicated tale

While it is unquestionable that "The Story of Henrietta" criticizes the cruelty of the slave trade and the inhumanity of its perpetrators, it is also crucial to address the extent to which "The Story of Henrietta" perpetuates racist depictions of black Africans and their descendants. As Paravisini-Gerbert puts it, "the terrors of the heroine's situation are exacerbated by her atavistic fears of Jamaica's African-derived magicoreligious practice of Obeah and the possibility of sexual attack by black males."[52] Common racist stereotypes fill the narrative: black men are often violent and sexually threatening, and black women are simple-minded and overly sexualized. Such depictions were common across late-nineteenth-century literature, including the source material Smith consulted for "The Story of Henrietta," Edward Long's deeply racist *The History of Jamaica* (1774).[53] Smith accepts his depictions of enslaved Africans as threatening and lascivious, heightening the terrors that Henrietta experiences. Smith's utilization of these racist stereotypes begs the question: to what degree does this narrative (or Smith personally) support the plight of the enslaved and Maroons if it perpetuates these stereotypes?

This question is a major point of contention among critics. Adrian Craciun, for instance, notes that while Smith portrays "an obvious discomfort" with West Indian slavery, she ultimately "did not take an abolitionist stance when exploring the slave plantations that her protagonists encounter, instead portraying slavery as morally ambiguous."[54] On the one hand, this seems like a sound argument. In addition to the racist stereotypes of black and Creole people within the novel, there is one point in the narrative in which Henrietta declares her father "has been used to purchase slaves and feels no repugnance in selling his daughter to the most dreadful of all slavery."[55] The marriage that her father contracts is certainly cruel and deeply embedded in notions of absolute male power, but it does not compare with the experiences of chattel

---

[51] *Ibid.*, 71.

[52] Paravisini-Gerbert, "Colonial and Post-Colonial Gothic," 229.

[53] Smith asked her associate James Upton Tripp for a copy of this in March 1793 (See Stanton, ed. 114).

[54] Craicun, "'Empire without end,'" 40.

[55] Smith, *Henrietta*, 121.

slaves: it is decidedly not "the most dreadful of all slavery." Historical documents and penal codes reveal the brutally violent treatment that displaced Africans and their descendants suffered. Reading Henrietta's statement uncritically is irresponsible.

There is also Smith's personal proximity to the slave trade to consider: despite Smith's popularity among scholars; it is a little-discussed fact that she owned enslaved people. Charlotte's father-in-law, Richard Smith, owned several sugar plantations in Barbados, which his wastrel son Benjamin took over upon his father's death. After Smith's separation from Benjamin, she dealt with the plantation agents herself: a task she found distasteful but necessary, given her constant poverty. Shortly before her death in 1806 she referred to "Barbados traders" as "Men who are notorious for their total want of honesty and who do not even affect the semblance of it."[56] Additionally, she blamed the Smith plantations for the death of her son Charles, who died there while looking into the plantation's mismanagement (Smith suspected someone was embezzling). In fact, in 1804 Smith suggested that her son was murdered by someone on the plantation, writing of Charles' dealings with a local agent in Barbados that: "of His death, the wretch took advantage, & such is my opinion from long & fatal experience of the people in Barbados that I should not be surprised if his death had been hasten'd."[57] So low was Smith's opinion of the men who ran the British West Indian sugar industry that she believed them capable of murder or for financial gain. It is no wonder, then, that in her fiction, such men are represented as the worst examples of corrupt and immoral power.

However, scholars must stop ignoring the fact that Smith benefitted from the slave trade: she was not an innocent bystander, despite her disdain for those who ran the plantations. For instance, in a letter she wrote in 1800, Smith lists the prices of several enslaved people she recently sold, including "one Slave named Bennah…a very old Woman worth nothing; her death therefore & that of the old Men is rather a relief than a disadvantage to the Estate."[58] It is difficult to grasp how Smith can express such radical opinions in her fiction yet also write this passage. How do readers come to terms with this? Was Smith pandering to abolitionist sympathies in her literature for commercial success? Did she believe in abolition in the abstract but not apply this belief to her personal life?

---

[56] Charlotte Smith, *Charlotte Smith, The Collected Letters of Charlotte Smith*, ed. Judith Phillips Stanton (Indiana UP, 2003), 738.
[57] *Ibid.*, 604.
[58] *Ibid.*, 404.

I suggest following the lead of Carol Fry, who sees the racism of Smith's texts and her involvement in the slave trade as indicative not of anti-abolitionism but of the racism inherent in the abolition movement itself. "A republican in all issues," she explains, "Smith opposed slavery. But despite her philosophical opposition to the institution, she reveals the same racial prejudice shared by many others committed to the abolition movement."[59] It is not just Smith who utilizes racist stereotypes in her treatment of black characters; racist understandings of racial hierarchies were embedded in the abolition movement itself.[60] This recognition that the British abolition movement was racist, I argue, is key in understanding the complex stance that Smith takes on slavery in "The Story of Henrietta." That is, ideologies from this period were often racist and abolitionist conterminously; just because an individual or organization advocated for the freedom of the enslaved that does not mean black persons were considered equal to white Europeans.[61] In *An Appeal to the Religion, Justice, and Humanity of the Inhabitants of the British Empire, in Behalf of the Negro Slaves in the West Indies* (1823), for instance, William Wilberforce – who is often hailed a white savior to the enslaved – claims that the enslaved are "below the level of human beings," an argument that supports hierarchal theories of race.[62] Abolitionists such as Wilberforce ultimately blame the plantation system and evils of the slave trade for keeping the enslaved in a degraded state, but twenty-first-century critics must acknowledge that most white Europeans believed Africans and their descendants were morally and intellectually inferior. Overlooking this fact does a disservice to the history of the enslaved and their descendants, whose path to freedom is more complicated than late-eighteenth-century abolitionists admit. Despite links fostered between Henrietta and the enslaved via their shared revolution, Smith's narrative inevitably supports larger theories of racial hierarchies that were so prominent in her period.

---

[59] Carol Fry, "'Misery is...the Certain Concomitant of Slavery': The British Anti-Slavery Movement in Charlotte Smith's Novels," *PMPA* 2002-2003, no. 27 (2002): 45.

[60] Here I use "abolition movement" to indicate the political movement lead by white Europeans, not the actions taken by the enslaved and their allies.

[61] See also Clare Midgley, "British Women, Women's Rights and Empire, 1790-1850," in *Women's Rights and Human Rights: International Perspectives*, ed. Grimshaw, Holmes, and Lake (Palgrave, 2001). She argues: "despite assertions of international and cross-race sisterhood" that comparing white women and black slaves created, "these comparisons tended to work against any notion of full equality. In both cases British social and cultural superiority is stressed, but there was a shift to a more racialised – a more racist – conception of the basis of this superiority" (164-5).

[62] William Wilberforce, *An Appeal to the Religion, Justice, and Humanity of the Inhabitants of the British Empire, in Behalf of the Negro Slaves in the West Indies* (London, 1823), 10.

Do these eighteenth-century notions of racial inferiority, then, negate any abolitionist arguments in "The Story of Henrietta"? George Boulukos would likely say yes, given his description of its abolitionism as "discouraging."[63] Arguing that Smith thought that the political climate in Jamaica – along with the inferiority of enslaved West Indians – was too corrupt to reform, he explains that "[b]rutalization," by which he means a position of extreme subjection, "can produce enlightenment in whites, but only serves to confirm the inherent brutality of Africans."[64] That is, he argues that in "The Story of Henrietta," white characters like Henrietta experience enlightenment and can excise tyranny from their lives, but black characters, due to their primitive natures and the demeaning circumstances of their bondage, are incapable of such self-enlightenment. In "The Story of Henrietta," Smith portrays black characters as intellectually and (frequently) morally inferior, yet the narrative still contains an argument for their freedom alongside a condemnation of the tyrannous system that encourages men like Maynard to value individual economic gain above all else.

Both this narrative and Smith's personal dealings with the slave trade shape it as a system that blights all in its path. However, it is also a system with immense political weight supporting it. As George's failed attempts to free their family's slaves shows, those in power will stay there unless extreme measures remove them. The "maxims of policy which the tyranny of custom has established" dictate, according to George, "that the strong may trample on the weak."[65] George's political reforms were destined to fail, leaving the more drastic revolutions enacted by the Maroons and enslaved as the only path forward. In "The Story of Henrietta," unauthorized rebellion, as opposed to institutional change, emerge as the only possibility for escaping unjust oppression. As Henrietta is justified in her refusal to obey her father's command that she marry Sawkins and in her decision to run away to escape his tyranny, so too are the enslaved and Maroons vindicated for escaping Maynard and for deposing the figurehead of the plantation system. In this sense, "The Story of Henrietta" can be read as a pro-abolition text, but one in which emancipation (from slavery and from tyrannical family ties) is initiated by the subjects themselves rather than through any institutional assistance.

---

[63] George E. Boulukos, "The Horror of Hybridity: Enlightenment, Anti-slavery and Racial Disgust in Charlotte Smith's Story of Henrietta (1800)," in *Slavery and the Cultures of Abolition: Essays Marking the Bicentennial of the British Abolition Act of 1807*, ed. Brycchan Carey and Peter J. Kitson (Woodbridge: Boydell & Brewer Ltd, 2007), 87.
[64] *Ibid.*, 102.
[65] Smith, *Henrietta*, 287-8.

Fighting against the "proud Lords of Traffic": Mary Robinson's *Angelina*

Given her formidable stage career and her infamous affairs with famous men like the Prince of Wales and Charles James Fox, Mary Robinson's personal life is often of greater interest to scholars than her writing. However, Robinson saw herself as a poet and novelist on par with the best of her day; critics have been slowly moving toward recognizing her literary accomplishments, primarily in terms of her poems, but more recently, her novels, as well.[66] Robinson was an outspoken advocate for women's rights who boldly depicted the sometimes-horrific realities that many poor, outcast women faced. Her novel *Angelina; A Novel* also adapts *Clarissa*'s forced marriage plot to explore the material connections between the slave trade and the subordination of women, showing the causal connection between the socio-economic power of the plantation owner and the continued need for women who are submissive to patriarchal authority.

Angelina; A Novel draws the reader's attention to the ways in which the capitalist ethos of wealth accumulation led to men using women as pawns in the pursuit of wealth and power. The epistolary novel begins with Lovelace-like Lord Acreland lamenting the fact that his aristocratic family has fallen on hard times. He writes to his friend Sir Fairford that his situation is a common one; he is confident that he will find a "wealthy upstart" on the watch for "needy nobility" with whom he can trade his title and associations for an influx of capital to save his estate.[67] Chapter one of this project analyzes the ways in which the emergent middle class, such as merchants like the Harlowe family, amassed enough wealth to buy considerable socio-political influence. The Harlowes want to buy a peerage for James since they recognize that a title is a stepping stone to power. Sir Edward Clarendon, the tyrannical father in this novel, can be seen as a manifestation of the Harlowe family's scheme. The "rich West India merchant," as Lord Acreland describes him, "not content with having received the dignity of knighthood, was eager in the pursuit of more substantial honors."[68] That is, even though Sir Edward has extreme wealth –

---

[66] Jennifer L. Airey, "'Abused, Neglected,—Unhonoured,—Unrewarded': The Economics of Authorial Labor in the Writings of Mary Robinson," ABO: Interactive Journal for Women in the Arts, 1640-1830 6 (1), 2016, https://doi.org/10.5038/2157-7129.6.1.1; Craciun, *Fatal Women*; Elizabeth Fay, "Mary Robinson: On Trial in the Public Court, *Studies in Romanticism* 45, no. 3 (2006); and Sharon M. Setzer, "The Marriage Market, the Slave Trade and the 'Cruel Business' of War in Mary Robinson's Angelina," in *Didactic Novels and British Women's Writing, 1790-1820*, edited by Hilary Havens (Routledge, 2017) have been crucial to the renaissance of Robinson studies.

[67] Mary Robinson, *Angelina; A Novel* (Dublin, 1796), 1:3.

[68] *Ibid.*, 1:5.

and was even able to purchase a title just as James Harlowe hopes to do – he is not content and seeks an alliance with one of England's most respected and ancient families will provide him with even more influence. The inverse circumstance applies to Lord Acreland, who has an ancestral title and estate but is running out of capital to maintain them. Rich upstarts like Sir Edward Clarendon, an absentee plantation owner, present an opportunity for liquid assets; Acreland hopes to marry Sophia, Sir Edward's daughter, who would bring a large dowry to the marriage. Daniel Defoe describes this dynamic as a common occurrence in his 1728 *A Plan of the English Commerce*, in which he explains:

> The ancient Families, who living wasted and exhausted their Estates, and being declin'd and decay'd in Fortune by Luxury and high Living, have restor'd and rais'd themselves again, by mixing Blood with the despis'd Tradesmen, marrying the Daughters of such Tradesmen, as being overgrown in Wealth, have been oblig'd, for want of Sons, to leave their Estates to their Female Issue…As thus the decay'd Estates of the Nobility and Gentry have been restored, and their Family Wounds heal'd by the Daughters of the richer Tradesmen.[69]

Gentility and nobility disdained the meteoric rise of tradesmen, according to Defoe (Sir Edward is elsewhere called an "illiterate grub"), but their wealth enticed the aristocracy to seek out inter-class marriages between their sons and daughters in order to undo generations of squandering wealth.[70] Or, as Lord Acreland puts it: "we constantly behold young women of little birth, and great fortune, as indelicately exposed to sale, as our horses or our hounds."[71] Women are commodified as objects of exchange between men: conduits for the transfer of wealth and influence. As Sir Edward puts it, "All's fair in the way of business…we buy honour, and they have little to sell, therefore the commodity is rare and demands a good price: coronets are often on sale in the city."[72] Plainly calling Sophia "the commodity," it is obvious that Sir Edward has no respect for her personhood. Anything done in the name of business is, to him, justified: Sophia is nothing but a pawn in their business dealings.

---

[69] Daniel Defoe, "A Plan of the English Commerce: Being a Compleat Prospect of the Trade of this Nation, as Well the Home Trade as the Foreign; in Three Parts [...]," in *The Novels and Selected Writings of Daniel Defoe*, ed. William K. Wimsatt Jr. and Ronald S. Crane, vol. 7 (Shakespeare Head Press, 1927), 349-480. 61.

[70] Robinson, *Angelina*, 1:71.

[71] *Ibid.*, 1:3.

[72] *Ibid.*, 2:122.

Sophia refuses this commodification, proving herself a strong-willed heroine. While Henrietta had to face the prospect of a forced marriage in order to awaken her own consciousness, the liberal education Sophia received from her Aunt Juliana, a radical Wollstonecraft-like figure who is "a perfect judge of the antique, and had read the most admired Greek and Latin authors in their original languages; to say the truth," and, Lord Acreland concludes, "an enlightened and intelligent female."[73] Juliana has "cultivate[d]" Sophia's "mental graces," which Acreland posits will "compensate for the ignorance and vulgarity of the good knight her father."[74] Instead of emphasizing physical allurements meant to attract a husband, Juliana develops Sophia's intellect, her "mental graces," as Acreland terms them, to foster reason and intelligence. Travel and the study of literature are the cornerstone of Sophia's education; Juliana has followed Wollstonecraft's notion that "[r]eading is the most rational employment, if people seek food for the understanding, and do not read merely to remember words; or with a view to quote celebrated authors...Judicious books enlarge the mind and improve the heart."[75] Wollstonecraft, whose writings regularly draw attention to the gender-based inequalities of enlightenment ideologies, advocates teaching women to exercise reason, seeing a young woman "who submits, without conviction, to a parent or husband" as possessing a "weakness of mind."[76] She echoes this more forcefully in her *A Vindication of the Rights of Woman*, where she urges women "to endeavor to acquire strength, both of mind and body, and to convince them that the soft phrases, susceptibility of heart, a delicacy of sentiment, and refinement of taste, are almost synonymous with epithets of weakness" that men intentionally foster to keep women submissive.[77]

Her non-traditional, Wollstonecraft-esque education inculcates Sophia with critical thinking skills and deep knowledge of her own personal value, which she knows is greater than the socioeconomic value her father sees in her. *Angelina*'s epistolary style allows readers to inhabit Sophia's independent mind and empathize with her reason and morals; from her first introduction to the readers, her sense of heroic disobedience is strong. "The wealth which Sir Edward has accumulated by days of labour and nights of calculation is at last appropriated – to what? To the purchase of a title for an only daughter! Thus

---

[73] *Ibid.*, 1:7.

[74] *Ibid.*, 1:7.

[75] Mary Wollstonecraft, *Thoughts on the Education of Daughters: With Reflections on Female Conduct, in the More Important Duties of Life* (London: J. Johnson, 1787), 49.

[76] *Ibid.*, 63.

[77] Mary Wollstonecraft, *A Vindication of the Rights on Women* (1792), ed. Janet Todd (Oxford World Classics, 2008) 73.

will he ennoble his family by a sacrifice of one, whose happiness ought to be his first consideration," she writes to her friend Mrs. Horton: "Oh! blind and mistaken parent; thou art the dupe of that ambition, which will only render thee an object of contempt to the wise, of pity to the compassionate."[78] She firmly declares: "I will not add to the degraded phalanx of mercenary victims."[79] Aware of her father's endless pursuit of wealth and status, she understands that she must defy his will: a task that will bring challenges. "My father has the free disposal of my fortune; but my mind is still unshackled. I may be driven from his house; – stung by his reproaches, condemned by the world; but will there not be virtue in my resistance?"[80] Because of the accepted notions of ideal femininity as submissive to patriarchal authority, many in her social sphere will condemn her perceived disobedience. However, Sophia has the intellectual acuity to know that resisting the patriarch is not a sign of disobedience but a marker of bravely privileging one's own values. She is one step ahead of Clarissa Harlowe and Henrietta Maynard, whom readers see come into an awareness of their right to make important life decisions.

Sophia comes out swinging against her father's demands. She begs, bargains, and tries to reason with Sir Edward. When he refuses to budge, she takes matters into her own hands and flees their rural mansion, hiding with various friends across the British countryside. The remainder of the novel consists of a cat-and-mouse chase between Sir Edward and Sophia; though she constantly moves between the homes of friends she thinks will be safe, he is always on her tail, causing chaos and fear wherever he shows up.

Sir Edward's gothic consumption

Angelina; A Novel contains many gothic motifs that harken back to earlier gothic novels, like Horace Walpole's *The Castle of Otranto* (1764) – crumbling castles, ghostly visions, haunted churches – that foster an eerie atmosphere. However, like Smith, the gothic atmosphere that Robinson employs in her writing of the forced marriage plot reveals that evil emanates not from the supernatural but from the patriarch. After Sophia runs away from home to escape the forced marriage, he pursues her across the countryside, doggedly hunting her. Like a true gothic villain, his pursuit is threatening Sophia's life and freedom. At one point, he jumps out of a carriage, exclaiming: "Have I caught you?" while grabbing Sophia at gunpoint.[81] The novel even contains a dramatic

---

[78] Robinson, *Angelina*, 1:12.
[79] *Ibid.*, 1:54.
[80] *Ibid.*, 1:12.
[81] *Ibid.*, 2:139.

chase scene: "I thought I should expire!" Sophia insists when her father finally catches her.[82] Like many a gothic heroine before her, Sophia "is made a prisoner" in the tower of a rural Abbey by her tyrannous father.[83]

A specific aspect of Sir Edward's characterization as a gothic monster comes from connections forged between him and a cannibal: his fixation on consumption. Sir Edward is a "blustering, rude, disagreeable, money-breeding savage" who "understands nothing but eating."[84] He "mistakes profusion for hospitality, and magnificence for taste: his attention fatigues, his conversation disgusts" and he "guzzles [wine] from morning to night."[85] In his own words, Sir Edward claims: "[l]ife is not life, my Lord, without good eating and drinking," as if his appetite were just an innocent indulgence.[86] When read in connection to the gothic cannibal, however, Sir Edward's appetite appears more sinister. Cannibal violation "evokes torture and murder, rape and incest – often in folklore involving the victimization of the most innocent, of children, boys, and young women," according to Howard L. Malchow.[87] Or, as Patrick Brantlinger puts it, the British "treat[ed] cannibalism as the nadir of savagery, the complete antithesis of civilization."[88] Such descriptions aptly apply to Sir Edward. For instance, after hunting the English countryside for Sophia, he barges in on the woman with whom she has been hiding. Wildly drunk, he declares: "here you are, my tasty ones," while insisting, "a city lady wouldn't deny a body a harmless kiss – I'm not going to eat you."[89] His demands for kisses and threats to eat the women are especially threatening since Sir Edward is also holding a gun and has locked the women in the room with him, promising to shoot anyone who tries to leave. While there is certainly humor in the scene (an absurd feathered headdress worn by one of the more obnoxious characters ignites in flames, and readers are eventually clued into the fact that the gun – unbeknownst to Sir Edward – is not loaded), the bottom line is that Sir Edward, with his creepy threats to eat the women, feels entitled to make demands from women and does not hesitate to hold them at gunpoint to obtain what he wants. Speaking of Robinson's poetry, Judith Pascoe argues: "Robinson juxtaposes tales of abjection with humorous tales, but the humor is of a dark variety" that expose

---

[82] *Ibid.*, 2:197.

[83] *Ibid.*, 2:237.

[84] *Ibid.*, 1:71, 74.

[85] *Ibid.*, 1:147, 149.

[86] *Ibid.*, 1:147-8.

[87] Howard L. Malchow, *Gothic Images of Race in Nineteenth-Century Britain* (Stanford University Press, 1996), 43.

[88] Patrick Brantlinger, *Taming Cannibals: Race and the Victorians* (Cornell UP, 2011), 66.

[89] Robinson, *Angelina*, 2:266.

abuses of power.[90] This same dynamic applies to *Angelina; A Novel*, as well. Readers are not likely to fear that Sir Edward will literally eat the women, but his violent threats liken him to a cannibal, underscoring his monstrous nature.

The version of cannibalism portrayed through Sir Edward, however, is unusual in that, typically, contemporary depictions of cannibalism villainized black or brown subjects (often of African descent), not white Europeans. Cannibals were commonplace in late eighteenth-and early nineteenth-century gothic fiction and were typically aligned with racialized depictions of an exotic, dark other. In Cynric R. Williams' *Hamel, the Obeah Man* (1827), a classic Caribbean gothic novel set against the backdrop of unrest in colonial Jamaica, for example, a white missionary who stumbles upon an Obeah ritual is attacked by a cannibal whose teeth have been sharpened "as to make them resemble those of a cat, and render them narrow and sharp as needles."[91] "He gnashed these in the face of his shuddering suppliant; and his brawny arm was already raised to strike."[92] Hamel spares the missionary's life but makes him drink blood.[93] A common indicator of cannibalism, drinking blood appears in literature claiming to be non-fiction, as well. The enslaved persons planning an uprising on a plantation in Jamaica, according to Lewis' *Journal of a West India Proprietor* (1834), were known to "assist it with all the usual accompanying ceremonies of drinking human blood, eating earth from graves, &c."[94] Such depictions, Malchow explains, were constructed by the pro-slavery lobby to dehumanize Africans and justify their enslavement.[95] Even when cannibalism is not explicitly mentioned, the inhumanity of Africans and their enslaved descendants was emphasized. For instance, Bryan Edwards' *A History, Civil and Commercial, of the British West Indies* (1793) describes rebels in Saint Domingue as "savage people, habituated to the barbarities of Africa...[who] fall on the unsuspecting planters, like so many famished tigers thirsting for human blood. Revolt, conflagration, and massacre, everywhere mark their progress."[96] Animality and cannibalistic qualities are emphasized, much like in the fictional

---

[90] See Robin Pascoe's "Introduction" in Robinson, *Mary Robinson: Selected Poems*, ed. Judith Pascoe (Broadview Press, 2000), 55.
[91] Cynric Williams, *Hamel the Obeah Man* (London, 1827), 125.
[92] *Ibid.*, 125.
[93] *Ibid.*, 125.
[94] Matthew Gregory Lewis, *Journal of a West India proprietor: kept during a residence in the Island of Jamaica* (London: John Murray, 1834), 225.
[95] Malchow, *Gothic Images of Race*, 41.
[96] Bryan Edwards, *The History, Civil and Commercial, of the British Colonies in the West Indies* (London, 1793), 67.

accounts. In Long's *History of Jamaica* (which Charlotte Smith consulted when writing "Henrietta's Tale"), the enslaved are depicted as:

> void of genius, and [they] seem almost incapable of making any progress in civility or science. They have no plan or system of morality among them. Their barbarity to their children debases their nature even below that of brutes. They have no moral sensations; no taste but for women; gormandizing, and drinking to excess; no wish but to be idle. Their children, from their tenderest years, are suffered to deliver themselves up to all that nature suggests to them.[97]

The barbarous, immoral, vice-ridden nature of Africans, according to Long's racist account, makes them less than human: simple-minded, dangerous, and in need of a firm (white) ruling hand.[98] In *Angelina; A Novel*, however, it is the slave owner – not the enslaved – who is the inhumane, cannibalistic monster. Obsessed with his social status rather than intellectual or moral refinement, a glutton, womanizer, and tyrannous father, Sir Edward fits Long's account of barbarity in every aspect.

While the connection between Sir Edward and cannibalism is palpable, his real power is derived not from eating humans, but from a more metaphorical type of human consumption: slavery. As Simon Gikandi explains, "institutions of high culture in the English eighteenth century were enabled by money made in West Indian plantations."[99] Similarly, Eric Williams points out that absentee slave owners could buy their way into local government and Parliamentary positions from which they were able to influence policy to their own benefit.[100] Sophia's lover Belmont sums up this cycle:

> The plodding citizen is educated in the laborious art of traffic; he passes the day in pursuit of riches; he dreams of profit and of loss. If fortune smiles upon his toils, his next hope is the aggrandizement of his name, by an alliance with some illustrious family. He then fancies himself ennobled; and in every society arrogates to himself something of superior distinction: talks of his daughter's consequence, or his son's nobility; lives in a sort of second rate magnificence.[101]

---

[97] Edward Long, *The History of Jamaica or, General Survey of the Antient and Modern State of that Island* (London: T. Lowndes, 1774), 353.

[98] The Long family were, according to Williams among the wealthiest absentee plantation owners in England; they obviously had a political interest in perpetuating these stereotypes (*Capitalism and Slavery*, 89).

[99] Simon Gikandi, *Slavery and the Culture of Taste* (Princeton University Press, 2011), 149.

[100] Williams, *Capitalism and Slavery*, 92-3.

[101] Robinson, *Angelina*, 1:67.

Society may not like men like Sir Edward, but his money buys his acceptance into influential circles. What *Angelina; A Novel* shows is the way in which, despite the geographical and social distances that appeared to exist between colonial plantations and English drawing rooms, there were close connections between the slave trade, polite society, and institutions like Parliament that empowered absentee plantation owners. Sir Edward is a tyrannous monster, but it is his society that enables him.

As in "The Story of Henrietta," *Angelina; A Novel* draws a direct line from the slave trade to the oppression of women in the metropole. Lady Watkins, her aunt, lashes out at Sir Edward, praising Sophia for running away from home to escape the forced marriage, noting that it shows an "independent spirit."[102] Lady Watkins means this as a compliment, but Sir Edward's reaction to his daughter's independence is telling. "Independence is the stalking horse for all sorts of absurdities," he exclaims, "I should like to know what would come of my plantations if such doctrines are encouraged... Hav'n't I made a fortune by slavery! and I warrant independence had nothing to do in the profits of *black* traffic."[103] In Sir Edward, Robinson pushes beyond the metaphorical linking of slaves and British women; Sir Edward provides a material connection between the slave trade and the forced marriages of young women. Both are done solely for profit and involve reducing whole groups of people to commodities. In her defense of Sophia, Lady Watkins moves between empathizing with Sophia's oppression and the oppression of the enslaved people forced to work on sugar plantations, further drawing the reader's attention to the fact that the source of that oppression is the same in both cases. She expresses a wish that men with "black hearts," like Sir Edward, would be exposed to the public and sent to Africa, where: "they would then behold the miseries they deride; they would then confess, that the poor negro can feel the scourge – can faint in the burning rays of noon – can hope, can fear – can shrink from torture and sigh for liberty as well as the European."[104] She humanizes enslaved persons, highlighting the miseries that men like Sir Edward perpetuate. She refers to both the physical "torture" they endure, the emotional trauma of the slave experience, and their innate desire for liberty. Humanizing enslaved Africans and their descendants in this way counters the dehumanizing rhetoric that anti-abolitionists (like Long) so often called upon to support slavery.

Passages such as those quoted above, in which slavery and greed for wealth and power drive the subjection of those who are without money and influence,

---

[102] *Ibid.*, 2:123.

[103] *Ibid.*, 2:123. Italics in original.

[104] *Ibid.*, 2.123.

echo many passages of Mary Wollstonecraft's *A Vindication of the Rights of Woman*, in which the author laments the systemic oppression wrought by the wealthiest members of British society. "[F]rom the respect paid to property flow, as from a poisoned fountain, most of the evils and vices which render this world such a dreary scene to the contemplative mind," she explains, [f]or it is in the most polished society that noisome reptiles and venomous serpents lurk under the rank herbage."[105] Wollstonecraft's argument here contains echoes of Adam Smith's observations in his *The Theory of Moral Sentiments*, in which he expresses an obvious concern over the corrupting nature wealth has on British society:

> When we consider the condition of the great, in those delusive colours in which the imagination is apt to paint it, it seems to be almost the abstract idea of a perfect and happy state. It is the very state which, in all our waking dreams and idle reveries, we had sketched out to ourselves as the final object of all our desires. We feel, therefore, a peculiar sympathy with the satisfaction of those who are in it. We favour all their inclinations, and forward all their wishes. What pity, we think, that any thing should spoil and corrupt so agreeable a situation![106]

Man idolizes the trappings of wealth, which leads to a misguided sympathy with those who possess wealth. It is not that the ultra-wealthy deserve adoration, according to Smith, but people love to imagine themselves in such a position and end up vicariously championing the wealthy. "To disturb, or to put an end to, such perfect enjoyment, seems to be the most atrocious of all injuries," Smith continues. "[t]he traitor who conspires against the life of his monarch, is thought a greater monster than any other murderer. All the innocent blood that was shed in the civil wars, provoked less indignation than the death of Charles I."[107] *Angelina*, then, shows the consequences of this dynamic. Sir Edward is a contemptable, crass, "illiterate grub," but understands the degree to which his wealth allows him to act with impunity. When Lady Watkins declares that "all the world will despise" Sir Edward for his cruel treatment of Sophia, he bluntly retorts: "not while I can command more money than my neighbors...tis money that makes the mare go."[108] This sentiment is confirmed by other characters in the novel: as one family acquaintance remarks on Sophia's forced marriage: "[y]oung women have no right to judge for themselves ...Sir Edward Clarendon, after having toiled so many years, had

---

[105] Wollstonecraft, *Rights of Women*, 221.
[106] Smith, *Theory of Moral*, 114.
[107] *Ibid.*, 114.
[108] Robinson, *Angelina*, 2:21.

unquestionably a right to dispose of his own."[109] It is this injustice – that money provides men with unfettered power over their subordinates – that is at the heart of forced marriage plot novels.

Writers as diverse as Adam Smith, Samuel Richardson, Mary Wollstonecraft, and Mary Robinson recognized this fact, but only the latter three acknowledged the specific ways in which women (and in the case of Wollstonecraft and Robinson, the enslaved) were particularly victimized by this socio-economic power dynamic. For instance, wealth accumulation is construed as a fundamental source of moral delinquency in British society throughout the *Rights of Woman*. Wollstonecraft links it to chattel slavery, to society's turning women into objects of male pleasure rather than thinking beings, and to the oppression of the English poor more widely. She argues that "one kind of despotism supports another"; tyranny of different forms, whether of white women or slaves, for instance, is inextricably linked to the type of estate building evidenced in Sir Edward.[110]

Independence and education are the keys to counteracting these structures. As Wollstonecraft writes, independence is "the grand blessing of life, the basis of every virtue," and the key to social reform.[111] That is, in *Rights of Woman* Wollstonecraft argues that "the most perfect education" is "to enable the individual to attain such habits of virtue as will render it independent. In fact, it is a farce to call any being virtuous whose virtues do not result from the exercise of its own reason."[112] In fact, even Sir Edward seems to recognize the link between education and independence; he laments that "[w]omen, now-a-days, are so confounded knowing…Women have no business either to write or to read, as I said before: the rank I designed my daughter to move in requires neither."[113] Knowledge is, quite literally, power; though he has tried to raise his daughter as a commodity who will dutifully – unquestioningly – accommodate his desire to be exchanged at his leisure, the education she has received from her aunt – heavily influenced by Classical history, philosophy, and poetry – has made her aware of the injustices her father imposes and provided a spirit of independence necessary to fight for her own rights. In *A Letter to the Women of England on the Injustice of Mental Insubordination* (published under the pseudonym Anne Francis Randall), Robinson argues that England will need "a legion of Wollstonecrafts to undermine the poisons of prejudice and malevolence"

---

[109] *Ibid.*, 2:189.
[110] Wollstonecraft, *Rights of Women*, 232.
[111] *Ibid.*, 65.
[112] *Ibid.*, 86.
[113] Robinson, *Angelina*, 1:87.

that women face.[114] Robinson has a deep admiration for Wollstonecraft, and in Sophia Clarendon, she uses the forced marriage plot to dramatize Wollstonecraft's radical philosophies to champion the fight against the money-based hegemonic power structure that kept women ignorant and subordinate.

Sharon Setzer, one of the few critics who analyzes *Angelina* at length, draws similar conclusions about slavery's function in the novel, writing:

> Robinson's Sophia...repeatedly expresses her aversion to being "bartered like a slave." The analogy, in her case, carries a particular force because her tyrannical father is also a "black trader" and the proud owner of plantations and slaves in the West Indies ...As Sophia's Aunt Juliana observes, there is not simply an analogy between Sir Edward's attitudes toward his slaves and his daughter but a causal connection.[115]

Setzer's commentary on the "causal connection" between slavery and Sir Edward's tyranny is apt, yet – I argue – can be pushed further, especially when the novel is read alongside "The Story of Henrietta" in that the happiness of both heroines is facilitated by turbulence on the plantations. As discussed above, the enslaved under Maynard's control band together with Maroons, killing Maynard in retribution for his cruel treatment of them. It is notable that, after capturing and imprisoning his daughter in their home, Sir Edward receives word of "losses of considerable consequence, news of the most unpleasant nature" from the West Indies that "require[s] his immediate attention."[116] Readers are not privileged with the exact nature of this "unpleasant" news, but from Sophia's reaction the situation is clearly dire: Sir Edward faces financial ruin.

Given the publication date of *Angelina; A Novel*, 1796, readers, I contend, are meant to associate this disturbance with a slave or Maroon uprising; the Haitian Revolution was in full swing in 1796, which was also the culmination of the Second Maroon War in Jamaica. Furthermore, Sir Edward's last name – Clarendon – also provides a link to slave rebellions. Clarendon is a county in Jamaica where one of the first major (British) slave uprisings took place; hundreds of enslaved people revolted against their masters in Clarendon in 1690. Though this took place over 100 years before the publication of *Angelina*, it was commonly cited in the many historical (or quasi-historical) accounts of Jamaican history that became so popular during the later eighteenth century.

---

[114] Mary Robinson, *A Letter to the Women of England and The Natural Daughter*, ed. Sharon Setzer (Broadview Press, 2002), 41.

[115] Setzer, "The Marriage Market," 61.

[116] Robinson, *Angelina*, 2:310.

Long, for instance, emphasizes the brutality and violence of the slaves and the swift, firm response of the British. Characterizing the black inhabitants of Clarendon by their "aversion to husbandry, and the martial ferocity of their disposition," he claims a planter named Sutton was killed by the people enslaved on his plantation, who then went on to challenge British forces.[117] His Majesty's troops, according to Long, easily defeated the rebels, who "threw down their arms, and begged for mercy; the rest were afterwards either slain, or taken prisoners; the ringleaders of the conspiracy hanged," mirroring in some ways the violent ending of Aphra Behn's 1688 *Oroonoko, or, The Royal Slave*. Long shapes the white colonists as morally and martially superior to the black rebels, creating a mythology of white supremacy in the Caribbean. Robinson's use of the surname "Clarendon" and the general popular interest in West Indian uprisings in the 1790s should clue readers into the fact that some sort of violent uprising took place on Sir Edward's plantation.

Ultimately, Sir Edward does not lose as much of his fortune as he initially believed, but for the remainder of the novel, he is a completely different man. He transforms from a cannibal-like gothic villain into a chastised, passive background figure. "His manner," Sophia remarks, "was less violent, his voice less harsh, his countenance seemed to lose much of its austerity."[118] Meekness becomes the new hallmark of this previously tyrannical villain as Sophia descends from the gothic tower in which he imprisoned her and marries her beloved Belmont, a marriage Sir Edward forbade before the West Indian disaster. Until this point, Sir Edward has been a constant source of violence and terror, but when his plantation and profits suffer a loss, so does his authority over Sophia. Meekness, in *Angelina*, emanates from the patriarch, not the daughter. Read in this light, the disaster on his plantation, though unspecified in the text, is coded as a rebellion that is a source of retribution for Sir Edward's violent tyranny. Violence, Adrian Craciun argues, is in fact, a significant theme across Robinson's work. She asserts that Robinson "rewrite[s] the seduction plot from *Clarissa* onwards, insisting that women enlarge their understanding of honor and take up arms to actively defend it and themselves."[119] Extending this argument further, I argue that *Angelina; A Novel* shows that violence is an effective tool for overcoming evil. Although the "violence" done to Sir Edward happens offstage, so to speak, and he is not subjected to the same bodily

---

[117] Long, *The History of Jamaica*, 446.

[118] Robinson, *Angelina*, 2:249.

[119] Adriana Craciun, "'Empire without end': Charlotte Smith at the Limits of Cosmopolitanism," *Women's Writing* 16:1 (2009): 52.

violence as Maynard, the theme is still present. After the pitfalls in the West Indies, Sir Edward is a chastised man.

Robinson and the slave trade

Robinson's views on the slave trade appear elsewhere in her body of writing in ways that support reading Sophia's resistance against her father alongside resistance to the slave trade. Kate Ferguson Ellis notes that "Mary Darby Robinson regularly published attacks on the institution [of slavery] throughout the 1770s, 1780s, and 1790s until her death in 1800."[120] For instance, her poem "The Negro Girl," first published in her 1800 collection *Lyrical Tales*, tells the story of a pair of African lovers, Zelma and Draco, who are so distraught at Draco's being captured into slavery that they both die by suicide. Calling on rhetoric like Josiah Wedgewood's famed "am I not a man and a brother" slogan, the speaker exclaims: "Whate'er their TINTS may be, their SOULS are still the same."[121] Much late-eighteenth-century discourse promoted viewing black persons as less human than white Europeans (even abolitionist theories, as seen above). Robinson's poem, however, presents a different argument: that black Africans have souls and inner lives just as developed as those of white Europeans, a fact that is absent from Charlotte Smith's writing. Furthermore, Robinson shows her knowledge of the sexual exploitation of enslaved black women. For instance, the line "Torn from my Mother's aching breast,/ My Tyrant sought my love" references the rape by the enslaver.[122] Though Zelma is kept as a sexual slave she hopes to return to her beloved Draco, even if it means death. She waits for an opportunity to escape and acts when she has the chance. "ZELMA, and Love contriv'd, to break the Tyrant's chain."[123] She is too late to meet Draco but feels triumphant in her escape from her enslaver.

In another abolition poem, Robinson also focuses on the possibility of liberty and freedom. "The African" (1798) ends with the stanza:

> OH LIBERTY! From thee the suppliant claims
> The meed of retribution! Thy Pure flame
> Wou'd light the sense opake [sic], and warm the spring
> Of boundless ectacy [sic]: while Nature's laws,
> So violated, plead immortal tongu'd,
> For her dark-fated children! Lead them forth

---

[120] Kate Ferguson Ellis, *The Contested Castle: Gothic Novels and the Subversion of Domestic Ideology* (University of Illinois Press, 1989), 175.
[121] Robinson, "The Negro Girl" in *Mary Robinson, Selected Poems*, line 54.
[122] *Ibid.*, lines 67-8.
[123] *Ibid.*, line 84.

> From bondage infamous! Bid Reason own
> The dignities of MAN, whate'er his clime,
> Estate, or colour. And, O sacred TRUTH!
> Tell the proud Lords of Traffic, that the breast
> Thrice ebon-tinted, owns a crimson tide
> As pure, – as clear, as Europe's son's can boast.[124]

This poem resonates with the warning that Charlotte Smith presents in *The Emigrants*. That is, the speaker addresses that the enslaved "meed," or deserve, retribution for the wrongs they have faced, which makes "The African" about slave rebellions as much as it as about abolition. Truth, reason, and liberty are all on the side of the enslaved, who are justified in their desire for freedom and vengeance over their oppressors. Though this poem was published two years after *Angelina*, reading Robinson's body of work helps scholars gain a fuller picture of the institutions that she wrote against in *Angelina; A Novel* and provides additional support for reading Sir Edward's chastisement after the event at his West Indian properties as retributive violence against him for his sins.

Conclusion

Angelina; A Novel ends with a letter from Sophia to her friend Mrs. Delmore that serves as a denouement. Sharing her plan to retreat from England to the Welsh countryside with her new, beloved husband, Sophia ruminates on her hopes for the future in verse:

> And now, my friend, to peaceful scenes I'll fly,
> As the poor swallow seeks a milder sky;
> Long on the mercy of the tempest cast,
> The genial season soothes my soul at last! [...]
> I'll seek the hermit PEACE! With him to stray,
> While modest twilight weeps retiring day [...]
> While conscious virtue prompts sublime repose,
> And on his pallet rude, his weary eyelids close!
> OH! Solitary SAGE! To Heaven allied!
> From Greatness banish'd, and estrang'd from Pride.[125]

Sophia presents the halcyon atmosphere of the rustic Welsh countryside as an antidote to the suffering caused by her corrupt, tyrannical father and the greedy society that enables him. She aligns the hermit and his lifestyle – the lifestyle

---

[124] Robinson, "The African" in *Mary Robinson, Selected Poems*, lines 24-35.
[125] *Ibid.*, 2:343.

she will emulate – as one of peace, wisdom, and virtuous contentment. Robinson makes it clear, however, that virtue already resides in Sophia and that this virtue is directly related to her resistance against her father's violence. In *Angelina; A Novel*, Robinson draws a throughline between the slave system and the unjust commodification of British women that goes beyond comparing the latter to the former but shows how these are two sides of the same coin. Abusing enslaved humans empowers men like Sir Edward, who then extend their humans-as-chattel attitude to their daughters in order to gain more money and power; a cycle that then feeds back into the plantation system. Importantly, the sense of selfhood that Sophia has is a strong, independent one; Sophia "was marked as a victim; her resistance was dictated by truth, and consistent with reason; she had to choose between a single act of disobedience, and the degradation of falsehood, perjury, meanness, sordid, legal prostitution."[126] Like Charlotte Smith, Robinson works to redefine virtue, concluding, like Mary Wollstonecraft does, that young women deserve an education that empowers their individual desires. Like their enslaved brethren, women possess an innate right to personal freedom. When this is denied, revolution – even if violent – is the only path forward for the oppressed.

Recognizing the potency of chattel slavery as a metaphor for the subjection of white British women, Charlotte Smith and Mary Robinson push the connection further than their peers in their explorations of the real-world connections between the two. That is, their writings show that there are specific material links between chattel slavery and the patriarchal structures of their period. Adapting the plot of *Clarissa*, Smith, and Robinson transport the struggle between a tyrannous father, who believes in his right to force his daughter into an unwanted marriage, into their own historical moment to expose the extreme degree to which young women were commodified for economic gain. These same powerful men, portrayed in the novels as classic gothic villains, are shown to be the same men profiting off the Atlantic slave trade, a fact that is closely tethered to their authoritarian brand of fatherhood. In addition to their shared oppressor, these narratives suggest a shared emancipation: the rebellions of the enslaved and (and Marooned, in the case is "The Story of Henrietta") depose the tyrants, ending their persecution of those under their power. Though Smith's "The Story of Henrietta" perpetuates racist stereotypes of black persons, mirroring the racist assumptions that pepper the abolitionist movement, Robinson advocates for seeing the shared humanity between black and white alike. In both cases, however, the right to fight against tyranny – by violence, if necessary – is supported and celebrated.

---

[126] *Ibid.*, 2:331.

Chapter Three

"Young Ladies that have no Money are to be pitied": Jane Austen and the Forced Marriage Plot

The first two chapters of this book examine forced-marriage-plot novels that dramatize capitalism's corrupting influence and its disastrous impact on women's autonomy. The disobedient heroines in *Clarissa, The Female Quixote,* "The Story of Henrietta," and *Angelina; A Novel* are all denied a say in who they will marry by the novels' villains: greedy father figures who seek to sell their daughters in *quid pro quo* arrangements. That using women as exchangeable objects was a lynchpin of this economy was obvious to Samuel Richardson, Charlotte Lennox, Charlotte Smith, and Mary Robinson; using iterations of the forced marriage plot, these authors expose this wrong and champion young, female characters who disrupt the system by refusing the mercenary marriages their patriarchs broker for them. Each heroine is empowered to create her own system of values, different from the monetary one, in which her sense of self takes precedence over the patriarchal expectations of her society and in which her right to consent – or not – to a matter as important as marriage is presented as a basic human right.

While there is not a significant time gap between Austen's novels and those examined in the previous chapter (Smith's "The Story of Henrietta" was published in 1800 and *Pride and Prejudice,* the earliest of Austen's novels discussed here, in 1813), the ways in which class and money are portrayed shift. That is, the simple good/evil dichotomy between money and morality used in earlier forced marriage plot novels dissolves into a more complex examination of the ways in which money, necessity, and morality interact. By Austen's period, class mobility was even more fluid; upward (or downward) mobility created ever-increasing gradations within the class structure and inter-class interactions. As Deborah Kaplan puts it, "social escalators" in Austen's period "went down as well as up" since "many professionals and rentiers were not men on the rise but younger sons, who were directed into professions while their older brothers inherited family estates. They were thus inextricably intertwined by kinship and patronage with their generally more prosperous, landowning neighbors."[1] While, as will be discussed below, many families still relied on patrilineal inheritance measures to consolidate their family's wealth, there were far more variances in the class system as observed by Austen, who, according to Vivian Jones, "is much more interested in the types of people who lived more precariously on the margins of the gentry proper, but whose connections, education, or role in the community gave them the right, like her father, the rector, to 'mix in the best society of the neighborhood.'"[2] In Austen's variances of the forced marriage plot, financial need – sometimes even poverty – hangs over the characters' heads in a way absent from earlier versions, and possessing extreme wealth does not necessarily equate to villainy. The following chapter will consider how the forced marriage plot intersects with her novels *Sanditon*, *Pride and Prejudice*, and *Mansfield Park*, in which female protagonists grapple with love, financial security, and social expectations. In these novels, women must trust their own sense of agency to find an acceptable combination of those characteristics within their limited parameters of possibility.

Pride and Prejudice reconsidered: or, why readers should give Mrs. Bennet a break

When one thinks of forced marriage within the context of Austen's 1813 novel *Pride and Prejudice*, the arranged marriage between Mr. Darcy and Anne de Bourgh is, understandably, likely what will come to mind. As Lady Catherine tells Elizabeth Bennet: "[t]he engagement between them is of a peculiar kind. From their infancy, they have been intended for each other. It was the favourite wish of *his* mother, as well as of her's. While in their cradles, we planned the union…Have you not heard me say, that from his earliest hours he was destined for his cousin?"[3] Though Lady Catherine speaks of the intended marriage between her daughter and nephew as providence, it is at its core a forced marriage brokered to safeguard the family's wealth, title, and influence, and Lady Catherine is a tyrant who wants to keep their family's wealth and bloodlines intact.

In her essay "Austen's Powers: Engaging with Adam Smith in Debates about Wealth and Virtue," Elsie M. Michie analyzes Lady Catherine alongside economic philosophers like Adam Smith and David Hume, arguing that they and Austen were interested in the same issue: how wealth impacts moral values. "[W]e could say that Austen's fictional characters embody the fears that haunt the

---

[1] Deborah Kaplan, *Jane Austen Among Women* (Johns Hopkins University Press, 1992), 9.
[2] Jones, "Appendix B: Rank and Social Status," in *Pride and Prejudice*, 291.
[3] Jane Austen, *Pride and Prejudice*, ed. Donald Gray and Mary A. Favret (New York: Norton, 2016), 242. Hereafter *PP*.

social imaginations of eighteenth-century political economists, specifically the fear of engrossment, the term writers like Smith and Hume used to define the negative effects of wealth," she explains.[4] The relationship between John Dashwood and his sisters in *Sense and Sensibility* is a good example of this: John and Fanny's desire for wealth leads them to disinherit the Dashwood girls in direct opposition to the late Mr. Dashwood's wishes. Instead, they hoard all the money and property for themselves even though Mr. Dashwood's widow and her daughters are in real financial need: an obviously immoral, unkind choice. Interestingly, though, in her assessment of Austen's exploration of money and morality, Michie posits that it is women – Lady Catherine, for example – who are to blame for economic immorality. "Associated with both the consolidation of land (the engrossment of estates) and the accumulation of money (the engrossment of monopolies), the principle of engrossment is represented in Austen's novels through rich women's assumption that ideal marriages are financial mergers, uniting one great estate and/or fortune with another."[5] That is, according to Michie, in Austen's earlier novels like *Pride and Prejudice*, "[t]he rich woman's drive to consolidate or engross rather than disperse wealth" is the root cause of socio-economic immorality.[6]

While I heartily agree that Austen's novels explore the impact that emergent capitalism had on the values of British society, I think it is a mistake to only consider this in terms of the wealthy women in the novel due to the clear patriarchal roots of mercenary economic attitudes. In Lady Catherine's case, the narrative ultimately reveals that she is utterly powerless in forcing a financially expedient marriage between her daughter and nephew. Mr. Darcy is an independently wealthy, mature man who is free (in legal, economic, and social terms) to marry whomever he wants: he is not subject to the same power structures to which the female characters are. Put simply, he does not have to do anything his aunt says.

Instead, the specter of a forced marriage plot haunts other families: the Bennets and Lucases. On the surface, *Pride and Prejudice* diverges from the strict forced marriage plot points depicted in the other novels analyzed in this project, including Austen's later novel *Mansfield Park*, discussed below, in that there is not necessarily a tyrannical father who has contracted a quid pro quo

---

[4] Elsie B. Michie, "Austen's Powers: Engaging with Adam Smith in Debates about Wealth and Virtue," *NOVEL: A Forum on Fiction* 34, no. 1 (Autumn, 2000): 6.

[5] *Ibid.*, 6.

[6] *Ibid.*, 6. Michie argues that over the span of her career Austen shifts perspectives, eventually creating more complex, "ambiguous" wealthy female characters, a stance that fails to take *Sanditon* and the patriarchal underpinnings of Regency economic into account.

marriage for his own socio-economic gain. If anything, it is Mrs. Bennet who appears to be trying to force her daughters into marriage while Mr. Bennet supports their right to autonomy. Thus, the proposed marriage between Mr. Collins and Elizabeth Bennet appears to be Mrs. Bennet's doing. Her bumbling eagerness to marry off her daughters is comedic, and her family often mocks her one-track mind. Mr. Bennet, for example, insists he has "a high respect for [Mrs. Bennet's] nerves. They are my old friends," he tells his wife, "I have heard you mention them with consideration these twenty years at least."[7] Half mocking, half exasperated, Mr. Bennet's attitude toward his wife has typically directed how readers understand Mrs. Bennet. Edward Copeland, for instance, falls into this trap when he describes Mrs. Bennet as "ambitious" due to her obsession with marrying off her daughters.[8] Similarly, Lisa Hopkins claims that Mrs. Bennet "suffers from an innate lack of restraint and good taste which has nothing to do with her financial situation."[9]

However, applying the principles of the forced marriage plot to *Pride and Prejudice* shows that Mrs. Bennet's anxieties about marriage are, in fact, quite rational and justified. The entail that looms over the head of the Bennet family is one of the most-discussed aspects of *Pride and Prejudice*. As Mrs. Bennet declares, "I do think it is the hardest thing in the world, that your estate should be entailed away from your own children; and I am sure if I had been you, I should have tried long ago to do something or other about it."[10] Jane and Elizabeth's frequent attempts to make their mother understand the "nature of an entail" have been futile, and Mrs. Bennet remains "beyond the reach of reason."[11] As with many of the family's reactions to Mrs. Bennet, there is a discernable note of exasperation at her inability – or refusal – to listen to their logic.[12] Her ever-changing opinion of Mr. Collins, who goes from "odious" to a highly-desirable son-in-law, also makes her insistence that Elizabeth accepts his proposal seem absurd.[13] However, Mrs. Bennett's begging her husband to force Elizabeth to marry Mr. Collins and subsequent attempts at forcing the

---

[7] Austen, *PP*, 4.

[8] Edward Copeland, "Money," in *The Cambridge Companion to Jane Austen*, ed. Edward Copeland and Juliet McMaster, 127-138 (Cambridge: Cambridge University Press, 1997), 127.

[9] Lisa Hopkins, "Jane Austen and Money," *The Wordsworth Circle* 25 (1994): 77.

[10] Austen, *PP*, 44-5.

[11] *Ibid.*, 45.

[12] This is perhaps heightened by the fact that Lady Catherine, usually full of pompousness and bluster, happens to agree with Mrs. Bennet: she tells Elizabeth "'I see no occasion for entailing estates from the female line. It was not thought necessary in Sir Lewis de Bourgh's family," Austen, *PP*, 115.

[13] *Ibid.*, 45.

marriage herself (she "talked to Elizabeth again and again; coaxed and threatened her by turns. She endeavored to secure Jane in her interest") should not be read as a sign of ambition, but rather as a sign of her fear for her daughters' socio-economic stability.[14]

As critics like Alistair Duckworth and Sandra MacPherson point out, the way that the Bennet family estate, Longbourne, is passed from male heir to male heir is "not merely a plot device designed to set in motion and to serve the marriage comedy" but is deeply political.[15] The concept of entails was, from its very inception, a patriarchal and classist practice that enabled landowners to protect their estates. According to Deirdre Gilbert, entails and similar provisions (such as fee tail, fee simple, and strict settlements, just to name a few) were natural outgrowths of primogeniture, meant "to prevent the disintegration of large estates through divisible inheritance."[16] The specific differences between these terms are so complicated that William Blackstone called inheritance law "the most intricate and most extensive object of legal knowledge [sic]. Thorough comprehension of these, in all their minute distinctions," he claims, "is perhaps too laborious a task for any but a lawyer by profession" – an opinion clearly shared by Mrs. Bennet.[17] In their case, when Mr. Bennet dies, the Longbourne home and living will revert to their distant cousin, Mr. Collins, since there is no male heir among Mr. Bennet's children. Part of Mrs. Bennet's – and quite probably Austen's – outrage over the entail is its sexist nature since, in practice, it was almost always sons who benefitted, leaving the women of the family at the mercy of familial charity or the marriage market for their economic security. This is, in part, no doubt to the patriarchal, exclusionary nature of inheritance practices in Austen's period; Mrs. Bennet is angry at and anxious toward the legal mechanisms that will disinherit her daughters.

There is more to Mrs. Bennet's anger at the entail, however: the very practical fact that upon Mr. Bennet's death, she and any unmarried daughters will be left in relative poverty. As the narrator lays out in great detail, the fault for this lies squarely with Mr. Bennet. "Mr. Bennet had very often wished before this period

---

[14] Austen, *PP*, 81.

[15] MacPherson, "Rent to Own" in *PP*, 382; see also Alistair M. Duckworth, *The Improvement of the Estate: A Study of Jane Austen's Novels* (Johns Hopkins University Press, 1971), 18.

[16] Deirdre Gilbert, "'Willy-Nilly' and Other Tales of Male-Tails: Rightful and Wrongful Laws of Inheritance in Northanger Abbey and Beyond," *Persuasions* On-Line 20, no. 1 (1999): n.pg.

[17] William Blackstone, "Introduction," in *Commentaries on the Laws of England*, accessed May 26, 2023, Yale Law Library: The Avalon Project, https://avalon.law.yale.edu/18th_century/blackstone_intro.asp, 1.7.

of his life that, instead of spending his whole income, he had laid by an annual sum for the better provision of his children and of his wife if she survived him. He now wished it more than ever."[18] Rather than provisioning for the family he has, Mr. Bennet counted on having a son to take care of his wife and daughters. The narrator continues:

> The son was to join in cutting off the entail, as soon as he should be of age, and the widow and younger children would by that means be provided for. Five daughters successively entered the world, but yet the son was to come; and Mrs. Bennet, for many years after Lydia's birth, had been certain that he would. This event had at last been despaired of, but it was then too late to be saving. Mrs. Bennet had no turn for economy, and her husband's love of independence had alone prevented their exceeding their income.[19]

As in other places within the novel, Mrs. Bennet's silliness (her certainty they will have a son, she has "no turn" for saving money) thinly veils her husband's failure to support his family. This passage makes it perfectly clear that Mr. Bennet has neglected an important aspect of his paternal duties: financial planning. Though he is aware of his shortcomings – his lack of any savings – he is content to write it off as a lost cause without any attempt at rectifying the situation. Mary A. Burgan helpfully describes Mrs. Bennet as a "convenient scapegoat" whom the family – and reader – can blame for the Bennet family's mishaps, explaining that: "Mrs. Bennet's extravagances provide a convenient blind for her husband, and he uses her to justify his continuous retreats to his library and to his satirical perspective on all that passes," but by the end of the novel both Elizabeth and readers see "signs of a crucial failure in her father," especially when it comes to providing for his daughters.[20]

This point is made even clearer by Robert Hume, who (drawing on the work of J. A. Downie) corrects a common misunderstanding of *Pride and Prejudice*: that the Bennet family has only modest financial means. Hume provides a formula for translating their wealth into twenty-first-century equivalencies. "Mr. Bennet's £2,000 projects to a present-day buying power between £200,000 and £300,000 a year" in twenty-first-century liquid assets, meaning that, as long as Mr. Bennet is alive, the Bennet family is wealthy.[21] "What Jane Austen shows

---

[18] *Ibid.*, 299.

[19] *Ibid.*, 209-10.

[20] Mary A. Burgan, "Mr. Bennet and the Failures of Fatherhood in Jane Austen's Novels," *The Journal of English and Germanic Philology* 74, no. 4 (October 1975): 539.

[21] Robert D. Hume, "Money in Jane Austen," *The Review of English Studies* 64, no. 264 (April 2013), 303.

but does not say in this novel is that Mr. Bennet has been grossly irresponsible," Hume continues, "[h]e has an income of £2,000 per annum, and he has saved nothing. Most present-day readers seem to assume that this is just too small an income on which to save anything, but this is manifestly untrue."[22] Though readers often enjoy Mr. Bennett's sarcasm and dry humor, Hume argues that Austen wanted her readers to be critical of the Bennett family patriarch, given his conscious neglect of his daughters. "A husband and father ought to have been setting something aside from the time of his marriage, as Mr. Bennet perfectly well knows...His complete failure to make any attempt to provide for his wife and daughters suggests that Austen is implicitly asking us to despise him."[23] Tapping into what Burgan describes as Mr. Bennet's "cynical inertia," other scholars, such as Deidre Gilbert, argue that Mr. Bennet could have, in fact, broken the entail if he were not such a "dead beat dad."[24] Perhaps not the obvious mercenary villain found in *Clarissa* or in the gothic-inspired forced marriage plot novels of the 1790s, Mr. Bennet's financial neglect has serious repercussions for his wife and daughters that he seemingly has no interest in rectifying. As he tells Mrs. Bennet: "when I am dead, [Mr. Collins] may turn you all out of this house as soon as he pleases," a fact which clearly weighs heavily on Mrs. Bennet.[25] In addition to being house-less, upon Mr. Bennet's death, the Bennet women's income will also be drastically reduced from a collective £200,000-£300,000 a year in twenty-first-century money to about £40 each per year (again, in today's currency): a dire situation, especially without any marketable skills or a brother to support them.[26] In the end, marriage is their only viable option to house and keep themselves.

There are many ways in which bumbling Mrs. Bennett is made the butt of the joke throughout the novel: she is constantly mocked by her husband and the

---

[22] *Ibid.*, 300.

[23] *Ibid.*, 308.

[24] Gilbert, "Willy Nilly," n.pg.; Gilbert argues: "By the date of *Pride and Prejudice*, had the arrangement been a simple entail, Mr. Bennet could have brought it to an end at any time. But because Mr. Bennet could not do so, the circumstances that plague and baffle his wife must describe a strict settlement rather than an entail. On the other hand, Austenites who label Mr. Bennet a 'dead-beat dad' might argue that Austen made no error: remaining steadfast in his library, Mr. Bennet simply could not be bothered to end the entail. In any event, given Austen's apparent confusion, perhaps readers should be less quick to judge poor Mrs. Bennet. As we remember, despite the attempts of Jane and Elizabeth to explain the nature of an entail, Mrs. Bennet always found the subject "beyond the reach of reason.""

[25] Austen, *PP*, 44.

[26] Hume, "Money," 294. As Hume points out, the girls will not receive this amount until after their mother's death.

Bingley women, her poor manners are an embarrassment to Elizabeth, and her mothering skills are at least partially to blame for Kitty and Lydia's flirtatious manners. However, the narrator makes it clear that silly as she is, Mrs. Bennet is not solely responsible for their family's shortcomings. In fact, readers are told that, when it comes to his attitude toward his wife, "[r]espect, esteem, and confidence, had vanished for ever [sic]," which is obvious through the way he treats her. The novel is filled with moments in which he is dismissive and demeaning to his wife and daughters. Even Elizabeth, his favorite daughter:

> had never been blind to the impropriety of her father's behaviour as a husband…[his] continual breach of conjugal obligation and decorum which, in exposing his wife to the contempt of her own children, was so highly reprehensible. But she had never felt so strongly as now, the disadvantages which must attend the children of so unsuitable a marriage, nor even been so fully aware of the evils arising from so ill-judged a direction of talents; talents which rightly used, might at least have preserved the respectability of his daughters, even if incapable of enlarging the mind of his wife.[27]

As she fears for Lydia's wellbeing – having been allowed to go to Bath without a proper chaperone – Elizabeth can no longer ignore the harm her father has done to their family unit. He has no patience or regard for his wife and three younger daughters; though humorous, his constant belittling of his wife is, in fact, quite mean. Constantly undermining Mrs. Bennet's authority over their children, he nevertheless shirks most of his own fatherly duties. Despite the affection she seems to feel for her father, Elizabeth recognizes these serious shortcomings and laments that he has wasted so much potential by spending his time mocking his wife or shut up in his library. Instead of finding a way to provide for his daughters, Mr. Bennett has exacerbated the problems within his marriage and family. There is a recognition within the text – within Elizabeth – that the near-disgrace into which Kitty falls with Wickham is ultimately her father's fault. As she tells the Gardiners, Wickham "might imagine from my father's behaviour, from his indolence and the little attention he has ever seemed to give to what was going forward in his family, that *he* would do as little, and think as little about it, as any father could do."[28] And while it is certainly understandable to applaud his decision to support Elizabeth's rejecting Mr. Collins (one can see how that plotline might have turned out differently if Mr. Bennet put more stock in socio-economic advancement), how exactly Elizabeth will be supported after his death is not a matter that ever

---

[27] Austen, *PP*, 162-3.
[28] *Ibid.*, 192. Italics in original.

concerns Mr. Bennet beyond the vague regret quoted above. The financial negligence he shows his daughters is bad enough, but Elizabeth's inner monologue goes further, describing a father who fails the women in his family on multiple levels. If there is a silver lining to Mr. Bennet's negligence, it is that Elizabeth is confident that her father will not support the forced marriage Mrs. Bennet tries to enact. When Mr. Collins refuses to take her rejection seriously, she: "determined that if he persisted in considering her repeated refusals as flattering encouragement, to apply to her father, whose negative might be uttered in such a manner as must be decisive."[29] Mr. Bennet's laziness as a father prevents *Pride and Prejudice* from becoming a forced marriage plot proper, but the problems that he causes within the family show echoes of the forced marriage plot Austen will employ in *Mansfield Park*.

"The pure and disinterested desire of an establishment": a case study of Charlotte Lucas

Elizabeth Bennet and Anne de Bourgh have narrow brushes with forced marriages that, ultimately, their mothers lack the power to enforce, but it is possible to see how marriage can be forced in other ways when considering Charlotte Lucas: a character who, like Mrs. Bennet, is typically seen unfavorably by twenty- and twenty-first-century readers. There is a tendency to see Charlotte through Elizabeth's perspective: that Charlotte has "sacrificed every better feeling to worldly advantage."[30] Applying the socio-economic context behind the forced marriage plot, however, allows a more historicized reading of Charlotte's marriage that reveals the many grey shades of forced marriage in Regency England. There is no question that Charlotte marries Mr. Collins out of "the pure and disinterested desire of an establishment," a blunt statement that, taken alone, casts Charlotte in a materialistic light.[31] "I am not romantic, you know," she insists to Elizabeth, who is shocked at the news, "I never was. I ask only a comfortable home; and considering Mr. Collins's character, connection, and situation in life, I am convinced that my chance of happiness with him is as fair as most people can boast on entering the marriage state."[32] However, over the course of her discussion with Elizabeth on the subject, it is revealed that Charlotte's sense of urgency toward finding a husband is based on the financial precarity she faces as a woman. Charlotte highlights the principle that, as Austen wrote to her niece Fanny, "[s]ingle women have a dreadful

---

[29] *Ibid.*, 79.
[30] *Ibid.*, 90.
[31] *Ibid.*, 87.
[32] *Ibid.*, 90.

propensity for being poor – which is one very strong argument in favour of Matrimony."[33] Between male-centered inheritance practices and the lack of employment opportunities for women like Charlotte, she has a palpable fear for her future economic stability that, like Mrs. Bennet, she must consider. "Without thinking highly either of men or of matrimony, marriage had always been her object; it was the only honourable provision for well-educated young women of small fortune, and however uncertain of giving happiness, must be their pleasantest preservative from want"; as a twenty-seven-year-old woman without great beauty, talents, wealth, or alternative prospects, she feels the "luck" of the connection.[34]

This feeling of luck is no doubt bolstered by Britain's shortage of eligible bachelors. This was partially due to the protracted Napoleonic wars Britain fought against France and the War of 1812; Laura Fairchild Brodie calculates that in the year 1810, one in six British men were away fighting – and most of these would have been around marrying age.[35] Additionally, as Deborah Kaplan explores at length:

> Women of more modest means had a hard time finding spouses even among younger sons. Patrilineal customs left younger sons, many of whom could not find professional niches that paid very well, with fewer inherited resources and therefore with a greater need for affluent brides or with less inclination to marry. The celibacy rate among younger sons of the aristocracy and gentry was over 20 percent at the end of the eighteenth century.[36]

More men were away fighting, and fewer men at home were getting married, leaving women with few options. Though Charlotte Lucas' marriage is not forced in the same way as Fanny Price's is in *Mansfield Park*, Austen's narrator makes it clear that, in a world with so few options, Charlotte feels compelled – gently forced – into accepting the first proposal that comes her way. Indeed, her brothers' reactions to her engagement – they are "relieved from their apprehension of Charlotte's dying an old maid" – suggests that she is right to worry about her own financial security since, as the Dashwood sisters learn, brothers were not

---

[33] Jane Austen, *Selected Letters*, ed. Vivien Jones (Oxford: Oxford University Press, 2009), 204-5. Interestingly, in this same letter, Austen advises Fanny to put off marriage to avoid "the business of Mothering quite so early in life" (205).

[34] Austen, *PP*, 88.

[35] Laura Fairchild Brodie, "Society and the Superfluous Female: Jane Austen's Treatment of Widowhood," *Studies in English Literature, 1500-1900* 34, no. 4 (1994): 699.

[36] Kaplan, *Jane Austen Among Women*, 22.

always a safeguard against penury.[37] "Sympathy for Charlotte is in short supply among twentieth- and twenty-first-century readers," Hume writes, "but from the vantage point of the early nineteenth century she was probably an object of empathy for some women."[38] As mentioned above, it is easy for Elizabeth to marry to suit herself since she knows her father will never deprive her of agency. As Hume concludes, her marriage to Darcy is analogous to a fairy-tale ending, while Charlotte Lucas' attitude toward marriage would likely be familiar to Austen's readers. This is not to argue that Austen's fiction encourages young women to marry the Mr. Collinses of the world. Rather, in *Pride and Prejudice*, Austen shows the legal and economic practices that backed women into a corner, leaving them with few options for sustaining themselves as they aged. In this light, Mrs. Bennet's apparent obsession with marrying off her daughters and Charlotte's resigning to marry Mr. Collins are logical reactions to the socio-economic precarity women faced, not faults for which they should be condemned.

Fanny Price's refusal: forced marriage in *Mansfield Park*

The contrast between Elizabeth Bennet's fairy tale marriage and Charlotte's less glamorous match is picked up in the opening passage of Austen's next novel, *Mansfield Park* (1814). When Maria Ward "had the good luck to captivate" and marries wealthy Sir Thomas Bertram, it is expected that her two sisters will make equally advantageous matches.[39] "But," the narrator laments, "there certainly are not so many men of large fortune in the world as there are pretty women to deserve them," leaving the eldest Ward sister "obliged to be attached to" Reverend Norris, and Frances, Fanny's mother, settling for a poor, drunken sailor.[40] The hard fact that there are not enough wealthy men for all of England's beautiful young women sets the tone for this forced marriage novel, which is unique among the forced marriage plots examined so far in that poverty hangs over the heroine in a way that is absent from the wealthy heiresses in *Clarissa*, *The Female Quixote*, "The Story of Henrietta," and *Angelina; A Novel*. In those earlier novels, the heroines were all born into privilege that sheltered them from the outside world. *Mansfield Park*, however, complicates this plot through its insertion of Fanny Price, who comes from a poor family, into the luxury of Mansfield: a narratological move that mirrors the increasing complexity of middle- and upper-class society in Austen's time. The proximity of the rich and poor in *Mansfield Park* signals a shift in the forced marriage plot that will be

---

[37] Austen, *PP*, 88.
[38] Hume, "Money," 294.
[39] Jane Austen, *Mansfield Park*, ed. Kathryn Sutherland (London: Penguin Classics, 2014), 5. Hereafter *MP*.
[40] *Ibid.*, 5.

seen throughout the Victorian period. That is, in *Mansfield Park* and subsequent forced marriage plot novels, there is a recognition that, though the mercenary accumulation of wealth lends itself to immoral behavior, people need money to survive; an issue, as Charlotte Lucas knows all too well, that is especially fraught for women. Fanny Price's struggle against the forced marriage to Henry Crawford that her uncle Sir Thomas Bertram tries to force is made more difficult by the liminal space she occupies in both the Bertram and Price households. Taught to believe she does not fully belong to the former and knowing that she no longer fits in the latter – and with her class and gender working against her – Fanny emerges as a heroically disobedient heroine for asserting her own desires against Sir Thomas' expectations.

Despite the charitability of the Bertrams' agreeing to take in poor Fanny, there are strict limits to her membership in the family. In fact, what Sir Thomas seems to fear the most is that one of his sons will eventually fall in love with her. Though Mrs. Norris assures Sir Thomas that including her in their household from a young age will give her the opportunity to find "a credible establishment" – a husband – and that growing up as a sibling to her cousins would prevent one of the Bertram sons from wanting to marry her, he still worries about her impact on the household.[41] It is salient to note that Fanny, whom they have yet to meet when the above comments are made, is only nine years old at this point, but that does not prevent Mrs. Norris and Sir Thomas from thinking of her in terms of her marriage prospects: how they will be able to dispose of her to another family while safeguarding the Bertram boys from the perceived degradation of marrying below themselves. Additionally, though he is willing to take Fanny on as a financial burden, Sir Thomas and Mrs. Norris agree that there is a strict hierarchy they must uphold within their home. "There will be some difficulty in our way," he tells Mrs. Norris:

> as to the distinction proper to be made between the girls as they grow up: how to preserve in the minds of my *daughters* the consciousness of what they are, without making them think too lowly of their cousin; and how, without depressing her spirits too far, to make her remember that she is not a *Miss Bertram*...they cannot be equals. Their rank, fortune, rights, and expectations will always be different.[42]

Many critics have pointed out the degree to which Fanny is mistreated by the women in the Bertram household, but it is less common to explore Sir Thomas' role in Fanny's treatment. That is, this conversation makes clear that, though Mrs. Norris is certainly guilty of cruelty to Fanny, it is Sir Thomas, as the family's

---

[41] *Ibid.*, 8.
[42] *Ibid.*, 2. Italics in original.

primary authority figure, who defines Fanny's inferior role in their family, enabling the others to follow suit. The above passage also betrays the shallow nature of Sir Thomas' benevolence. That is, he agrees that their poor relative may come to Mansfield Park, but if she fails to meet certain standards of behavior, she will be sent back to her parents, much like an unwanted pet shuffled between unenthusiastic caretakers. While he – so far – lacks the same maniacal tyranny of earlier forced marriage plot villains, from the very beginning of the novel Sir Thomas is pin-pointed as an autocratic father figure who has serious limits to how he treats people outside of his own nuclear family.

Sir Thomas' debts

Of course, any discussion of Sir Thomas as a villain must consider his role as an absentee plantation owner who relies on the forced labor of enslaved people. Critics have understood this connection in a myriad of ways. Some, like Edward Said and Moira Ferguson, believe that Austen uses Sir Thomas "to legitimize the ruling class in light of the French Revolution" by "transform[ing] Sir Thomas Bertram of Mansfield Park...into a benevolent, reforming landowner."[43] Others, like Jane Sturrock, see the plantation as a convenient method for furthering the plot since "Sir Thomas, the controlling parent, must absent himself from home for a period long enough to allow his family to entangle themselves with Crawfords, Rushworths, and Mr. Yates; problems with an Antiguan estate provide a perfectly convincing rationale for such an absence."[44] It is also possible to understand Sir Thomas' status as a wealthy plantation owner – wealth derived from the suffering of the enslaved – as a sign of his "essential depravity," to borrow Susan Fraiman's terminology.[45] In fact, Fraiman's analysis

---

[43] Edward W. Said, *Culture and Imperialism* (Vintage Books, 1994), 62; Ferguson, *Colonialism and Gender*, 66; George Boulukos makes a similar argument in his essay "The Politics of Silence: *Mansfield Park* and the Amelioration of Slavery," in which he claims that critics should not read the Bertram family's silence (in response to Fanny's question about the slave trade) as an inditement of their involvement in the immoral human trafficking business, but "if we imagine that Fanny asks her uncle about the 'slave trade' enthusiastically, because she sees him as a morally exemplary slave-owner, the exchange as Austen represents it makes far more sense." See George E. Boulukos, "The Politics of Silence: Mansfield Park and the Amelioration of Slavery," *Novel* 39, no. 3 (November 2006): 362.

[44] June Sturrock, "Money, Morals, and Mansfield Park: The West Indies Revisited," *Persuasions* 28 (2006), 178.

[45] Susan Fraiman, "Jane Austen and Edward Said: Gender, Culture, and Imperialism," *Critical Inquiry* 21, no. 4 (1995): 813.

of Sir Thomas is analogous to my argument about Charlotte Smith's Maynard and Mary Robinson's Sir Edward Clarendon in the previous chapter: that the wealth Sir Thomas amasses from his plantation enables him to act with impunity at home and also serves as a symbol of his general lack of morals.

While I tend to agree with Fraiman's assessment of Sir Thomas, a point that is often misunderstood or ignored by critics – and that is crucial to the novel's forced marriage plot – is the seriousness of Sir Thomas' financial trouble. As Katherine Sutherland explains, Antigua was one of the earliest West Indian sugar islands Britain colonized, but by the time *Mansfield Park* is set, it was failing. By the late eighteenth century, "soil exhaustion and competition from more recently settled islands (notably the French island of Saint Domingue) had seriously eroded the previous wealth of the British planters. In 1800 sugar profits were only at 2.5 percent, and in 1807 the British planters were producing at a loss."[46] Writing in the same vein, Ruth Perry notes, "Antigua was particularly hard hit during the period that Austen sends Sir Thomas to see to his affairs there, for in addition to the falling price for sugar, an unusual drought had withered the crop to a third of its usual size," and – additionally – British markets were flush with sugar to the point that sugar's market value saw a sharp decline.[47] Low production and non-existent profits were further complicated by Britain's abolishing the slave trade, which J. A. Downie convincingly argues happens during Sir Thomas' visit to Antigua."[48] In addition to curbing the steady flow of free labor to the sugar islands, the ending of the slave trade also meant spending more on one's existing population of enslaved people, since "the human property...could not be abused or worked to death but would have to be handled so as to encourage [their] health and reproduction."[49] Taken individually, each of these issues was a serious problem for Antiguan planters. Cumulatively, there were catastrophic. Mrs. Norris' assertion that "Sir Thomas's

---

[46] Sutherland, in *MP*, 465, see endnote no. 2.

[47] Ruth Perry, "Austen and Empire: A Thinking Woman's Guide to British Imperialism," *Persuasions* 16 (1994): 99.

[48] J. A. Downie, "Who Says She's A Bourgeois Writer? Reconsidering the Social and Political Contexts of Jane Austen's Novels," *Eighteenth-Century Studies* 40, no. 1 (2006): 78. Downie draws on Chapman's dating of Fanny's coming out ball to 22 December 1808 and works backwards with the novel's plot to conclude that Sir Thomas was in Antigua from 1805-1807.

[49] Perry, "Jane Austen and British Imperialism" p. 241; NB: where I have used "[their]" to refer to "the human property," Perry uses "it" – a dehumanizing pronoun that emphasizes enslaved people as objects rather than individual humans. I point this out to raise awareness of the white supremacy that can be found in academic texts – whether intentional or accidental.

means will be rather straightened if the Antigua estate is to make such poor returns" is perhaps one of the few instances in which her anxiety about money is not exaggerated; Sir Thomas sees the "necessity of the measure" – going to Antigua himself – "in a pecuniary light," and whatever compelled his travel there (mismanagement, drought, debts, etc.) would have been a separate issue from abolition, which would have been a new problem arising while he was there.[50] Readers never get precise numbers, but these issues on Antiguan plantations suggest serious financial losses for Sir Thomas.[51]

This economic strain is compounded by another financial issue that gets even less discussion than the Antigua matter: Tom Bertram's debts. Though Copeland downplays the importance of Tom and his debts, calling them a "prominent irritant" but claiming "Austen seems little interested in them or Tom," they are crucial in understanding Sir Thomas' motivations.[52] Theresa Kenney gives Tom's character more credit, arguing: "Tom has failed at all the things he as eldest brother should be mindful of," but "[h]is story, which seems so peripheral at a casual first reading, is deeply interwoven into Fanny and Edmund's, and even Mary and Henry's."[53] And, I would add, Sir Thomas' relationships with Maria and Fanny. Though readers are not privy to precisely how high Tom's debts are, they are significant enough that Sir Thomas must sell off the lucrative parish living he was saving as Edmund's inheritance. "Tom's extravagance," readers are told, "had…been so great as to render a different disposal of the next presentation necessary, and the younger brother must help to pay for the pleasures of the elder."[54] Sir Thomas admonishes him: "you have robbed Edmund for ten, twenty, thirty years, perhaps for life, of more than half the income with ought to be his," which, knowing the little we do about the Mansfield living, must be a great sum – possibly the equivalent of over half a million pounds in twenty-first-century currency.[55] That is, during the Rev. Mr.

---

[50] Austen, *MP*, 29, 31.

[51] See Downie, "Who Says," 78; Downie uses historical research to show that the Bertrams likely acquired their estate and title during the seventeenth century and bought the plantations later, which could suggest that they had other income available (from rents, for example).

[52] Copeland, "Money," 134.

[53] Theresa Kenney, "Why Tom Bertram Cannot Die: 'The Plans and Decisions of Mortals,'" *Persuasions* Online 35, no. 1 (Winter 2014): n.pg.

[54] Austen, *MP*, 23.

[55] Austen, *MP*, 23; Sir Thomas has two livings set aside for Edmund. If we assume that by robbing Edmund of over half of his income, he refers to losing the Mansfield living (and retaining Thornton Lacey) for the next twenty years of the next clergyman's tenure, the £700 pounds per year received by Norris over twenty years is £14,000 lost by Edmund.

Norris' lifetime, the Norrises had "very little less than a thousand a year."[56] Assuming that all three Ward sisters had the same fortune, about three hundred pounds per year, it is safe to estimate that the Mansfield living – the one originally meant for Edmund – amounted to an annual income of about seven hundred pounds.[57] According to the British National Archives, seven hundred pounds in 1800 (roughly the year Norris died) would be roughly equivalent to £31,000 in today's money: a far cry from the average income of a clergyman in England at that time. Eileen Sutherland explains that clergymen's incomes varied widely but were rarely anywhere close to Mansfield's £700 per annum: Austen's clergyman father made only a modest income, and her cousin Edward Cooper was assigned to a position valued at about £140 per year. The living that Col. Brandon intends for Edward Ferrars in *Sense and Sensibility* is about £200 per year, which is considered generous. Their salaries were derived mostly from tithes paid by farmers within the parish. However, as Sutherland notes, the £700 per year that the Norrises began with probably increased during his tenure: "[i]t would be interesting to know how much the [Mansfield] living had improved during the twenty years or so of Mrs. Norris's management, and what it was worth after the indolent Dr. Grant's incumbency."[58] This is just to say that at the point when Sir Thomas sells the Mansfield living to cover the costs of Tom's "extravagance," it would have been a highly-sought, lucrative position able to fetch a fair amount of money. By extension, it suggests that Sir Thomas' need for fast cash is significant: he is not as flush as is typically assumed.

This financial strain directly impacts Fanny: both in terms of her daily life and how Sir Thomas views her role within their family. Once Mr. Norris dies

> "[t]he time was now come when Sir Thomas expected his sister-in-law to claim her share in their niece...and as his own circumstances were rendered less fair than heretofore, by some recent losses on his West India estate, in addition to his eldest son's extravagance, it became not undesirable to himself to be relieved from the expense of her support, and the obligation of her future provision.[59]

As with the amount of Tom's debt and Sir Thomas' West Indian losses, the text is not precisely clear on Sir Thomas' meaning here. Thinking back to his earlier

---

According to the National Archives currency calculator, this translates to £617,000 in today's money.

[56] *Ibid.*, 5.

[57] Readers learn in the opening paragraph of the novel that Lady Bertram's had a £7,000 inheritance: the interest of which would have amounted to about £300 annually.

[58] Sutherland, "Tithes and the Rural Clergyman," 51.

[59] Austen, *MP*, 24.

conversations with Mrs. Norris, it seems probable that in sending Fanny to her aunt, he wants Mrs. Norris to fulfill her promise to find a husband for Fanny since it is Mrs. Norris who takes charge of the Bertram girls' social life and will presumably do the same for Fanny. If this is the case, his desire to be released from "the obligation of [Fanny's] future provision" means finding a husband who will support Fanny, thus relieving himself of the burden. However, given the phrase "it became not undesirable to himself to be relieved from the expense of her support," is followed by "and" – indicating there are two separate reasons for the change, makes one wonder if perhaps, in addition to wanting a husband for her, Sir Thomas is in such dire need of liquid assets that removing whatever minor expenses she brings on his household is a welcome relief. Dwelling on this passage, and Tom's debts in general, highlight his financial need and his motivations behind the marriages he forces, aligning him not with a kind, gentle patriarch but as a cold, financially motivated villain.

Mansfield Park's multiple forced marriages

Within this financial context, Sir Thomas' need to marry off his biological and pseudo- daughters advantageously is obvious. When it comes to Maria's alliance with insipid Rushworth, "[n]ot all his good-will for Mr. Rushworth, not all Mr. Rushworth's deference for him, could prevent [Sir Thomas] from soon discerning some part of the truth – that Mr. Rushworth was an inferior young man, as ignorant in business as in books, with opinions in general unfixed, and without seeming much aware of it himself."[60] What is perhaps worse than his own dislike of the man is his awareness of Maria's disdain for her betrothed: "[l]ittle observation there was necessary to tell him that... [s]he could not, did not like him."[61] His one feeble attempt at helping her break the engagement notwithstanding, Sir Thomas' knowledge that the "alliance" would be "advantageous" prevents real intervention.[62] "Sir Thomas was satisfied," the narrator explains:

> too glad to be satisfied, perhaps, to urge the matter quite so far as his judgment might have dictated to others. It was an alliance which he could not have relinquished without pain...happy to secure a marriage which would bring him such an addition of respectability and influence,

---

[60] *Ibid.*, 186.
[61] *Ibid.*, 186.
[62] *Ibid.*, 186.

and very happy to think anything of his daughter's disposition that was most favourable for the purpose."[63]

While there is some measure of genuine concern in his discussion with Maria, the advantages he would gain through having Mr. Rushworth as a son-in-law justify the match to him. As Burgan puts it, "Sir Thomas can sacrifice his daughter to the exigencies of family aggrandizement, justifying the possible drawbacks on the basis of family bonds."[64] While Maria's decision to go through with the marriage is a reaction to Henry Crawford's scorn, Burgan also points out that she is heavily motivated by "an hatred of home, restraint, and tranquillity [sic]" that is even more pronounced since her father's return from Antigua.[65] Similarly, Moira Ferguson argues that Maria is a "victim of Sir Thomas's mercantilist attitudes," in that he "manipulated" her into a marriage with Rushworth, "a man whom her father desires financially."[66] Or, as Fraiman puts it, "[t]he father at Mansfield intimidates, exploits, and also ignores his daughters" in a way that is detrimental to their lives.[67] An association with Rushworth's 700 acres at Sotherton and £12,000 per year has an allure that Sir Thomas will not turn down, even if it means letting his daughter marry a man whom she obviously hates.

If Sir Thomas' mercenary materialism begins to surface as a reaction to Maria's engagement, it is through Fanny's forced marriage that his role as a villain comes to fruition. He is not, as Said suggests, Austen's mouthpiece in the novel, advocating for patriarchal control of plantation and home, but an opportunist who tries to use Fanny's gender and class against her for his own benefit. Noticing the attention Crawford pays to Fanny at her coming out ball, Sir Thomas begins his campaign gently by advising Fanny to leave her own ball and go to bed early. "'Advise' was his word," the narrator notes, "but it was the tone of absolute power…In thus sending her away, Sir Thomas perhaps might not be thinking merely of her health. It might occur to him that Mr. Crawford had been sitting by her long enough, or he might mean to recommend her as a wife by showing her persuadableness."[68] The narrator's facetious tone suggests the last reason is foremost in Sir Thomas' mind, and it is here that his sense of authority over Fanny's marriage emerges.

---

[63] *Ibid.*, 186-7.

[64] Burgan, "Mr. Bennet and the Failures of Fatherhood," 546.

[65] Austen, *MP*, 188.

[66] Moira Ferguson, *Colonialism and Gender Relations from Mary Wollstonecraft to Jamaica Kincaid: East Caribbean Connections* (Columbia University Press, 1993), 79.

[67] Fraiman, "Jane Austen and Edward Said," 810.

[68] Austen, *MP*, 259.

Later, unable to comprehend why Fanny turns down Crawford's proposal given the young man's geniality and fortune (he has a "good estate in Norfolk" and four thousand pounds a year), Sir Thomas confronts Fanny in a way that highlights his tyrannical nature.[69] Stammering that her rejection "is beyond me" and "requires explanation," Sir Thomas berates Fanny before concluding: "I am half inclined to think, Fanny, that you do not quite know your own feelings."[70] The text indicates that his disbelief is a cover for his long-held fear of Tom or Edmund's marrying Fanny and his fear of losing the two-fold connection to the Crawfords (though Fanny's marrying Henry and Edmund's marrying Mary). On the heels of what must have been significant losses in Antigua, combined with his worry about Edmund's future without the Mansfield settlement, maintaining the Crawfords as lucrative in-laws is no doubt foremost in Sir Thomas' mind. In fact, he confronts Fanny several times during their confrontation about her cousins, such as when he says: "Edmund I consider from his disposition and habits as much more likely to marry early than his brother. *He*, indeed, I have lately thought has seen the woman he could love, which, I am convinced, my eldest son has not. Am I right? Do you agree with me, my dear?"[71] His goal – forcing Fanny to agree that neither of her cousins is interested in marrying her – echoes Lady Catherine's demand to Elizabeth that she renounces any connection to Darcy. Elizabeth has confidence in herself as "a rational creature speaking truth from the heart," but Fanny has been raised by the Bertrams to always submit to their demands.[72] That, combined with her general fear of Sir Thomas, she only feels capable of uttering a disheartened "Yes, Sir" in response to his question.[73]

Even beyond the self-centered financial motives that prompt his anger at Fanny's rejecting Crawford, Sir Thomas is also motivated by a wave of more general anger that Fanny – a charity case and a young woman, two strikes against her – broached the family hierarchy when she made her decision without consulting him. "[Y]ou have disappointed every expectation I had formed and proved yourself of a character the very reverse of what I had supposed," he berates Fanny as she sits "in trembling wretchedness," clearly afraid of her uncle's anger.[74] "For I had, Fanny, as I think my behaviour must

---

[69] *Ibid.*, 40; according to the National archives, this would be equivalent to almost £200,000 pounds in 2017 currency – he has means.

[70] *Ibid.*, 292.

[71] *Ibid.*, 93. Italics in original.

[72] Austen, *PP*, 79.

[73] Austen, *MP*, 292.

[74] *Ibid.*, 293.

have shewn, formed a very favourable opinion of you from the period of my return to England," he continues:

> I had thought you peculiarly free from wilfulness [sic] of temper, self-conceit, and every tendency to that independence of spirit which prevails so much in modern days, even in young women, and which in young women is offensive and disgusting beyond all common offence. But you have now shewn me that you can be wilful [sic] and perverse; that you can and will decide for yourself, without any consideration or deference for those who have surely some right to guide you, without even asking their advice... You think only of yourself...and are, in a wild fit of folly, throwing away from you such an opportunity of being settled in life, eligibly, honourably, nobly settled, as will, probably, never occur to you again.[75]

Singling out "independence," "wilfulness [sic]," and a lack of "deference" toward himself as Fanny's main sins, he clearly sees her refusing the marriage as an act of insubordination. That he pegs "that independence of spirit which prevails so much in modern days" as "offensive and disgusting beyond all common offence," particularly when found in women, indicates an anger larger than this specific situation: one directed at women who presume to think for themselves. To him, this is a monstrosity worse than, say, Thomas' degenerate lifestyle or Maria's marrying an imbecile for money. Fanny has circumvented his authority in favor of her own will – an act that he deems unacceptable. This aspect of Sir Thomas' anger parallels the dynamic between Clarissa Harlowe and her father discussed in chapter one. That is, while Mr. Harlowe is angry that Clarissa's refusal to marry Solmes jeopardizes his self-aggrandizing plans, Mrs. Harlowe makes it clear to Clarissa that he sees her refusal as a usurpation of his authority for which he will not stand: she describes her husband as a "jealous Father, needlessly jealous, I will venture to say, of the prerogatives of his Sex...and still ten times more jealous of the authority of a Father."[76] In both forced marriage plot novels, the conflict between the fathers and daughters explicitly gestures beyond the immediate problem of the forced marriages in question to larger issues of gender- (and in Fanny's case) class-based oppression. Sir Thomas continues his rant: "You do not owe me the duty of a child. But, Fanny, if your heart can acquit you of *ingratitude—*.'"[77] He makes it clear that she is less to him than his own daughters while, paradoxically, reminding her that she owes him a debt – of

---

[75] *Ibid.*, 293-4.
[76] Richardson, *Clarissa*, 1:109.
[77] Austen, *MP*, 294. Italics in original.

gratitude, obedience, respect – for the home he has provided her: a debt to be repaid by marrying to please him. Even though he married Lady Bertram because he was "captivate[d]" by her —not for money – he thinks of his dependents' marriages as tools to be used for material benefit.[78]

Fanny Price: an unlikely heroine

Despite Fanny's palpable fear of her uncle (indeed, she "tremble[s]" in "terror" when she hears him coming to talk to her) and inability to explain why she turned down Crawford, she exhibits herculean bravery in her quiet but firm refusal of Crawford.[79] Fanny Price has been variously described as: "quivering and shy," "innocent of accomplishment," "meek, self-deprecating, pious, sickly, and self-righteous," and, perhaps most bluntly, "a wimp," just to name a few descriptors used by twenty-first-century critics.[80] However, reading her narrative arc as a forced marriage plot shows the depth of her bravery and strength – her heroic disobedience. It is because of her fear of Sir Thomas – who also intimidates his biological children – that her disobedience is so courageous. Hearing his endorsement of Crawford with "the utmost perturbation and dismay," Fanny, who is usually loth to contradict Sir Thomas, confronts him directly: "'[y]ou are mistaken, sir,' cried Fanny, forced by the anxiety of the moment even to tell her uncle that he was wrong; 'you are quite mistaken.'"[81] Three consecutive times he asks her if she really refuses Crawford, and each time responds with a determined "yes, Sir."[82] Each time he comes at her with a reason why she should be more amenable to his attentions – she is friends with Mary, Crawford procured a promotion for William, she would be able to help her family, etc. – but she holds strong, not letting Sir Thomas' bullying sway her. She does her best "to harden and prepare herself against farther questioning" since "[s]he would rather die than own the truth; and she hoped, by a little

---

[78] *Ibid.*, 5.

[79] *Ibid.*, 288.

[80] See: Stephanie M. Eddleman, "Mad as the Devil but Smiling Sweetly: Repressed Female Anger in Mansfield Park," *Persuasions* 28 (2006): 41; Allison Shea, "'I am a wild beast': Patricia Rozema's Forward Fanny," *Persuasions* 28 (2006): 52; Katheryn L. Shanks Libin, "Lifting the Heart to Rapture: Harmony, Nature, and the Unmusical Fanny Price," *Persuasions* 28 (2006): 137; and Lynda A. Hall, "Addressing Readerly Unease: Discovering the Gothic in Mansfield Park," *Persuasions* 28 (2006): 208. In all of these examples, the authors listed are quoting or paraphrasing other critics' negative opinions of Fanny before taking a more nuanced look at her character. Nevertheless, these quotes hint at the general attitude toward Fanny by a large portion of her readership.

[81] Austen, *MP*, 290.

[82] *Ibid.*, 291.

reflection, to fortify herself beyond betraying it."[83] Bullied into meekness by the whole Bertram clan, Fanny was never taught to recognize the validity of her own feelings, yet she knows that when it comes to Crawford's proposal, she must not give in to Sir Thomas' expectations.

Sir Thomas' attempt to force the marriage of Fanny and Crawford, however, does not end with her saying "no." Like so many women before and after her, Fanny's lack of consent means nothing to the man in charge – he simply changes his tactic from overt force to covert coercion. "Intreaty [sic] should be from one quarter only," he strategizes, "[t]he forbearance of her family on a point, respecting which she could be in no doubt of their wishes, might be their surest means of forwarding it."[84] Blatantly lying to Fanny, Sir Thomas promises, "from this hour, the subject is never to be revived between us. You will have nothing to fear, or to be agitated about. You cannot suppose me capable of trying to persuade you to marry against your inclinations," while he is at that very moment hatching a plan to do exactly that.[85] In sending Fanny back to Portsmouth to visit her parents, Sir Thomas "wished her to be heartily sick of home before the visit ended." [86] He considers this manipulative plot a "medicinal project upon his niece's understanding, which he must at preset consider diseased," since living in Mansfield Park's luxury has "a little disordered her powers of comparing and judging. Her Father's house would, in all probability, teach her the value a good income," he reasons.[87] Essentially, Sir Thomas wants to scare Fanny into accepting Crawford's proposal by reminding her of the poverty from which she came – and could return to – should she fail to secure economic stability through a husband. Though he does not say it outright, there is also the hint of a threat: that perhaps Sir Thomas is implying a failure to live up to his expectations of her could result in the loss of his support, along with the fact that seeing her family's financial distress could compel her to help them through the Crawford fortune. In fact, Hume points out that the ten pounds Sir Thomas gives Fanny for her journey are equivalent to somewhere between 1,000 and 1,500 pounds in twenty-first-century money.[88] It would be nearly impossible for Fanny to ignore the ease with which the Bertrams can give away money when contrasted to her parent's strain, and

---

[83] *Ibid.*, 292.
[84] *Ibid.*, 304-5.
[85] *Ibid.*, 305.
[86] *Ibid.*, 342.
[87] *Ibid.*, 342.
[88] Hume, "Money in Jane Austen," 304; he also notes: "Tom Bertram says dismissively that the theatre he orders built 'might cost a whole twenty pounds' (150), but as Wiltshire points out, £20 was a year's salary for a butler."

Sir Thomas expects that her sense of duty to them will override her aversion to Crawford.

Sir Thomas' understanding of class difference, and the way he uses this to manipulate Fanny, begins to show measured success. That is, after spending some time in Portsmouth, Fanny finds her parents' home "in almost every respect, the very reverse of what she could have wished. It was the abode of noise, disorder, and impropriety…She could not respect her parents."[89] Harsh words, but between the general chaos of the home, her father's sloth and heavy drinking, and her mother's indifference to her further endear Mansfield Park, with its abundance and relative tranquility, to Fanny's mind. However, in the end, Sir Thomas' scheme backfires; the longer he forces her to stay there, the more her eyes are opened to the cruelty of what he is doing. Knowing Fanny's desire to return to Mansfield – which is also what Lady Bertram desires – Sir Thomas insists he must be the one to bring Fanny home, but he purposefully extends her banishment again and again. "I never will, no, I certainly never will wish for a letter again," Fanny thinks after receiving news of another delay, "she was within half a minute of starting the idea that Sir Thomas was quite unkind, both to her aunt and to herself."[90] This is the earliest example of Fanny giving a mental voice to a negative thought about her uncle. For so long, her sense of duty to him prevented these thoughts, but this situation gives her the mental clarity necessary to confront the inequity of their relationship.

Thinking her uncle "quite unkind" may not be the dramatic confrontation or declaration of independence seen in earlier iterations of the forced marriage plot, but, as Stephanie M. Eddleman notes, Fanny – like many women in the eighteenth and nineteenth centuries – is taught by society and the Bertrams that anger is not an appropriate emotion for women to feel. Drawing on the research of Cox, Bruckner, and Stabb, Eddleman deftly applies their observation that "although anger is a legitimate emotion that serves the very important purpose of 'endow[ing] its owner with emotional energy and intellectual clarity for making needed life changes,' women, through the centuries, have learned that it is inappropriate, unladylike, even sinful, to express anger."[91] The result of this historical-emotional process is generations of women internalizing or denying anger as a reaction to injustices (especially gender-based injustices). This eventually strips a woman's identity away in a process that "psychotherapist

---

[89] Austen, *MP*, 361.

[90] *Ibid.*, 393.

[91] Eddleman, "Mad as the Devil," 41-2; Eddleman quotes from Cox et. al., *The Anger Advantage*, 11.

Harriet Lerner calls 'de-selfing'"[92] Fanny has, in short, internalized her society's belief that, to quote the Bible, "it is better to dwell in a wilderness, than with a contentious and an angry woman."[93] Despite this social conditioning against anger, Eddleman is able to point to moments when Fanny shows glimpses of anger toward Crawford; applying this lens to her thoughts on Sir Thomas is instructive, as well. Between the cruel confrontation surrounding her relationship with Crawford and the forced separation from Mansfield Park, Fanny is awakened to Sir Thomas' faults as a father figure. This realization, then, opens the door for Fanny to doubt his authority over her. "She had hoped that, to a man like her uncle, so discerning, so honourable, so good, the simple acknowledgment of settled *dislike* on her side would have been sufficient. To her infinite grief, she found it was not."[94] If a "good," "honourable" guardian would trust his niece's judgment on this important matter, extending Fanny's logic implies her realization that perhaps her uncle is not very good or honorable. It is an awareness that mirrors Mary Wollstonecraft's argument that: "I love man as my fellow; but his scepter, real, or usurped, extends not to me, unless the reason of an individual demands my homage; and even then the submission is to reason, and not to man."[95] That is, Sir Thomas' behavior towards Fanny is governed by neither reason nor kindness; he wants her blind obedience in a situation she knows would compromise her self-respect, and Fanny is unwilling to make this compromise.

It is a subtle moment, but Fanny's internal criticism of Sir Thomas represents a shift in the power he holds over her. After this point, there are no instances in the novel in which she sees him with fear and awe. After three agonizing months, Sir Thomas calls her home to comfort the family in the wake of Julia's elopement and Maria's affair; from this point forward, Fanny holds a different position in the Bertram home and the dynamic changes between her and Sir Thomas. Long denied a real place within the inner family circle, she is now Edmund's "only sister – [his] only comfort now" and has even managed to broach Lady Bertram's formerly-impenetrable self-obsession: "when Lady Bertram came from the drawing room to meet [Fanny]; came with no indolent step; and, falling on her neck, said, 'Dear Fanny! now I shall be comfortable'" – the only time in the novel when Lady Bertram does anything without her usual languid manner.[96] Fanny knows that this family disaster vindicates her against

---

[92] *Ibid.*, 42; Eddleman quotes Lerner, *The Dance of Anger*, 11.
[93] *The Bible* (Christian), Proverbs 21:19.
[94] Austen, *MP*, 293. Italics in original.
[95] Wollstonecraft, *Rights of Women*, 103.
[96] Austen, *MP*, 413, 415.

all of Sir Thomas' unfair allegations: "[h]is displeasure against herself she trusted, reasoning differently from Mrs. Norris, would now be done away. *She should be justified. Mr. Crawford would have fully acquitted her conduct in refusing him.*"[97] All along, she has known that her stance was the correct one, and now she knows that Sir Thomas knows this too and must face his own shortcomings as a parent. "Sir Thomas, poor Sir Thomas," the narrator laments, "a parent, and conscious of errors in his own conduct as a parent, was the longest to suffer. He felt that he ought not to have allowed the marriage; that his daughter's sentiments had been sufficiently known to him to render him culpable in authorising it; that in so doing he had sacrificed the right to the expedient, and been governed by motives of selfishness and worldly wisdom."[98] Fully admitting that he prioritized financial advantage over his daughter's emotional well-being, Sir Thomas knows that, ultimately, he is to blame for Maria's disastrous marriage: knowing it – and suffering from it – are his penance.

There is a triumphant irony in the fact that Fanny becomes a daughter to Sir Thomas, given the lengths he (and his henchperson Mrs. Norris) took to prevent Fanny from having equal status as his biological children. Marriage between Fanny and one of his sons was Sir Thomas' greatest fear, especially when facing economic precarity: his main goal was to use his children's marriages to pursue social status and wealth. "Sick of ambitious and mercenary connexions [*sic*], prizing more and more the sterling good of principle and temper," Sir Thomas undergoes a complete change of heart and is genuinely happy at the prospect of Fanny and Edmund's marriage. "Fanny was indeed the daughter that he wanted…on really knowing each other, their mutual attachment became very strong."[99] The tyrannical patriarch's coming-to-god moment, in which he learns that his moral framework and treatment of women were wrong and learns to change his ways, is a plot arc that becomes more common throughout nineteenth-century forced marriage plots, indicating that concrete changes within gender-based oppression are possible. In *Mansfield Park* Fanny is finally considered an equal, full member of the family and gets the previously forbidden marriage that she desires – all the result of standing by her own moral code even in the face of forced marriage.

---

[97] *Ibid.*, 420. Italics in original.
[98] *Ibid.*, 428-9.
[99] *Ibid.*, 437-8.

The *Sanditon* fragment and unfettered capitalism

Before concluding this chapter, I would like to spend a few moments dwelling on Austen's final, unfinished novel *Sanditon*. The fact that only twelve chapters exist (researchers have yet to find any tangible evidence regarding the intended plot arc) is likely to blame for the relative lack of existing scholarship, but the chapters that do exist suggest Austen's increasing interest in capitalism's impact on the lives of women and in using the forced marriage plot to explore the topic. The novel follows Charlotte Heywood's introduction to Sanditon, a small coastal village where two of the other main characters, Mr. Parker and Lady Denham, are determined to transform into a profitable resort town. Mr. Parker, readers are told, is a kindly man "with more Imagination than Judgement" who seems to love Sanditon above all else in his life – including, at times, his family.[100] Sanditon "was his Mine, his Lottery, his Speculation and his Hobby Horse; his Occupation his Hope and his Futurity."[101] Though what exists of the novel does not explicitly state whether his "Speculation" will be a success, the narrator's constant hints that Parker depends on its success for his livelihood (and that Mrs. Parker is "not of a capacity to supply the cooler reflection which her own Husband sometimes needed") suggest disaster ahead.[102]

His business partner is a local dowager, Lady Denham, whose singular goal in life is hoarding wealth. Twice widowed, the narrator makes it clear that Lady Denham, "born to Wealth but not to Education," married her first husband for his money and her second husband for his title.[103] Connecting the wealthy merchants of chapters one and two of this project with the greedy speculators of chapters four and five, she exemplifies the extreme wealth that concerned Adam Smith and which Marx and Engels will decry later in the century. From a stylistic point of view, she shares characteristics of Charles Dickens' Mrs. Skewton or a female Ralph Nickleby in that her over-the-top obsession with money melds dark humor with social satire. Having "so well nursed and pleased" her (elderly) first husband that he left her his entire property outright (much to the detriment of his relatives), she keeps this money to herself when she marries again.[104] "The late Sir Harry Denham, of Denham Park in the Neighborhood of Sanditon," readers are told, "had succeeded in removing her

---

[100] Jane Austen, *Sanditon*, in *Northanger Abbey, The Watsons, and Sanditon*, ed. James Kinsley (Oxford: Oxford University Press, 2003), 302.
[101] *Ibid.*, 302.
[102] *Ibid.*, 302.
[103] *Ibid.*, 304.
[104] *Ibid.*, 304.

and her large Income to his own Domains, but he could not succeed in the views of permanently enriching his family, which were attributed to him"[105] In fact, she is known to boast that "that though she had *got* nothing but her Title from the Family, still she had *given* nothing for it."[106] Socio-economically speaking, Lady Denham is something of an anomaly; I suspect if *Sandition* were finished, the inheritance practices in it would likely be as widely discussed as the entail in *Pride and Prejudice* since it was rare for women to inherit such large fortunes, and married women who did have their own money (typically by way of legacy or marriage settlements) did not commonly enjoy full control over the entirety of these sums. Furthermore, as Martha Bailey points out, "marriage settlements often provided that a wife would give up her dower rights, a life interest in one-third of all land owned by the husband during the marriage, and receive instead a jointure, a specified sum for her separate use that would be her support if she survived her husband."[107] In terms of its legal history, dower rights can be seen as a casualty of primogeniture in the race to fortify estates, and it also makes it all the more remarkable that Lady Denham is able to maintain control over her own money through two marriages. Upon marriage, a woman's legal status changed from an individual to what was called a *feme covert*. As William Blackstone defines in *Commentaries on the Laws of England*:

> the very being or legal existence of the woman is suspended during the marriage, or at least is incorporated and consolidated into that of the husband: under whose wing, protection, and cover, she performs every thing [sic]; and is therefore called in our law-French a *feme-covert*; is said to be covert-baron, or under the protection and influence of her husband, her baron, or lord; and her condition during her marriage is called her coverture.[108]

While this absorption of her legal identity into her husband's did have some potential benefits for a married woman (for instance, her husband was responsible for any debts acquired – even before the marriage), mostly it resulted in the wife's losing the few financial freedoms she had as a single woman. According to Bailey, "[o]ne implication of coverture was that the husband

---

[105] *Ibid.*, 304.

[106] *Ibid.*, 304. Italics in original.

[107] Martha Bailey, "The Marriage Law of Jane Austen's World," *Persuasions* 36, no. 1 (Winter 2015): n. pg.

[108] Blackstone, *Commentaries*, 440. Italics in original.

became entitled to his wife's property and income."[109] Any money or property that she owned became her husband's legal property upon their marriage.

While it is tempting to read Lady Denham's circumventing patriarchal inheritance practices as empowering, her vanity and rough manners make her an object of mockery to Charlotte (and, by extension, the reader), and her miserliness has significant negative impacts on the people around her. A keen observer, Charlotte is quick to identify the cruelty that results from Lady Denham's obsession with wealth and, like *Clarissa*'s Rodger Solmes, her refusal to share anything with her impoverished family members. In fact, this is where the novel's forced marriage plot originates. The three relatives that live near Lady Denham all exhibit financial needs despite their relation's extreme wealth. Young Sir Edward inherited his title from Lady Denham's second husband, but there was no money left to accompany it. "For though I am *only* the *Dowager* my Dear, and he is the *Heir*, things do not stand between us in the way they commonly do between those two parties," Lady Denham boasts, "Not a shilling do I receive from the Denham Estate. Sir Edward has no Payments to make *me*. He don't stand uppermost, beleive [*sic*] me. – It is *I* that help *him*."[110] The only "help" she has ever given him is a gold pocket watch (which his late uncle planned to give him anyway) and – when it suits her – a room in which to stay during visits. However, her wealth and local influence keep Sir Edward and his sister bound to her in their hope for greater financial support. Whom they will marry is a subject on which she, therefore, feels entitled to control. "[H]e is very well to look at," she says of Sir Edward, "and it is to be hoped that some lady of large fortune will think so – for Sir Edward *must* marry for Money," though she regrets that "[h]eiresses are monstrous scarce."[111] Of Esther she says much the same thing, that the young woman "must marry somebody of fortune too – She must get a rich Husband. Ah! young Ladies that have no Money are very much to be pitied."[112] It is hard to say if Lady Denham's position on her niece and nephew's marriages has the same *quid pro quo* benefits to her that are present in other forced marriage plot novels – given that only a few chapters exist – but at the very least it is clear that they must marry for wealth so that she does not have to provide for them.

The unfinished nature of the novel leaves many unanswered questions. Was Lady Denham meant to be the novel's villain? Would Sir Edward and Esther

---

[109] Bailey, "The Marriage Law of Jane Austen's World," n.pg.
[110] Austen, *Sanditon*, 234. Italics in original.
[111] *Ibid.*, 234-5. Italics in original.
[112] *Ibid.*, 325.

have given into her demands and married to please her, or would Lady Denham have been scorned by her relatives? Would her character have shown any redeeming qualities, or, like Austen's earlier character Lady Susan, been able to be read as rebelling against her society's patriarchal capitalism?[113] One thing that is certain, as Roger Ebbatson has pointed out, is that commerce, capitalism, and class anxieties are at the heart of *Sanditon*, in which "the logic of capital," the desire for self-enrichment, caused "[t]he increasing threat to customary relations."[114] I would emend his statement to point out that, when understood as part of the forced marriage plot heritage, it is obvious that Austen's era is not the first to see the impact of self-enrichment on interpersonal relationships, but that Austen identified shades of complexity that emerge in her texts.

Conclusion

As I have argued above, understanding the ways in which capitalism – and the changes it brought to British social classes – is a crucial context in understanding Jane Austen's novels. The complex ways in which British socio-economic classes were developing created more challenges for women who lived within this system. Moving away from the simplistic alignment of money acquisition and evil found in the forced marriage plots of her predecessors, Austen engages with questions asked by economic philosophers like Adam Smith and David Hume about the connections between wealth, morality, and – unique to Austen – the difficult ways in which women must navigate the turbulent path between economic stability and autonomy over their own life decisions: a pairing that was elusive for many women. Using the forced marriage plot as a framework, Austen shows the many ways in which the expanded wealth accumulation enabled by capitalist markets was detrimental to women's freedom. The genteel women about whom she writes were (purposefully) denied access to money through education and inheritance practices, leaving them dependent on men. Continuing the examination of changes to family dynamics wrought with evolving economies common to forced marriage plot novels, novels like *Pride and Prejudice* and *Mansfield Park* contain father figures who abuse the trust their daughters have in them, forcing Elizabeth, Maria, and Fanny, respectively,

---

[113] See Deirdre Le Faye, "Sanditon: Jane Austen's Manuscript and Her Niece's Continuation," *The Review of English Studies* 38, no. 149 (Feb. 1987). Le Faye argues: "It is apparent, therefore, that although Jane had to some extent discussed the characters of Sanditon with Anna in the early months of 1817, she had told neither her nor Cassandra how she intended to develop the plot" (59). It is possible that Austen herself had no clear idea how the plot would conclude.

[114] Austen, "Sanditon," 46-7.

to face the threat of economic precarity. This, in turn, forces the women of the novel to make difficult choices between following their society's social norms – consenting to the situations their patriarch has caused – or listening to their desires and moral systems to fight for their own best interests.

Chapter Four
"Selling a girl": Charles Dickens, Elizabeth Stone, and Post-Industrial Patriarchy

The previous chapter ended with a brief look at the possible forced marriage plot present in *Sanditon*, Austen's last unfinished novel, in which the language of post/industrial capitalism impacts the lives of the characters. Commercial wealth, speculation, and the discourse of improvement (and profit) pervade the existing pages of that novel in a way that I feel safe assuming would have impacted the novel's burgeoning forced marriage plot(s). This chapter, then, picks up those socio-economic threads and shows the prominent role they played in post-industrial Britain. I analyze Charles Dickens' *Nicholas Nickleby* (1838-9) and *Dombey and Son* (1846-8) and Elizabeth Stone's *William Langshawe, the Cotton Lord* (1842) as forced marriage plot novels that provide insights into the ways in which England's precarious post-industrial capitalist boom of the 1830s and 40s fostered an environment that encouraged the use and abuse of women in the name of financial gain. This specific socio-economic period fostered an environment in which a man's worth was tethered to his income; mid-nineteenth-century discourses often linked a hearty work ethic to virtue and thus to ideal masculinity. This glorification of work then segued into a glorification of wealth. It is no coincidence that this period also saw the rise of speculation and joint-stock corporations: practices that encouraged the rapid accumulation of wealth outside of typical labor/wage exchange (though very much enabled by it).

Adapting the forced marriage plot to their historical moment, Dickens and Stone dramatize the oppressive, gender-based power hierarchy upon which those at the top of the socio-economic food chain relied to grow and maintain their individual wealth. Like their contemporaries, Karl Marx and Frederich Engels, Dickens and Stone recognized that dehumanizing fellow humans into objects of self-enrichment was an important feature of post-industrial capitalism, but – unlike the latter duo – the novelists understood the specific functions of women and family dynamics in this economy. Utilizing the forced marriage plot to expose this disparity (and often adopting literal and figurative manifestations of sex work to do so), *Nicholas Nickleby*, *Dombey and Son*, and *William Langshawe, the Cotton Lord* offer an innovation on the genre in that they all portray the importance of community – chosen family – in circumventing the male-centered power structures that were enabled by capitalist practices.

Money, masculinity, and the Victorian family

Dickens' oeuvre is filled with novels that explore the intersection between money and marriage. For instance, Thomas Gradgrind's obsession with Utilitarianism teaches his daughter Louisa that love is a frivolous feeling and that Bounderby's ability to provide for her makes the match a good one, despite her obvious dislike of the man. In *Our Mutual Friend*, John Harmon's father stipulates that he must marry Bella Wilfer to inherit his sizable fortune, though as a man with marketable employment skills, Harmon has other options available to him. Many of the relationships in *Bleak House* pivot on the outcome of the *Jarndyce v. Jarndyce* trial; Richard Carstone pins all his hopes on a lucrative outcome, and the decisions he makes based on this hope have tragic implications for Ada Clare. *Little Dorrit* villainizes Fanny and Mr. Dorrit's obsession with wealth and the ways in which this obsession leads them to abuse Amy, whose nickname, "Little," is a nod to her malnourished body, reminding readers of the many times she goes hungry while her father feasts on sumptuous meals. Though a forced marriage plotline does not feature prominently in *Little Dorrit*, Dorrit makes it clear that he expects his daughter to marry "eligibly."[1]

In all but one of these examples, the problematic attitude toward wealth is presented in the form of a father who makes a choice to tend to his own sense of material self-interest over that of his children. Given the pervasiveness of this dynamic in Dickens' *oeuvre*, it is worth considering the socio-economic changes that inspired so many dysfunctional fathers. One of these factors is changing attitudes toward the *nouveaux riches*. For instance, in the novels discussed in chapters one and two, which were written in the eighteenth century, new-money merchants like Harlowe, Solmes, Maynard, and Clarendon are still, to an extent, social pariahs. As thinkers as diverse as Adam Smith and Eric Williams express, these men can buy socio-political clout but are still, to some degree, marked as vulgar for the fact that they made their money through trade. A shift in this attitude is perceptible by Jane Austen's period, in which the stark class differences have become more complex; *Sanditon*'s Lady Denham, for instance, is rude and selfish but is so wealthy (due to commerce and strategic marriages) that her neighbors consider her "[t]he great lady of Sanditon." Mr. Gardiner in *Pride and Prejudice* has elevated himself through his trade and is also perfectly respectable.[2] All of which is to say that Austen experienced and recorded a class system that was both more complex and

---

[1] Charles Dickens, *Little Dorrit*, ed. Helen Small (Penguin Classics, 2004), 638.

[2] Austen, *Sanditon*, 304.

ambiguous, and a character's socio-economic status was not an accurate indicator of their personal qualities.

By the time Dickens wrote *Nicholas Nickleby*, however, the shift first seen in Austen had grown more pronounced; making one's own wealth had grown to have more positive associations. As Eric Hobsbawm puts it, there was a belief that: "wealth was not due to economic banditry but, as it were, to the generosity with which society rewarded its benefactors."[3] The myth of the self-made man as a national hero loomed large in this period. This is an idea that Samuel Smiles perpetuates in his 1859 guide *Self-Help; with Illustrations of Character, Conduct, and Perseverance*, in which he includes anecdotes about some of England's most famous titans of industry, claiming they "are almost equivalent to gospels – teaching high living, high thinking, and energetic action for their own and the world's good."[4] He goes on to claim that "[h]onorable industry travels the same road with duty; and Providence has closely linked both with happiness."[5] The pursuit of wealth is linked to godliness; those who made their fortune through the industry are celebrated as heroes, while those who are not wealthy are encouraged that their own hard work will lead to their own moral and financial success.

However, as Dickens' many corrupt father figures show, this narrative lacked a basis in truth; according to John Tosh, this "characteristically Victorian valorization of work as both moral duty and personal fulfillment" was little more than a façade used to justify greed, acting like "a camouflage for moneymaking and self-advancement."[6] In *Nicholas Nickleby*, for instance, Ralph Nickleby grows up hearing his father extoll the luxuries that money can buy. From this, Ralph "deduced the often-repeated tale the two great morals that riches are the only true source of happiness and power, and that it is lawful and just to compass their acquisition by all means short of felony."[7] That obtaining money is life's primary goal is a lesson he learns in his own home, from his own family – and, as the excerpts from Smiles show – was pervasive within his society. His culture celebrates the capitalist ethos so much that Ralph and his partner Bonnie are cheered out of the House of Commons on the shoulders of Parliament members after making a pitch for what is very

---

[3] Eric Hobsbawm, *The Age of Capital: 1848-1875* (Abacus Books, 1975), 174.

[4] Samuel Smiles, *Self-help: With Illustrations of Character, Conduct and Perseverance* (1859; London, 1878), 27.

[5] *Ibid.*, 49.

[6] John Tosh, "Masculinities in an Industrializing Society: Britain, 1800–1914," *Journal of British Studies* 44, no. 2 (2005): 332-3.

[7] Charles Dickens, *Nicholas Nickleby*, 1838-9, ed. Mark Ford (Penguin Classics, 2003), 18-9. Hereafter *NN*.

obviously a scam corporation. For Ralph, Parliament, and much of their larger society, the pursuit of wealth was not just tolerated – it was glorified.

Speculation and joint stock corporations in Victorian England

Another historical context worth lingering over before discussing Dickens' forced marriage plots is the reemergence of joint-stock companies in Victorian England. Joint-stock corporations, companies owned by groups rather than individuals, experienced a boom in England during the 1830s and 40s. After the disastrous stock market crash caused by the bursting of the South Sea Bubble in 1719, Parliament passed the Bubble Act of 1720, which prohibited the creation of joint stock companies without Parliament's approval. As James Taylor explains, joint stock companies enjoyed legal privileges that were unavailable to other types of privately-owned companies. They "had an existence distinct from their members: they could sue and be sued in the courts, own property, and lived on after their founders had died" and were, in some cases, granted the rights to monopoly in their respective fields.[8] In short, joint stock corporations established a layer of separation between businessmen and businesses that shielded individual board members from potential problems, like lawsuits or financial losses, that in private partnerships would likely have negative repercussions for the business owners.

For many decades after the Bubble Act, Parliament granted few charters for joint stock companies; a few giants, such as the East India Company, held monopolies over certain goods, but it was not until the turn of the century that joint stock companies underwent a renaissance. The Industrial Revolution fed the desire for more joint stock companies to the point that in 1844 Parliament passed the Joint Stock Companies Act, which eliminated the need for Parliamentary approval, opening the floodgates to a tide of joint stock companies in the British market. Some sold shares that brought a return on investment, but there were many, like the banking firm Overend, Gurney, and Company, that failed extravagantly.[9] Some of these failures were so dramatic that some wondered if that had been their goal the whole time. In fact, as early as 1776, Adam Smith cast doubt on joint stock companies. "[B]eing the managers rather of other people's money than of their own, it cannot be well expected,

---

[8] James Taylor, *Creating Capitalism: Joint-Stock Enterprise in British Politics and Culture 1800-1870* (The Boydell Press, 2006), 3.

[9] For decades a highly respected bank, in the 1860s Overend and Gurney overextended itself and was denied a bailout from the Bank of England. This triggered a rush on the bank and a highly publicized collapse that had wide scale ramifications and is considered a major factor in the financial Panic of 1866. For more, see Geoffrey Elliot, *The Mystery of Overend and Gurney: A Financial Scandal in Victorian London* (Methuen, 2006).

that they should watch over it with the same anxious vigilance with which the partners in a private copartnery frequently watch over their own," he wrote in *The Wealth of Nations*, "[n]egligence and profusion, therefore, must always prevail, more or less, in the management of the affairs of such a company."[10] As the early decades of the nineteenth century progressed, Smith's claims of negligent money managers morphed into charges of outright predation, as people began to believe shareholders purposefully preyed on investors: taking their money for self-enrichment while neglecting the claimed goals of the project. As one reporter put it in *Fraser's Magazine for Town and Country*, the London Stock Exchange was a "temple of vice," and speculators (those who sold shares for joint stock companies) were "the vampires of the stock market."[11] There was growing animosity toward joint-stock corporations as the public suspected such businesses existed solely to lure in unwary investors and disappear with their hard-earned money, yet their grand promises of large returns lured in thousands of investors who hoped to amass personal wealth.

Ralph Nickleby, "the Capitalist"

Dickens brings the vampiric figure of the evil speculator to life through Ralph Nickleby, who applies the methods he uses as a mercenary stock jobber to all facets of his life, especially in terms of how he treats women. In addition to his role as the pseudo-father figure to Nicholas and Kate after their father's death, Ralph is also a founding member of the United Metropolitan Improved Hot Muffin and Crumpet Baking and Punctual Delivery Company, and it is through this role as a speculator that Ralph gains power over others. As the novel opens, Ralph and his business partner Mr. Bonney scheme to raise five million pounds by selling 500,000 ten-pound shares for their scam corporation.[12] "'And when they are at a premium,' said Mr. Ralph Nickleby, smiling," as the two discuss their business model, "'[w]hen they are, you know what to do with them as well as any man alive, and how to back quietly out at the right time,' said Mr. Bonney, slapping the capitalist familiarly on the shoulder."[13] The Improved Hot Muffin Company is a scam that solicits investments before dissolving, allowing Ralph and Bonney to pocket the investments. As John Bowen explains in

---

[10] Smith, *Wealth of Nations*, 3:259.

[11] "Stock Exchange No. 1," *Fraser's Magazine For Town and Country* (London, vol. 4, no. 20, September 1831), 577-80.

[12] According to the British National Archives, £5,000,000 in 1840 would have the same purchasing power as over £300,000,000 in today's currency. £10 (the cost of individual shares) is equal to about £600 in today's purchasing power, which is a considerable amount of money to solicit from common people.

[13] Dickens, *NN*, 25.

Nicholas Nickleby: "[w]e are presented with capitalist and entrepreneurial activity in its purest, most speculative and exploitative form...Ralph is not a hoarder of loot, counting his pots of gold in squalor" like Ebenezer Scrooge, "but an entirely contemporary figure, a master-manipulator of the new complexities of publicity, monopoly, and speculation."[14] Rooting his villain's identity in the socio-economic practices of his own moment allows *Nicholas Nickleby* to explore the real-world impacts of these present to society at large. Previous chapters have explored the ways in which socio-economic developments relied on women as commodities: exchangeable objects to help move money between men. This trend, which persisted into the nineteenth century, relied on women's compliance within this "systemic social apparatus," to borrow Gayle Rubin's term, that actively worked to prevent women from developing their own sense of identity and acting with autonomy.[15]

In *Nicholas Nickleby*, readers witness two forced marriages that dramatize how money-hungry men treated women as objects of exchange for their own financial gain. The primary forced marriage plot, in which Ralph uses his niece Kate to make money for himself, will be considered at length below, but there is another, perhaps more minor, forced marriage plot worth mentioning, as well, especially since it highlights Ralph's eagerness to exchange women between men. Mr. Bray, a bad-tempered invalid, owes Ralph and Arthur Gride (another of the novel's villains) a collective debt of £2,600, and the two worry that Bray will die before they can collect repayment. Not one to let debts go unpaid, Ralph concocts a scheme in which Bray will give Madeline to Gride as a wife in exchange for a reprieve from some of his debts. For his role as a middleman, Ralph gets a fee and rights to the fortune Madeline will inherit upon her father's death.[16] "You have money," Ralph says to Gride, "and Miss Madeline has beauty and worth. She has youth, you have money. She has not money, you have not worth. Tit for tats – quits – a match of Heaven's own making."[17] Bray loves Madeline "with the utmost affection of which he was capable," which is to say not very much, "yet he loved himself a great deal better."[18] Like many of the mercenary fathers previously discussed in this book,

---

[14] John Bowen, "Performing Business, Training Ghosts: Transcoding Nickleby," *ELH* 63, no. 1 (1996):158-9.

[15] Gayle Rubin, "The Traffic in Women: Notes on the Political Economy of Sex," in *Toward an Anthropology of Women*, edited by Rayna R. Reiter (Monthly Review Press, 1975), 158.

[16] This fortune was willed in such a way to keep Bray from accessing any of it; knowing of his gambling and lavish tastes, Madeline's maternal grandparents are protecting Madeline's fortune from her own father – she cannot access any of it until he is dead.

[17] Dickens, *NN*, 587.

[18] *Ibid.*, 582.

"Selling a girl"

Bray sees his daughter as an exchangeable commodity to be used for his own benefit rather than an individual with her own desires; he has no scruples selling his daughter to the elderly money lender to increase his own comfort.

Madeline is caught between what she sees is her duty to serve her father and her abhorrence toward Gride to the point that she finds herself trapped by the social customs of her period. As Paul Jarvie notes, *Nicholas Nickleby* explicitly shows the psychological trauma that capitalist practices cause children, which is apt, but he problematically defines both Madeline Bray and Kate Nickleby as children in the same category as the young students whom Wrackford Squeers abuses at his school. Madeline and Kate are not naïve children like Squeers' pupils: they are grown women. In fact, Madeline understands the role into which her father forces her quite clearly. Nicholas tells her: "You are betrayed, sold for money – for gold, whose every coin is rusted with tears, if not red with the blood of ruined men, who have fallen desperately by their own mad hands," assuming that she is unable to understand the full dynamic of the situation.[19] Madeline rejects this notion: "I am impelled to this course by no one," she retorts, "but follow it of my own free will."[20] She admits: "I do *not* love this gentleman; the difference between our ages, tastes, and habits forbids it. This he knows, and knowing, still offers me his hand."[21] Madeline has been groomed to sacrifice her own happiness for her father's sake: a sacrifice, as will be discussed in more detail below, that conduct guides and other popular discourse taught women was their moral duty. Ralph's belief that Madeline is "devoted to the support and maintenance, and was a slave to every wish, of her only parent, who had no other friend on earth" is proved to be unfortunately true.[22] It is obvious to readers that Bray does not deserve such a devoted daughter, but her obedience to her father is complicated by her belief, planted by Ralph, that her father is so sick that he will die unless he can acquire better lodgings and care – things that Gride's wealth can easily provide. Playing on the same understanding of class and gender that Sir Thomas Bertram does in *Mansfield Park* when he sends Fanny back to her impoverished family in Portsmouth, Ralph knows that Madeline's socially prescribed understanding of feminine duty will not allow her to reject a marriage she thinks is necessary to save her father's life. "By accepting [Gride's hand in marriage], and by that step alone, I can release my father who is dying in this place, prolong his life, perhaps for many years," she tells Nicholas before bluntly admitting "[d]o not think so poorly of me as to

---

[19] *Ibid.*, 657.
[20] *Ibid.*, 658.
[21] *Ibid.*, 658. Italics in original.
[22] *Ibid.*, 582.

believe that I feign a love I do not feel...If I cannot in reason or in nature love the man who pays this price for my poor hand, I can discharge the duties of a wife."[23] What Madeline here describes is her resignation to a marriage that closely resembles sex work – exchanging her wifely "duties" for her father's comfort, transforming her into a tragic figure who is portrayed as a victim of post-industrial male greed.

Nicholas Nickleby's second forced marriage plot features many similarities to Madeline's but involves a female character – Kate Nickleby – who fights back against the forced marriage (and thus the power structures this marriage represents), modeling heroic disobedience that saves her and Madeline from certain misery. It begins with a foolish young Lord, Sir Frederick Verisopht, who will one day inherit a fortune; until he receives this payout, however, he has been borrowing heavily from Ralph. Not one to settle for scamming someone out of a portion of his inheritance when the whole inheritance can be obtained, Ralph decides to use Kate as a tool to keep Verisopht around – borrowing more money from Ralph – until Ralph decides to collect the debt and its exorbitant interest. Kate, Ralph believes, "will keep the boy to me, while there is money to be made" as a metaphorical carrot dangling in front of a donkey.[24] Interestingly, Ralph occasionally feels a pang of guilt for treating his beautiful young niece in such a manner: "[s]elling a girl," he thinks to himself, "throwing her in the way of temptation, and insult, and coarse speech. Nearly two thousand pounds profit from it already though. Pshaw! Match-making mothers do the same thing every day."[25] Knowing full well the debauched characters to whom he is exposing Kate, he nevertheless justifies filling his pockets by comparing himself to "[m]atch-making mothers." Though the discussion of *Dombey and Son* (below) shows that occasionally mothers do act in this manner, readers are likely to see the logical fallacy of Ralph's argument. It is worth noting that, despite his comment about match-making mothers, marriage does not actually seem to figure anywhere in Ralph's plan. His language around "selling" Kate – exposing her to "temptation" and "insult" suggests he is imagining a scenario in which he is selling her as a sexual object to Verisopht.

Marx famously referred to money as "the pimp between man's need and the object" he wants, inscribing those who possess it, like Ralph, with power over those, like Kate and Madeline Bray, who lack it.[26] While Marx's pimp analogy is

---

[23] *Ibid.*, 658-9.

[24] *Ibid.*, 329.

[25] *Ibid.*, 329; note that according to the National Archives, £2,000 in 1830 money would have the same purchasing power as (about) £130,000 today.

[26] Marx and Engels, *Economic and Philosophic Manuscripts*, 136.

meant to underscore the nefarious nature of what an excess of money can produce, it also speaks – if inadvertently – to the sexual dynamic that underpins the treatment of women in this post-industrial economy. In the novel, this becomes apparent in the resigned way Madeline agrees to marry Gride in exchange for her father's wellbeing and in Ralph's trafficking of Kate against her will to lascivious Verisopht. At one point, Ralph stops his crony Sir Mulberry Hawk from sexually assaulting Kate. Hawk asks Ralph: "[d]o you mean to tell me that your pretty niece was not brought here as a decoy for that drunken boy downstairs?... Do you mean to say that if he had found his way up here instead of me, you wouldn't have been a little more blind, and a little more deaf, and little less flourishing than you have been?"[27] Ralph admits that Hawk is right: he brought Kate to dinner to set up a romantic – likely sexual – encounter between Frederick and the unsuspecting Kate. This, Ralph claims, is just a "matter of business," making it obvious that his plan was to force Kate into some semblance of sex work, exchanging her for his own profit.[28]

Kate's importance in the novel has largely been ignored or downplayed by critics since Dickens' own time. Both Richard Ford in *Quarterly Review* (1839) and an anonymous reviewer for *Fraser's Magazine* (1840) dismiss Kate as a lifeless, flat character.[29] More recently, Hilary M. Schor has argued that Kate's most significant role in the plot is her silence. "Kate's chief 'value' in the novel (as the character and plot device) is her silent work in the marriage plot. She is the subject of her mother's and everyone else's fantasies in the novel," Schor contends, adding that Kate's plot arc "suggests that the world of patriarchal exchange is every bit as deadly to women."[30] Schor's argument that Kate highlights the dangers of patriarchal exchange is apt, but I challenge her notion that Kate's character is marked by her silence. Kate speaks up against Ralph early and often, consistently providing the novel's most blistering critiques of his methods; she is vocal in her condemnation of Ralph and firm in her resolve to break out of her role as his victim.

While Nicholas and Mrs. Nickleby gullibly trust Ralph, wasting their time creating "air-built castles" about the grand opportunities he will bring them, Kate immediately recognizes the mercenary motivations that compel his introduction into their lives.[31] In fact, during their first meeting after the death

---

[27] Dickens, *NN*, 238.

[28] *Ibid.*, 238.

[29] Philip Collins, ed., *The Critical Heritage of Charles Dickens* (Routledge, 1995), 83, 88.

[30] Hilary M. Schor, *Dickens and the Daughter of the House* (Cambridge University Press, 2000), 44.

[31] Dickens, *NN*, 42.

of Mr. Nickleby, Kate repeatedly raises concerns about Ralph's plans for the Nicklebys, only to be hushed by her family. For instance, when Ralph presents Wrackford Squeers' job ad, Kate points out that the £5 per year salary is "so small" and the school "such a long way off," but her mother interrupts her, insisting: "[h]ush, Kate my dear…your uncle must know best."[32] Suspicious of Ralph from the beginning, Kate recognizes that his charity is simply self-interest masquerading as concern. Unlike Madeline, who feels compelled to submit to his plan, Kate resists Ralph's oppression at every chance she gets. For example, recognizing that Ralph is using her as a pawn in his financial dealings with Lords Hawk and Frederick, Kate confronts Ralph directly: "If they were no friends of yours," she admonishes him after narrowly avoiding Sir Mulberry Hawk's sexual assault, "and you knew what they were, –, the more shame on you, uncle, for bringing me among them…if you did it – as I now believe you did – knowing them well, it was most dastardly and cruel."[33] Demeaning as Hawk's and Frederick's treatment of her is, it is Ralph's role as the enabler that most angers Kate. "[C]ome what may, *I will not*, as I am your brother's child, bear these insults longer," she declares.[34] Resisting the role into which Ralph forces her, Kate cuts ties with him:

> I am to be the scorn of my own sex, and the toy of the other; justly condemned by all women of right feeling, and despised by all honest and honourable men; sunken in my own esteem, and degraded in every eye that looks upon me. No, not if I work my fingers to the bone, not if I am driven to the roughest and hardest labour…I will hide myself from [Verisopht and Hawk] and you, and, striving to support my mother by hard service, I will live, at least, in peace, and trust God to help me.[35]

Vowing to respect the terms of her current employment as a lady's companion – she needs the money, after all – Kate tells Ralph in no uncertain terms that she is done with him, his associates, and their threatening machinations. She is intelligent enough to understand the manipulative, abusive way in which he is treating her, and she stands up to him with the authority of a woman who knows she is worth more than the price tag for which Ralph sees her. Kate refuses to be used as a tool for Ralph's personal enrichment. Rather than characterizing Kate by silence, as Schor does, Kate's verbal sparring – and the actions she takes to extricate herself from Ralph's schemes – is her character's

---

[32] *Ibid.*, 40.
[33] *Ibid.*, 355.
[34] *Ibid.*, 355. Italics in original.
[35] *Ibid.*, 357.

hallmark. She openly rebels against the unjust authority with which money imbues men, breaking with Ralph's and her family's expectations of obedience.

"Lets...take care of each other":
extended kinship networks as anti-patriarchy

Before moving on to my discussion of *Dombey and Son*, I'd like to include one last note on the methods of resisting patriarchal hegemony in *Nicholas Nickleby*. An important theme that emerges in Dickens' and Stone's portrayals of heroic disobedience – and the path to women's increased autonomy – is the importance of empowering friendships: friendships that enable women caught in the web of mercenary capitalism to fight their way out of their oppressive conditions. Holly Furneaux has written of the importance female friendships have in Dickens' fiction, arguing: "[w]hile domesticity is undoubtedly at the emotionally invested heart of Dickens's work, offering a fanaticized panacea to wider social suffering, it is a rigorously defamiliarized domestic that Dickens persistently recommends."[36] That is, domestic life is presented as a salve for the many troubles of the world, but, according to Furneaux, the family unit itself often looks quite different from the heteronormative nuclear family unit consisting of a man, a wife, and their biological offspring. This, I suggest, reflects Dickens' understanding of how capitalism fractured the family unit, something Marx addressed in *Capital*. "Machinery, by throwing every member of that family on to the labor-market spreads the value of the man's labor-power over his whole family... In order that the family may live, four people must now, not only labor, but expend surplus-labor for the capitalist," he explains, adding that "[c]ompulsory work for the capitalist usurped the place, not only of the children's play, but also of free labor at home within moderate limits for the support the family."[37] Every member of the nuclear family must labor outside the home in order to survive. This exploitative environment, according to Marx, causes a gamut of problems even beyond the fact that the family, instead of residing in a nurturing domestic environment, is now worked to the bone outside the home; it becomes necessary for the patriarch to exploit his own family for the sake of survival. "But now the capitalist buys children and young persons under age," Marx writes, "[p]reviously, the workman sold his own labour-power, which he disposed of nominally as a free agent. Now he sells wife and child. He has become a slave-dealer."[38] Marx is clear that the ultimate fault

---

[36] Holly Furneaux, *Queer Dickens: Erotics, Families, Masculinities* (Oxford University Press, 2009), 23.

[37] Karl Marx, *Capital: A Critical Analysis of Capitalist Production*, ed. Frederick Engels (1887; London, 1889), 391-2.

[38] *Ibid.*, 393.

for this exploitation of the family (especially women and children, since their labor was cheaper) lies with the capitalist since capitalists have created conditions in which the "workman" father has no other choice but the result is nevertheless catastrophic for the nuclear family unit.

This toxic family environment is precisely what is on display in *Nicholas Nickleby*; despite his immense wealth, Ralph seeks to exploit his niece's femininity for his own ends. With her mother's unhelpfully optimistic temperament and Nicholas away dealing with his own problems, Kate would have been left to deal with Ralph's abuse alone were it not for her friendship with Madame La Creevey. La Creevey, who paints miniatures for a living, is described as "an odd little mixture of shrewdness and simplicity," and offers Kate the support she so desperately needs.[39] La Creevey finds Ralph a "cross-grained old savage" and recognizes the cruel way he treats his brother's family. "[M]ightn't he, without feeling it himself, make you and your mama some nice little allowance that would keep you both comfortable until you were well married, and be a little fortune to her afterwards? What would a hundred a year for instance, be to him?" she asks Kate, echoing Kate's understanding that Ralph is not the benevolent savior Nicholas and Mrs. Nickleby believe him to be.[40] Her talents and shrewd observations show an understanding of the world that she puts to good use, supporting Kate. "I shall see you very often," she promises Kate, "and come and hear how you get on; and if, in all London, or all the wide world besides, there is no other heart that takes an interest in your welfare, there will be one little lonely woman that prays for it night and day."[41] The genuine affection she has for Kate goes beyond prayers into the realm of action. La Creevey chastises Ralph for his treatment of Kate and tries to convince Nicholas and Mrs. Nickleby see that "that old bear," as she calls him, does more harm than good.[42] When she discovers Ralph's attempt to traffic Kate, it is Madame La Creevey who helps Kate and Mrs. Nickleby sneak out from under Ralph's thumb, providing them with the logistical support – including a comfortably furnished cottage – needed to escape. Even her engagement to Tim Linkinwater toward the novel's close is unconventional. As a self-described "old" person, La Creevey's first marriage coming late in life is unusual, and Tim's proposal sets them apart even more. "'Let's be a comfortable couple, and take care of each other!'" he tells her, "'And if we should get deaf, or lame, or blind, or bed-ridden, how glad we shall be that we have somebody we are fond of,

---

[39] Dickens, *NN*, 122.
[40] *Ibid.*, 122.
[41] *Ibid.*, 135.
[42] *Ibid.*, 241.

always to talk to and sit with! Let's be a comfortable couple.'"⁴³ The two strive for a life full of companionship and contentment, which they extend outward to those around them; Tim proposes a vision of them living in communal happiness with Kate, Nicholas, their respective spouses and children, Newman Noggs, and the Cheeryble brothers. The friendship and chosen family that exists among the characters at the end of the novel, which La Creevey showed to Kate all along, is presented as an alternative to the traditional nuclear family unit free from the oppressive trappings of speculation, made possible by the fact that they treat each other as autonomous individuals, not possessions to exploit.

Dombey and daughter

One of the first things readers learn about Mr. Dombey, the patriarch in *Dombey and Son*, is the extreme degree to which his identity and purpose in life revolve around his family business:

> Dombey and Son. Those three words conveyed the one idea of Mr. Dombey's life. The earth was made for Dombey and Son to trade in, and the sun and moon were made to give them light. Rivers and seas were formed to float their ships; rainbows gave them promise of fair weather; winds blew for or against their enterprises; stars and planets circled in their orbits, to preserve inviolate a system of which they were the centre.⁴⁴

Business is Dombey's whole world; he has spent the past twenty years running it alone and obsessing over having a son to whom he can pass it down. On the surface, he fills many of the components of idealized Victorian masculinity: he works hard, makes a substantial income, runs his business in an above-board manner, and provides material comforts to his family, but the narrative shows how living up to this ideal comes at a terrible cost. The novel's forced marriage plot will be discussed at length below in terms of Dombey's second wife, Edith, but it is nevertheless important to linger on Dombey's relationship with his daughter since it evidences a variation of capitalism's impact on the family. Interestingly, Dickens saw a stage adaptation of *Clarissa*, the prototype for forced marriage plot novels, while writing *Dombey and Son*, perhaps inspiring Dickens to adapt the genre in his own fiction, especially via the father/daughter relationship.⁴⁵ Dombey is a capitalist, not a laborer, so he does not have to sell

---

⁴³ *Ibid.*, 762.

⁴⁴ Charles Dickens, *Dombey and Son*, ed. Andrew Sanders (Penguin Classics, 2002), 12. Hereafter *DS*.

⁴⁵ "'Clarissa Harlowe' is still the rage," Dickens wrote in a letter after the performance, "[t]here are some things in it rather calculated to astonish the ghost of Richardson, but

his child for profit to survive in the way that Marx describes, but as a wealthy, status-obsessed business owner, Dombey only sees his two children in terms of their economic potential: a mindset that leads him to abuse his daughter for years before causing their family unit to crumble.

As the narrator introduces Dombey to the reader in the novel's opening chapter, readers learn that, despite ten years of marriage, Dombey "had no issue."[46] Or, at least, none "[t]o speak of; none worth mentioning. There had been a girl some six years before," the narrator explains, "But what was a girl to Dombey and Son! In the capital of the House's name and dignity, such a child was merely a piece of base coin that couldn't be invested – a bad Boy – nothing more."[47] Slipping into Dombey's consciousness, this passage reflects his negligent attitude toward his daughter Florence. Dombey and Son is the only thing he cares about, and since he considers women and girls irrelevant to business, Florence is worthless to him. To be clear, Dombey sees both Florence and Paul only as material objects; Florence is a "base" coin – one that is defective or counterfeit – and therefore useless to him, while Paul is "capital" that Dombey believes will uphold the dignity of Dombey and Son. Over the course of the novel, Florence tries desperately to win her father's affection, but as time passes, his melancholy over the loss of his heir turns into a grudge against his living daughter, which escalates to physical violence against her. "[I]n his frenzy, he lifted up his cruel arm and struck her, crosswise, with that heaviness, that she tottered on the marble floor," the narrator describes the moment Dombey hits Florence.[48] Like other heroically disobedient daughters described in this project, being hit by her father provides a moment of clarity for Florence:

> She did not sink down at his feet; she did not shut out the sight of him with her trembling hands; she did not weep; she did not utter one word of reproach. But she looked at him, and a cry of desolation issued from her heart. For as she looked, she saw him murdering that fond idea to which she had held in spite of him. She saw his cruelty, neglect, and hatred, dominant above it, and stamping down. She saw she had no father on earth, and ran out, orphaned, from his house.[49]

Clarissa is very admirably played, and dies better than the original to my thinking." See: Charles Dickens, *The Letters of Charles Dickens*, ed. Mary "Mamie" Dickens and Georgina Hogarth, 2 vols. (New York, 1879), 1:201.

[46] Dickens, *DS*, 13.

[47] *Ibid.*, 13.

[48] *Ibid.*, 721.

[49] *Ibid.*, 721.

Raised in a culture that venerates men like Dombey, whose commercial success is equated with moral greatness, Florence lived the early years of her life desperate for him to accept her as a dutiful, loving daughter. When he hits her, however, Florence can no longer hide the truth from herself: that within Dombey's capitalist world, a person's value is only seen in economic terms. This realization inspires a moment of heroic disobedience in young Florence, who rejects the dominant father/daughter paradigm by leaving her father's home. The narrator indicates that Florence is now "orphaned," indicating her self-liberation from Dombey.

If the portrayal of Dombey and Florence's father/daughter relationship highlights the constantly evolving ways in which the capitalist ethos infected British family life, it also, like *Nicholas Nickleby*, speaks to the necessity of friendships in helping women break free from patriarchal understandings of value. For instance, after fleeing from her father's house, Florence experiences the challenge of navigating London alone. She desperately searches for "[s]omewhere, anywhere, to hide her head! somewhere, anywhere, for refuge, never more to look upon the place from which she fled!"[50] In a daze, Florence makes her way to Sol Gill's shop, where Captain Cuttle welcomes her into his home. Grieving the disappearance of Sol and the (misreported) drowning of Walter at the same time Florence is grappling with her new reality, the two form an extra-familial care network; Captain Cuttle cooks and cares for Florence while she comforts him in his time of loss. This friendship between the two represents an alternative family dynamic that provides support to both during their time of need. "[E]ven as her tears made prismatic colors in the light she gazed at, so, through her new and heavy grief, she already saw a rainbow forming in the far-off sky," according to the narrator, "[a] wandering princess and a good monster in a story-book might have sat by the fire-side, and talked as Captain Cuttle and poor Florence thought – and not have looked very much unlike them."[51] Readers familiar with *Clarissa* will remember that Clarissa Harlowe's family turn their backs on her after Lovelace lures her away from home; even though it was in many respects beyond her control, when she leaves the family home Clarissa suddenly finds herself without support – a major problem that precipitates her death ("[i]s it not a sad thing," Clarissa writes, "as beloved as I thought myself so lately by every one [sic], that now I have not one person to plead for me, to stand by me, or who would afford me refuge, where I to be under the necessity of seeking for it").[52] With the exception of Anna Howe, none of Clarissa's friends are willing to break social protocol and

---

[50] *Ibid.*, 722.
[51] *Ibid.*, 740.
[52] Richardson, *Clarissa*, 2:37-8.

help her, and even Anna's support is limited to emotional support since she lives under her mother's rule. In *Dombey and Son*, however, Captain Cuttle provides the runaway daughter with comfort, shelter, and food. With him, Florence is free to be open and honest about her experiences, feelings, and desires. Providing women in need with sincere friendships and material aid is presented as a political act in Dickens' novels: a way for those left out of – and abused by – power structures to escape from this system, necessarily undermining it at the same time.

Urania Cottage

Dicken's belief in the power of friendship and community as an avenue to freedom was not just a theoretical concept he wrote about in his fiction but a plan he tried to put in motion by co-establishing Urania Cottage with philanthropist Angela Burdett-Coutts. Burdett-Coutts, who came from a family of radical politicians, contacted Dickens in 1846 about setting up a haven for outcast women such as sex workers, those who committed petty crimes, or who had otherwise struggled to find stability. After initially trying to dissuade Burdett-Coutts from such an undertaking, Dickens eventually became involved in the day-to-day operation of Urania Cottage. In his essay "A Home for Homeless Women," Dickens describes some of the women and girls who came through the Home, as he calls it. Almost all their stories highlight the social inequalities that predestined them to poverty. One girl, estimated to be sixteen or seventeen, had been abandoned by her parents and was forced to fend for herself on the streets from the age of six or seven. She was arrested for "making a disturbance" at the gates of a workhouse "on being refused relief."[53] Most of the women were forced to turn to sex work to avoid starvation. According to Dickens, the House was a shelter for these women who had nowhere else to turn. They received an education, a clean environment, a little money to take with them when they emigrated to Australia, and – importantly – a community of peers who understood and empathized with their hardships. A letter from one of the Home's graduates to her friends still there reads: "Honnoured [sic] Ladies I can never feel grateful enough for your kindness to me and the kind indulgences which I received at my happy Home, I often wished I could come Home and see that happy place again once more and all my kind friends which I hope I may one day please God."[54] A former sex worker

---

[53] Charles Dickens, "Home for Homeless Women," in *The Works of Charles Dickens, Miscellaneous Papers* (Chapman and Hall, 1908), 379.

[54] *Ibid.*, "Home," 382.

and rape survivor, this young woman, now a happily-married homeowner in Australia, is still grateful for the utopia-like shelter she found at Urania Cottage.

To be fair, Dickens' relationship with Urania Cottage should be examined with a critical eye. By twenty-first-century standards, there are certain aspects of the operation that seem troubling. Already-vulnerable women were required to agree to terms of conduct before being accepted into Urania Cottage; they earned modest wages but were denied access to this money until their emigration; they had to make the clothes they wore but did not own these clothes; if a woman wanted to leave she was locked in a room by herself for 24 hours as a cooling-down period; and everyone's incoming and outgoing mail was read, just to name a few questionable practices, and there are also perceptible traces of ego and voyeurism in Dickens' descriptions of the House.[55] While these practices raise obvious red flags by twenty-first-century standards, if we look at Urania House by nineteenth-century practices, it was indeed a more empathetic atmosphere than other so-called "Magdalene Houses," which were often an extension of the prison system. That is, in a time when women in general – and sex workers in particular – were constantly devalued by their society, Dickens saw an inherent value in these women as individuals whom society had wronged and who deserved another chance at a better, more stable life. He resisted the urge to condemn women whose backgrounds included sex work, arrests, destitution, and other taboo, impolite aspects, but recognized the oppressive nature of Victorian moral codes and strove to help women who defied these morals to extreme lengths. He, Burdett-Coutts, and the Matrons of the House certainly kept a tight order over the inhabitants, but in Dickens' descriptions of Urania Cottage, there is something especially redemptive about the community of women that was formed there.

"[T]o replace young women who had already lost their characters and lapsed into guilt, in a situation of hope" is the central goal of the Home, according to Dickens, who also wrote in his essay "Home for Homeless Women" that after living at Urania Cottage for even a short amount of time, "a refining and humanising alteration is wrought in the expression of the features, and in the whole air of the person, which can scarcely be imagined."[56] As Dickens describes them, women who have engaged in sex work and petty crimes to survive are not irrevocably "lost" but just in need of support to help them return to a dignified human state. Though Kate Nickleby and Florence Dombey are narrowly spared the necessity of crime or sex work to support themselves, there is, I think, a line that can be drawn from their fictional situations to the

---

[55] See Rosemarie Bodenheimer, *Knowing Dickens* (Cornell University Press, 2007), 136-40.

[56] Dickens, "Home," 376.

inhabitants of Urania Cottage. That is, Kate and Florence – like the inhabitants of Urania Cottage – are victims of their circumstances who require material and emotional support from others, like Madame La Creevy and Captain Cuttle, to escape the oppressive situations into which they are forced.

Dickens' mercenary mothers

While Dombey spends most of the novel willfully blind to his daughter's worth, there are mothers in *Dombey and Son* who, as poor women, see their daughters as highly valuable commodities. One of these mother/daughter duos, Mrs. Skewton and Edith Granger (later Edith Dombey), enact the novel's forced marriage plot in a way that highlights Marx and Engel's claim that capitalism, especially as it was manifested in the Victorian period, ruined the nuclear family unit. "On what foundation is the present family, the bourgeois family, based? On capital, on private gain. In its completely developed form, this family exists only among the bourgeoise. But this state of things finds its complement in the practical absence of the family among the proletarians and in public prostitution," Marx writes in *The Communist Manifesto*:

> The bourgeois claptrap about the family and education, about the hallowed co-relation of parent and child, becomes all the more disgusting, the more, by the action of modern industry, [in which] all family ties are torn asunder and their children transformed into simple articles of commerce and instruments of labor.[57]

Many of Marx's critics took special offense to his calls to abolish the traditional family structure. Addressing such critics in the above passage, Marx points out that the traditional family dynamic has already been obliterated by capitalism. The bourgeoisie has so alienated the proletariat from any notion of self-worth beyond its economic connotation that parents only see their children for their potential labor value. While this is, in a general sense, the basic dynamic behind the forced marriage plot, most of the forced marriage plots examined so far focus on what Marx would do doubt call the bourgeoise – but Dickens shifts the focus to families who are alienated from the means of production: particularly poor women. *Dombey and Son* is unique in its portrayal of mercenary mothers, whose corrupting influence over their daughter represents the cyclical nature of capitalist-based oppression.

The novel's primary mercenary mother, Mrs. Skewton, is characterized by a falseness that defines her whole being. Called "Cleopatra" by the narrator due to her attempt to stylize herself like the ancient Queen, Mrs. Skewton's face

---

[57] Marx and Engels, *Economic and Philosophic Manuscripts*, 223-4.

features: "false curls and false eyebrows...false teeth, set off by her false complexion."[58] In some ways, this description links her to the tyrannical fathers discussed in earlier chapters, like Sir Edward and Maynard, who are characterized by their lavish conspicuous consumption. Instead of fine wines or rare pineapples, though, Mrs. Skewton's consumption is linked to her physical appearance and her pathetic attempts to appear young and beautiful. She is, one might say, a monstrous manifestation of what capitalism enabled.

Appearances mean more to her than relationships, and she understands that Edith, who is beautiful, is a commodity she can exchange for her own comfort. From the time Edith was a child, she explains, her mother "taught" her "to scheme and plot when children play; and married in my youth – an old age of design – to one for whom I had no feeling but indifference."[59] Mrs. Skewton understands the desirability of single, beautiful young women and realizes the economic opportunity this presents. This is not to say that mercenary mothers like Mrs. Skewton or Mrs. Brown, who is discussed below, are meant to be sympathetic characters, but neither is Mrs. Skewton, who is very poor and "chiefly lived upon the reputation of some diamonds and her family connections," is not culpable in the same way that the wealthy fathers of other forced marriage plot novels are.[60] *Dombey and Son* presents in Mrs. Skewton a more extreme, repulsive version of Mrs. Bennet. That is, just as the latter attempts to force Elizabeth to marry Mr. Collins out of a (justified) concern for her daughters' future economic stability, so too does Mrs. Skewton understand a beautiful woman's economic potential. To be clear, it is not my position that readers are meant to empathize with Mrs. Skewton's attitude the way that we are with Mrs. Bennet. Rather, Mrs. Skewton and Mrs. Brown are the monstrous by-products of a capitalist society vis a vis Marx, in which children are only seen as products. These mothers understand Marx's maxim that a capitalist knows: "I am ugly, but I can buy for myself the most *beautiful* of women. Therefore I am not *ugly*, for the effect of *ugliness* – its deterrent power – is nullified by money."[61] Possessing wealth provides power, including buying the companionship of beautiful women. With no other form of economic support, Mrs. Skewton teaches Edith to see herself as a sexualized object for male consumption. "The license of look and touch," Edith asks rhetorically, "have I submitted to it, in half the places of resort upon the map of England? Have I been hawked and vended here and there, until the last grain of self-respect is dead within me, and

---

[58] Dickens, *DS*, 317.

[59] *Ibid.*, 432.

[60] *Ibid.*, 319.

[61] Marx and Engels, *Economic and Philosophic Manuscripts*, 138, italics in original.

I loathe myself?"[62] She signals not just her compliance within the market but the broader way in which her mother's teachings have dulled her sense of self to the point of disappearing: she has been treated as a sexualized object of exchange for so long she cannot see herself as anything else.

Looking at the relationship between Alice Marwood and her mother, Mrs. Brown, helps to underscore the extent to which Mrs. Skewton is essentially trafficking her daughter in the sex trade (even if it does happen to be sanctioned by marriage). After returning from a prison colony abroad, Alice frames her life story:

> '[t]here was a child called Alice Marwood,' said the daughter, with a laugh, and looking down at herself in terrible derision of herself, 'born, among poverty and neglect, and nursed in it. Nobody taught her, nobody stepped forward to help her, nobody cared for her…The only care she knew,' returned the daughter, 'was to be beaten, and stinted, and abused sometimes…yet she brought good looks out of this childhood. So much the worse for her. She had better have been hunted and worried to death for ugliness.'[63]

According to Alice, beauty is her greatest downfall since it can be traded away to men willing to pay to possess it. Like Edith, Alice is groomed by her mother to exchange her looks for the financial support of men, first as Carker's mistress and then, after Carker abandons her, as a sex worker. In both cases, men are willing to pay for access to a woman's body, and the laws of supply-and-demand allowed their scheming mothers, needy themselves, to teach their daughters that society had no other options available to them. Like Madeline Bray in *Nicholas Nickleby*, these women know there are few distinctions between "prostitution, but public and private," as Marx puts it: public prostitution meaning sex work like Alice undertakes, and private prostitution, as the marriage Edith contracts.[64] In such cases, as with the inhabitants of Urania Cottage, readers are urged to be sympathetic to the women and girls who are the victims of this exchange.

Alice comes back from prison angry at the circumstances that precipitated her "fall,' but it takes Edith longer to reanimate her will to live according to her own dictates – a feeling that laid dormant during the many years of her mother's trafficking her. Arguing about a mother's needing to be "dutiful" to her daughter, Alice remarks: "It sounds unnatural, don't it?... I have heard some talk

---

[62] Dickens, *DS*, 432.

[63] *Ibid.*, 530-1.

[64] See Marx and Engels, *Economic and Philosophic Manuscripts*, 228.

about duty first and last; but it has always been of my duty to other people. I have wondered now and then—to pass away the time—whether no one ever owed any duty to me."[65] Her life experiences have taught her that "duty" is the rhetoric of the oppressor and that, moving forward, she is going to live by her own agenda. Similarly, Edith comes to resent the beliefs her mother taught her:

> ...there is no slave in the market: there is no horse in a fair: so shown and offered and examined and paraded, Mother, as I have been, for ten shameful years...Have I been made the bye-word of all kinds of men? Have fools, have profligates, have boys, have dotards, dangled after me, and one by one rejected me, and fallen off, because you were too plain with all your cunning: yes, and too true, with all those false pretenses: until we have almost come to be notorious.[66]

Hyperbolic as Edith's comparisons of herself to slaves and horses are, they nevertheless reify the connection to mercenary, immoral, capitalist markets where, with enough money, anything is for sale. She sees her mother trying to indoctrinate young Florence with the same ideas about beauty and marriage or even awaken Dombey to the benefit a forced marriage could have on his business and wants to save her young stepdaughter. "Leave her alone," Edith tells her mother, "[s]he shall not, while I can interpose, be tampered with and tainted by the lessons I have learned."[67] Though not a typical mother figure, Edith's sincere love for her stepdaughter helps her see the pernicious impact Mrs. Skewton had over her own life, and she fights to break the cycle from being handed down to another generation.

The Dombey disaster

Dombey, accustomed to thinking of everyone in terms of the use they provide for him, assumes that, once married, Edith will function as the subservient wife he desires; it never even occurs to him that a woman might have her own will. "Towards his first wife...he had asserted his greatness during their whole married life, and she had meekly recognized it," the narrator explains, but Edith's growing sense of self, awakened as the result of watching her mother reenact Edith's indoctrination on Florence, prohibits her from following this paradigm.[68] Confronting what he sees as her insubordination, Dombey demands: "I am to be deferred to and obeyed. That I must have a positive show

---

[65] Dickens, *DS*, 530.
[66] *Ibid.*, 432.
[67] *Ibid.*, 474.
[68] *Ibid.*, 608.

and confession of deference before the world, Madam. I am used to this. I require it as my right...I consider it no unreasonable return for the worldly advancement that has befallen you."[69] This is a telling passage in the sense that Dombey explicitly describes their marriage in terms of exchange: Edith gets material wealth, and he gets a beautiful object whose "deference before the world" he considers a sign of his dominion. Dombey fits Eric Hobsbawm's definition of Victorian bourgeois manhood, which was predicated on being obeyed by all in his domain: "the bourgeois was not merely an independent, a man to whom no one (save the state or God) gave orders, but one who gave orders himself...the monopoly of command – in his house, in his business, in his factory – was crucial to his self-definition."[70] It is not just important for him to possess a beautiful wife, but he takes pleasure in forcing her to enact submission as both an homage to his authority over her in private and in a more performative sense to display his power in public, as well. As Marx notes, it is not only proletarian families that are broken by capitalist methods of wealth accumulation, arguing "[t]he bourgeois sees in his wife a mere instrument of production."[71] To Dombey, a wife is an instrument to produce a male heir and reflect his own greatness.

Long resigned to playing her prescribed social role, the drama that unfolds in her marriage to Dombey awakens a spirit of resistance in Edith. She tries bargaining with Dombey to set equitable guidelines for their relationship, suggesting that "some friendship, or some fitness for each other, may arise within us," but that, under no circumstances will she submit to the demeaning role he expects of her.[72] "Do you think you can degrade, or bend or break, *me* to submission and obedience?" she asks rhetorically.[73] Dombey's pride prevents him from entertaining anything less than a subservient wife, terms Edith is unwilling to accept. During an especially rancorous fight, she casts off the expensive diamond necklace that Dombey gave her as a wedding gift and walks out of his home forever: a free woman.

Critical interpretation of Edith tends to be harsh; many align her with traditional fallen woman characters, emphasizing Edith's decision to leave Dombey. To many critics, the fact that she ends the novel estranged from the nuclear family unit signals her fallen status. For example, Rita Lubitz claims: "Edith is never forgiven for her actions and must remain alone for the rest of

---

[69] *Ibid.*, 613.

[70] Hobsbawm, *Age of Capital*, 288.

[71] Marx and Engels, *Economic and Philosophic Manuscripts*, 227.

[72] Dickens, *DS*, 617.

[73] *Ibid.*, 616. Italics in original.

her life."⁷⁴ Andrew Miller makes a similar claim, finding a parallel between Dombey and Edith's fates. "As we have seen in Dombey," he argues, "shame brings isolation with it, the construction of barriers."⁷⁵ To these critics, the Victorian glorification of the family as a cohesive, stable unit is so strong that any failure of prescribed family roles can only be seen as a condemnation. As Lisa Surridge's assertion that *Dombey and Son* "excludes and vilifies Edith" highlights, there is an assumption that in Dickens' novel, participation in the nuclear family unit is the ultimate – and only – measure of a character's worth.⁷⁶

Instead of understanding Edith's perceived failures as wife and mother as indications of narrative condemnation of her actions, an encounter between Edith and Florence that occurs near the novel's end highlights the sound moral reasoning behind Edith's decision to leave Dombey. During this meeting, Florence is under the mistaken assumption that Edith left Dombey to have an affair with his crony Carker; she repeatedly begs Edith to ask for Dombey's forgiveness for this (perceived) sin and for leaving him. "If you would have me ask his pardon, I will do it, Mama. I am almost sure he will grant it now if I ask him. May Heaven grant it to you, too, and comfort you! ... I am sure you wish that I should ask him for his forgiveness. I am sure you do."⁷⁷ Gently but firmly correcting the rumor about the alleged affair, Edith explains that the only crime she's "guilty" of is "a blind and passionate resentment, of which I do not, cannot, will not, even now, repent."⁷⁸ Edith knows that leaving Dombey was the direct result of his thoughts and actions, and as such is justified. "I do not repent of what I have done," she explains, "for if it were to do again to-morrow, I should do it...But that being a changed man, he knows, now, it would never be. Tell him I wish it never had been."⁷⁹ Willing to admit that the marriage was a mistake, Edith is firm in her belief that leaving was, for her, the moral choice, and she exhibits a profound sense of personal growth when she tells Florence:

> When he loves his Florence most, he will hate me least. When he is most proud and happy in her and her children, he will be most repentant of his own part in the dark vision of our married life. At that time, I will be repentant too—let him know it then—and think that when I thought so

---

⁷⁴ Rita Lubitz, *Marital Power in Dickens' Fiction* (Peter Lang Press, 1996), 88.

⁷⁵ Andrew H. Miller, *The Burdens of Perfection: On Ethics and Reading in Nineteenth-Century British Literature* (Cornell University Press, 2008), 188.

⁷⁶ Lisa Surridge, *Bleak Houses: Marital Violence in Victorian Fiction* (Athens: Ohio University Press, 2005), 47.

⁷⁷ Dickens, *DS*, 935-6.

⁷⁸ *Ibid.*, 937.

⁷⁹ *Ibid.*, 939.

much of all the causes that had made me what I was, I needed to have allowed more for the causes that had made him what he was. I will try, then, to forgive him his share of blame. Let him try to forgive me mine![80]

It is critically important to understand that she is not apologizing to Dombey for leaving him, but she allows Florence to pass on a message of repentance, as she terms it, for the unhappiness that existed between them. This message includes a crucial caveat: it is only to be delivered on the condition that he is a changed man who also feels remorse for the way he treated the women in his life, especially Florence. Dictating the terms in this way creates a sense of equality between the two that did not exist during their marriage but which Edith knows she deserves. Her language indicates a newfound understanding that the socio-economic forces that commodified her also impacted him, conditioning Dombey to see women as objects: a profound understanding of the insidious practices on which capitalism is based. That is, as Edith understood that there were socio-economic reasons why she was taught to see herself as an object instead of an individual, so too did Dombey learn to think of fellow humans as instruments of labor. The peace of mind that Edith achieves, I suggest, is the direct result of the recognition that neither she nor Dombey is inherently bad but that they were simply playing the roles to which they were assigned. By the end of the novel, Edith is neither a jaded, abused commodity nor a fallen woman; she is confident, content, and finally living a life of peace.

Kelly Hager is one critic who also diverges from reading Edith as a fallen woman, calling her "a Dickensian heroine who looks more like a New Women than an Angel in the House."[81] Helpfully, she points out that Edith's narrative arc ends with her traveling to Italy with her cousin Feenix, whose name is an obvious allusion to the mythical phoenix bird; constantly reborn from its own ashes, the phoenix symbolizes the new, happier life that awaits.[82] In fact, this relationship with Feenix has other implications for Edith's fate: it is an alternative, somewhat unexpected, configuration of the family unit that provides the mutual support that the traditional family model did not. In his customarily loquacious manner, Feenix explains:

...as I mentioned to my friend Dombey, I could not admit the criminality of my lovely and accomplished relative until it was perfectly established. And feeling, when [Carker] was, in point of fact, destroyed in a devilish horrible manner, that her position was a very painful one—and feeling

---

[80] Ibid., 940.
[81] Kelley Hager, *Dickens and the Rise of Divorce: The Failed-Marriage Plot and the Novel Tradition* (Ashgate, 2010), 97.
[82] Hager, *Rise of Divorce*, 97.

besides that our family had been a little to blame in not paying more attention to her, and that we are a careless family—and also that my aunt, though a devilish lively woman, had perhaps not been the very best of mothers—I took the liberty of seeking her in France, and offering her such protection as a man very much out at elbows could offer.[83]

This speech reveals a lot about Feenix's attitude toward women. That is, while the rest of their social circle was abuzz with rumors of Edith and Carker's alleged affair, Feenix refuses to believe the rumors, going so far as to stand up for her to Dombey. He also recognizes that, having left her husband, Edith lacks any financial support and admits that their family –especially her mother – failed her in the past. Feenix takes active measures to find her and offer her the support she so desperately needs. He goes on to say that Edith "put herself under my protection. Which, in point of fact, I understood to be a kind thing on the part of my lovely and accomplished relative, as I am getting extremely shaky and have derived great comfort from her solicitude," and he promises to be "a father to her."[84] Like Captain Cuttle to Florence and Madame La Creevey to Kate Nickleby, Feenix provides the emotional and practical support Edith needs when she is at her most vulnerable: he models the genuine sort of friendship that can exist when family structures, so often marred by the reach of capitalism, crumble.

These redemptive relationships are mutually beneficial, indicative of what Sally Ledger describes as Dickens' rejection of paternalism and the value he places on "the solidarity of the poor."[85] Arguing that after *A Christmas Carol* (1843), in which Scrooge – a wealthy patriarchal figure – swoops to the rescue of the downtrodden, Dickens moves away from this model of narrative closure, replacing it with narratives in which underprivileged characters ban together to help each other and create their own communities (such is in his 1844 holiday tale *The Chimes*). A similar dynamic is at work in *Dombey and Son*. Edith and Feenix's earlier relationship can be described as superficial at best. However, when Edith is in trouble – alone in France after leaving Dombey and scorning Carker – he seeks her out to offer his assistance, though, in the end, he derives as much benefit from their newfound relationship as she does. After a lifetime of commodification and abuse, first by her mother and then by Dombey, this friendship with her cousin provides an alternative path to fulfillment that frees Edith from the pressures of mercenary attitudes toward

---

[83] Dickens, *DS*, 937.

[84] *Ibid.*, 938, 941.

[85] Sally Ledger, *Dickens and the Popular Radical Imagination* (Cambridge University Press, 2007), 129.

women. Though this exchange is the last scene with Edith, readers are ensured that her character ends the novel feeling both at peace and empowered: a far cry from a fallen woman.

Interestingly, *Dombey and Son* goes further in countering the typical fallen woman narrative by applying a fallen-woman-like narrative to Dombey's narrative arc. Some, such as Hilary Schor, argue that the father/daughter reunion at the end of the novel signifies Florence's belief that she failed in her daughterly duty to her father.[86] However, such an analysis overlooks the degree to which Dombey, like Sir Thomas Bertram in Jane Austen's *Mansfield Park* forced marriage plot novel, must acknowledge and atone for his past treatment of Florence to earn the reunion. Dombey's transformation into a doting grandfather includes some key concessions on his part that flip the balance of power in Florence's favor. Dombey hits rock bottom; because the firm Dombey and Son was a partnership, not a joint-stock company, Dombey's personal assets are seized when Carker embezzles company funds, and the business fails. Dombey and Son was the primary love of Dombey's life and the locus of his authority. Like Mary Robinson's Sir Edward, once his financial success is undercut, Dombey is left metaphorically impotent. He is a "ruined man," as the narrator puts it, "[t]he house is such a ruin that the rats have fled, and there is not one left."[87] It is "[i]n agony, in sorrow, in remorse, in despair!" that he remembers the night he hit Florence.[88] What haunts him more than anything – even the loss of his beloved business and fortune – is how he treated Florence; Dombey finally understands that:

> He was fallen, never to be raised up any more [*sic*]. For the night of his worldly ruin there was no to-morrow's sun; for the stain of his domestic shame there was no purification; nothing, thank Heaven, could bring his dead child back to life. But that which he might have made so different in all the Past—which might have made the Past itself so different, though this he hardly thought of now—that which was his own work, that which he could so easily have wrought into a blessing, and had set himself so steadily for years to form into a curse: that was the sharp grief of his soul.[89]

---

[86] See Schor, In *Dickens and the Daughter of the House*, in which Schor argues: "her realization of how much she loves her child has demonstrated anew to Florence how much she should have loved her father, and not how much he should have loved her" (65).

[87] Dickens, *DS*, 903-4.

[88] *Ibid.*, 904.

[89] *Ibid.*, 904.

In his grief, Dombey understands that the losses he has experienced are his own fault, especially when it comes to his relationship with Florence. The narrator's frequent references to Dombey as a "ruined" and even "fallen" man mimic the language so often applied to sex workers and other women perceived as immoral by their peers in the Victorian period. While Edith maintains a sense of dignity through her isolation from her nuclear family, Dombey is represented as degraded, guilty, and remorseful for his actions. In fact, he is even on the brink of suicide when Florence, after her own recent near-death experience during childbirth, returns to her childhood home to reconnect with Dombey, who further humbles himself by begging Florence for forgiveness: "[o]h my God, forgive me, for I need it very much!" he begs while showing a "docile submission to her" that is new in him.[90] In the end, he is not a Mr. Harlowe, blaming everyone else for his sins, but accepts the culpability and can thus turn into the father Florence deserves. Notably, the novel ends with Dombey kissing Little Florence and stroking her hair – loving gestures indicating his newfound appreciation of girls. Dombey has to lose everything in order to appreciate those around him as people, not commodities, which serves as a lesson for readers: the intangible value of personal connections is more important than economic gains.

The Cotton Lord's coercion

Elizabeth Stone is one of many writers who has fallen through the cracks of literary memory; by including her in this chapter, I hope that other critics will examine her work – and the work of other women writers like her – that have historically been excluded from the canon. Like Dickens' novels, Stone's *William Langshawe, the Cotton Lord* shows the dangerous consequences capitalist greed has on girls' and women's autonomy.

Since *William Langshawe* is likely unfamiliar to many readers, a brief plot summary will be useful. The novel tells the story of Edith Langshawe; a beloved and dutiful daughter whose first clash with her parents comes when her father contracts a marriage between Edith and a man she finds morally repulsive. William, Edith's father, is a wealthy textile manufacturer and a kind father until Edith is old enough to be exploited as an exchangeable commodity. He and John Balshawe Sr., a fellow cotton lord, discuss to the following plan: Balshawe's son, John Balshawe Jr., will marry Edith and get her 100,000-pound inheritance: a sum that would equal over six million pounds purchasing power in today's currency.[91] In return, the families would merge their two businesses, creating a

---

[90] *Ibid.*, 911.
[91] Source: British National Archives currency converter

monopoly with immense potential for profit. Edith, unaware of this plan, is the lynchpin that holds the whole deal together. However, their grand plan is complicated when Langshawe makes bad speculation that – he believes – can only be remedied through this marriage, at which point William sees the marriage as an absolute necessity that must happen immediately. The coercive measures he takes to force Edith into the marriage place it firmly in the forced marriage plot tradition; Langshawe tells Edith she will inherit a fortune "provided – *pro-vid-ed* you marry to please me."[92] Additionally, a last-minute effort by Edith's chosen, non-nuclear family that saves her from the marriage underscores an idea present in both Dickens' novels and Marx's arguments against capitalism: that capitalist greed infects every facet of family life, for which non-familial friendships can provide a way out.

Though there are few scholarly engagements with Stone, the few that exist tend to focus on the insights it provides into life in Manchester during its manufacturing heyday. Sally Mitchell's *Dictionary of National Biography* entry for Stone calls this the first novel about industrial Manchester written by a resident, hinting at the unique insights that Stone's work provides.[93] Rosemarie Bodenheimer makes a similar argument about Stone's novel in her 1988 book *The Politics of Story in Victorian Social Fiction* – one of the only in-depth analyses of Stone's fiction – claiming that Stone's portrayal of Manchester life is more nuanced than earlier social reform texts. However, Bodenheimer emphasizes the novel's limits, arguing that the novel wavers uneasily between "social satire and highly conventional imitations of the sentimental novel."[94] Joseph Kestner emphasizes the social justice present in *William Langshawe, the Cotton Lord*. Around this period, Kestner notes, the findings of Parliament's investigative committees became available to the public, many of which exposed inhumane working conditions. These accounts provided inspiration for writers like Stone, whose novels include representations of the working classes derived from these reports. Indeed, at several points, the narrator of *William Langshawe* breaks the fourth wall to address the factual nature of the text, and Stone also includes occasional footnotes indicating real events she is fictionalizing. Stone stove to "combine uniqueness with factuality in the portrayal of workers' lives," Kestner claims, "in both the operative and

---

[92] Elizabeth Stone, *William Langshawe, the Cotton Lord* (London, 1842), 1:18. Hereafter *WL*; italics in original.

[93] Sally Mitchell, "Elizabeth Stone [née Wheeler], (1803–1881), novelist and historian," *Oxford Dictionary of National Biography*, 2004-09-23, Oxford University Press.

[94] Rosemarie Bodenheimer, *The Politics of Story in Victorian Social Fiction* (Cornell UP, 1988), 72.

managerial classes."[95] Like Dickens, Stone created fiction inspired by real-life occurrences, creating relatable subjects meant to foster empathy and inspire social change.

What *William Langshawe* highlights so well is the immense power that business owners had in "company towns," as Eric Hobsbawm calls them, like Manchester.[96] " [T]he fate of men and women depended on the fortunes and goodwill of a single master, behind whom stood the force of law and state power, which regarded his authority as necessary and beneficial," Hobsbawm elaborates.[97] Men like Langshawe and Balshawe, his co-conspirator in concocting the forced marriage between their children, were seen as something akin to overlords who reigned over their laborers, their power derived from their money and the influence they held over the lives of their workers. As *William Langshawe* makes clear, this type of power breeds greed and vanity. The narrator explains of Langshawe and Balshawe that:

> [t]heir whole souls were wrapped up in mercantile speculation; and while they were indeed of an age to require relaxation, and had in reality no earthly motive for extraordinary exertion, since they yearly laid aside a much larger sum than they spent, did still toil day after day as regularly, as elaborately, as if they really had to earn their daily food.[98]

Their whole identities are consumed with greed; they are not motivated by actual financial need but want riches for the sake of riches – and the power that it can buy. Balshawe Sr. has turned the profits from his mill into a Parliament seat which will, he presumes, eventually belong to his son John. Langshawe hopes that, with John as his son-in-law, the partnership between the families will lead to even more socio-economic power for himself.

As the plot unfolds, it becomes obvious that the values of their capitalist society – wealth, greed, power, and pride – have infected the way that these men see the world around them. As Marx ventriloquizes a capitalist: "I am bad, dishonest, unscrupulous, stupid; but money is honored, and therefore so is its possessor. Money is the supreme good, therefore its possessor is good...Does not my money therefore transform all my incapacities into their contrary?"[99] This parallels the argument Adam Smith made in *The Theory of Moral*

---

[95] Joseph Kestner, *Protest and Reform: The British Social Narrative by Women, 1827-1867* (University of Wisconsin Press, 1985), 78.

[96] Hobsbawm, *The Age of Capital*, 251.

[97] Stone, *WL*, 1:251.

[98] *Ibid.*, 1:128.

[99] Marx and Engels, *Economic and Philosophic Manuscripts*, 138. Italics in original.

Sentiments almost a century earlier: that people idolize wealthy, powerful people so much that the lower classes will condone anything the wealthy do, no matter how self-serving or immoral. This enables men like Langshawe and Balshawe to act in their own best interests, and, more broadly, it forces other people to live by their self-serving values. In *William Langshawe*, for instance, Edith loves (and is loved by) a kind, caring man named Frank. Though Frank comes from a wealthy mercantile family himself, he received a liberal arts education instead of training in the family's factory, which Langshawe uses as an excuse to ban Edith from marrying him. "Show me a young man with his business in his fingers, a clear head, a calculating mind, and industrious, frugal, hardworking habits," he instructs Edith, "there's solidity in such a character as that – and on such a one, if he had not a guinea in his purse nor a second coat to his back, I would not look askance." [100] Preventing his daughter from marriage with the man she loves is rooted in his belief that her husband is, first and foremost, a business decision; Frank's worldview differs from Langshawe's materialist one and therefore deems him unworthy in Langshawe's eyes.

Additionally, because of the benefits that Langshawe believes he would reap through a marriage alliance with the Balshawes, Langshawe is willfully blind to his intended son-in-law's evil behavior, especially the way he takes sexual advantage of the young women who work in his father's factory. John is characterized as a Lovelacean rake, "a low-lived libertine, carrying, in the indulgence of his brutal pleasures, shame, and sorrow to the lowly hearths of those to whom his father was bound by every tie of decency and morality to protect and cherish."[101] Raised with every luxury he desires and the knowledge that he will one day possess his father's power and fortune, John's sense of entitlement extends to seducing and then dumping vulnerable young women who work in his father's factory. Readers watch his predation at work when he seduces Edith's cousin Nancy, whom John promises to marry, impregnates, then abandons. "Too often," Stone's narrator exclaims, "is this the case with the half-fledged sons of these secluded petty princes, who carry on a wasting warfare upon the morality and domestic comfort of their petty localities."[102] That is, wealth breeds entitlement, power, and depravity: a dangerous combination. John is a predator whom Langshawe tries to force his own daughter into marrying. The wealth and its concomitant power that a marriage with the Balshawe heir presents willingly blinds Langshawe to John's many flaws.

---

[100] Stone, *WL*, 1:19.
[101] *Ibid.*, 1:124.
[102] *Ibid.*, 1:124-5.

William Langshawe depicts the havoc that this realignment of values – the turn away from moral goodness toward greed – wrought on the lives of women, bringing setbacks to their fight for more freedoms over their own lives. Like Clarissa Harlowe, Edith vacillates between a sense of duty toward her father and the insult of being treated as an exchangeable commodity. "And was it for this," she muses, "for a mercenary bargain with the son of a vulgar, profligate man – himself I fancy by no means immaculate – was it for this that such a man as Mr. [Frank] Walmsley was to be treated with scorn," she asks herself.[103] Edith sees the situation for what it is: her father's selling her off for cash, and understands the inherently demeaning nature of this act. "I suppose he would make a bill of parcels of me, as he would of a bale of goods."[104] Being treated as an object for sale is demeaning to Edith, and she initially refuses to participate in such a transaction. She calmly and confidently tells her father: "I will work for you, beg for you, starve for you; but I will not marry John Balshawe," asserting her right to marry by choice.[105] In this moment of heroic disobedience, Edith follows in the footsteps of her literary predecessor Clarissa Harlowe by refusing to consent to the proposition. Beyond her love for Frank, Edith possesses a sense of authority over her own life that she is unwilling – for now, at least – to give up.

Despite her keen understanding of the situation in which her father has put her (and the repugnance she feels toward John as a person), capitalism's reach into women's lives is shown to be many-pronged. For instance, Langshawe deploys extreme coercion tactics to guilt his daughter into the unwanted marriage, especially after his ill-advised speculation results in a significant loss of fortune. "[W]ith regard to the matter of starving, since that is the gentle term you choose to select," Langshawe tells Edith when she says she would rather starve than marry John, "remember that you will not starve alone. Be this reverse [in fortune] as it may, more or less severe, your mother must share it with you."[106] Edith is close to her mother, which Langshawe uses against her in an attempt to threaten her into acquiescing. Previously, he saw her marriage to John as a lucrative business opportunity, but in the wake of his speculation, Langshawe begins to see it as his only hope for survival.[107] Shaping himself as

---

[103] *Ibid.*, 1:214.

[104] *Ibid.*, 2: 8.

[105] *Ibid.*, 2:9.

[106] *Ibid.*, 2:9.

[107] Langshawe believes that, upon becoming his son-in-law, John will provide him enough cash to bail him out of the hole he dug himself. Later, John learns of this expectation and states he would not help Langshawe. The narrator tells readers that, once

a martyr, Langshawe also tells Edith he hopes he dies rather than face disgrace. While he does not explicitly threaten suicide, the possibility hangs in the air during this conversation. This marriage, according to Langshawe, is not just about Edith's wishes but about the basic survival of her parents, as well. His methods mirror what Elizabeth Kowaleski-Wallace calls "new-style patriarchy," in which patriarchal agents utilize methods beyond brute force to govern young women, especially through inciting feelings of "guilt and obligation" as methods of control, which the novel explicitly articulates as an effective method of reaching patriarchal end goals.[108]

Under "new-style patriarchy," Edith has been socially conditioned to view self-sacrifice for the sake of the *paterfamilias* as a noble component of femininity: conduct guides and religious instruction regularly taught girls this lesson from a young age. Sarah Stickney Ellis' *The Women of England, their social duties, and domestic habits* (1838), in fact, explicitly discusses the British economy's impact on female behaviors. Quoting Napoleon Bonaparte's observation that England is "a nation of shopkeepers," Ellis expresses her concern that the expanding middle classes' upward mobility is, in short, degrading the character of English women. Of particular concern to Ellis is what she perceives to be decreased domesticity in young women, who look for entertainment outside the home and can afford servants to perform domestic duties, since a comfortable home was what kept men connected to the moral values that were lacking in public, commercial world. As Leonore Davidoff and Catherine Hall explain, Ellis and other conduct-guide authors believed the domestic space was an antidote to the turbulent world. Domestic women, whose singular identity came from ministering to their family, were the key to upholding both the sanctity of the home and the English national character at large.[109] "Time was when the women of England were accustomed, almost from their childhood, to the constant employment of their hands," Ellis claims,

> I would write in characters of gold the indisputable fact, that the habits of industry and personal exertion thus acquired, gave them a strength and dignity of character, a power of usefulness, and a capability of doing good... Their sphere of action was at their own firesides, and the world in which they moved was one where pleasure of the highest, purest

---

married, John thinks "he should bring [Edith's] proud notions down a peg" (Stone, *WL*, 2: 5). He does not intend to be a kind husband or helpful to Langshawe.

[108] Elizabeth Kowaleski-Wallace, *The Father's Daughters: Hannah More, Maria Edgeworth, and Patriarchal Complacency* (Oxford University Press, 1991), 110.

[109] Leonore Davidoff and Catherine Hall, *Family Fortunes: Men and Women of the English Middle Class, 1780-1850*, 2nd edition (Routledge, 2003), 180.

order, naturally and necessarily arises out of acts of duty faithfully performed.[110]

Though it is unsurprising that a Victorian conduct-guide author sought to keep women tethered to service within the domestic space, it is of note that, in Ellis' case, this advice is given within the context of the changing British economy and changing class structures; she even gives specific advice to women, like Edith Langshawe, "whose fireside comforts are broken up by the adverse turn of their pecuniary affairs"; arguing that in such circumstances: "we see the importance of having cultivated the moral faculties, of having instilled into the mind those sound principles of integrity, usefulness, and moral responsibility," since women can apply these skills to earn an income by working for another family; she later notes that "where duty is most irksome, the moral responsibility [to serve her family] is precisely the same, as where it is most pleasing."[111] This is, girls owe a duty to their families even when what is required of them does not align with their own preferences. By this logic, it does not matter how distressing Langshawe's demands are: Edith must comply no matter what. As she says in *The Daughters of England: Their Position in Society, Character and Responsibilities*, the "object of a daughter is to soothe the weary spirit of a father when he returns home from the office or the counting-house, where he has been toiling for her maintenance," Ellis dictates.[112] Father/daughter relationships are transactional even to Ellis: a father works hard to support his family, and in exchange, he is entitled to a dutiful, doting daughter.

William Langshawe: the Cotton Lord shows the pernicious ways in which this conduct-guide family ideology leeched throughout British society, causing women to self-police to avoid breaking social protocol. In the novel, Edith connects with the kindly spinster Mrs. Halling, a "sympathetic and judicious friend," who knows Edith's aversion to John and the coercion behind the match but has been so indoctrinated by the glorification of subservient femininity that she is reluctant to warn Edith against what she knows will be a miserable marriage.[113] The dictates of polite society prevent Edith and Mrs. Halling from laying their real feelings on the matter bare; "Mrs. Frances Halling abhorred the idea of interference," the narrator explains, which leads her to advise Edith in

---

[110] Sarah Stickney Ellis, *The Women of England, their Social Duties, and Domestic Habits* (London, 1838), 14-15.

[111] *Ibid.*, 127, 136.

[112] Sarah Stickney Ellis, *The Daughters of England: The Position in Society, Character and Responsibilities* (1842; New York, 1843), 61.

[113] Stone, *WL*, 2:43.

vague platitudes that mirror the advice found in Ellis' conduct guides.[114] "Show me a person in the wide world whose career is one of unbroken misery," she tells Edith, "Suffering is the lot of all; nor may you look to escape."[115] Though her words do not match her true thoughts, Mrs. Halling believes she cannot broach social norms and advise Edith according to her feelings. Mrs. Halling tells Edith how, in her youth, she gave up her beloved fiancé to a friend instead of fighting for him – modeling meekness instead of standing up for her own feelings – Edith muses: "If Mrs. Halling sacrificed the cherished hope of her earthly existence in order to promote the happiness of a mere schoolday friend, shall I hesitate when my father's happiness is at stake?"[116] Readers are made to see the self-policing nature of patriarchal power: though both know the marriage will bring misery, they believe it is Edith's duty to help her father rather than act on her own desires.

In *William Langshawe*, feminine submission to the *paterfamilias* is not represented as a noble sacrifice for a good cause but a demeaning form of coercion done to placate an old man's inflated sense of pride, especially when Langshawe admits: "'[t]here will be no 'starving' in the case. We shall still have enough to support us in respectability, but I shall lose the high place which for nearly forty years I have toiled and striven unweariedly to attain.'"[117] That is, despite Langshawe's earlier claims, the family welfare is never on the line, just his pride – he simply lied to her in a desperate bid to coerce her to marry John to save his own reputation since he is embarrassed that he was hoodwinked by bad speculation. Even Edith's mother urges her to marry John to appease her father's hubris: "[y]our father's weak point is his standing in trade," she tells Edith, "if he were to lose the high position he has acquired, as a successful cotton merchant, whose exertions have raised himself to eminence – Edith, he could not bear it."[118] Protecting the patriarch's sense of superiority is the sole motivating factor in coercing Edith's consent; she is simply expected to submit her will to his because she is a woman.

Redemptive friendship

Edith's reluctant agreement to marry John demonstrates the coercive power that parents could wield over their daughters using popular notions of feminine self-sacrifice. Like Madeline Bray, Edith is made to think that she has no other

---

[114] *Ibid.*, 2:44.
[115] *Ibid.*, 2:46.
[116] *Ibid.*, 2:71.
[117] *Ibid.*, 2:12.
[118] *Ibid.*, 2:39.

option than to relent. *William Langshawe*, however, also shows the redemptive power of friendships in up-ending women's lack of autonomy. Though Mrs. Halling initially fails Edith by giving her bad, socially acceptable advice, Edith's unlikely friendship with the good hermit Bladow provides the support she needs to avoid the forced marriage and live her life on her own terms. William Deresiewicz explains that friendships between men and women were not always socially acceptable or even possible. In addition to the threat of scandal-mongering that could arise from young women spending extended periods of time with a man, cross-sex friendships presume intellectual and social equality between the sexes, which was unthinkable to many in the nineteenth century since "mental companionship, freedom of choice, equality, and mutual respect" were the foundations of friendship.[119] While some believed that these could not exist between men and women, those with more egalitarian understandings of gender embraced such friendships. For example, Bladow is the only person who actively discourages Edith from agreeing to the engagement; disavowing the materialism and obsession with profit margins of Langshawe, Bladow instead favors fostering meaningful relationships with his fellow man – and woman. According to Bladow, there is a simple explanation for the world's strife:

> what induces to crime? and what leads to misery? – Money. What makes a man overreach his neighbour? – Money. What tempts him to murder a fellow-creature? – Money. What shuts his heart to affection, and his ears to every cry of virtue and honour? – Money. What makes a father sacrifice his child at the altar? – Money – money – money.[120]

Serving as the novel's voice of reason, Bladow knows that money causes the blind self-interest that leads to a gamut of crimes, including John Langshawe's sexual "crimes" and the "sacrifice" of a beloved daughter. The double meaning of "altar" in Bladow's speech connects the marriage altar to a sacrificial altar at which Edith's life will be forfeited for the sake of her father's pride. Edith tries convincing him that she has consented to her own free will, but Bladow knows the truth. "She may have consented," he muses, "she may have consented, certainly; but has she been fairly and openly dealt by? – I doubt – I doubt."[121] Bladow recognizes the ease with which her parents can take advantage of her loving, dutiful nature and wants Edith to live her life on her own terms.

---

[119] William Deresiewicz, "Thomas Hardy and the History of Friendship Between the Sexes," *The Wordsworth Circle* 38, nos. 1-2 (2007): 59.

[120] Stone, *WL*, 2:185.

[121] *Ibid.*, 2:191.

Dramatically disrupting Edith's wedding with pregnant Nancy in tow, Bladow exposes John's profligacy and saves Edith from certain misery. Knowing that Edith has been coerced by her parents and her society's misguided attitudes toward the acquiescent role women are expected to play within the mercenary capitalist system, Bladow acts to help save his friend. As a hermit – someone who lives outside the confines of polite society – Bladow does not feel bound by the same rules of social decorum that initially prevented Mrs. Halling from giving Edith straightforward advice. Publicly exposing John's womanizing even awakens Langshawe to the error of his ways. "To the last day, to the last hour of my life," he tells young Balshawe, "I shall thank God that my child had a friend less improvident than her father, and that her marriage with you has been prevented."[122] Within the novel, Bladow shows how having true friends can provide an escape from the confines of capitalist oppression. Women need friends – allies – who are willing to act in each other's best interest to create support systems that lie outside of the family unit, which has been so marred by the capitalist ethos.

One of the important themes that both *William Langshawe, the Cotton Lord*, and *Dombey and Son* have in common that makes them unique among the forced marriage plot novels analyzed so far is the capacity for real change, not just for the heroines, but for their oppressors. That is, Dombey's fall from grace makes him realize the cruelty with which he treated Florence; not only does he acknowledge his faults and apologize for the harm he caused, but he also changes the way he thinks about women in general. He comes to value Florence and her daughter above anything else, changing his opinion that a girl is "merely a piece of base coin that couldn't be invested – a bad Boy – nothing more," as he learns to cherish them as beloved fellow humans.[123] Langshawe exhibits similar changes; he: "did not shut his heart to this lesson; he felt truly and earnestly, that house and land were as nothing to him compared with the happiness of his only daughter."[124] In fact, Langshawe takes his newfound appreciation for people over profits and pays it forward. He encourages his niece Nancy to reunite with her family and sets them up as proprietors of a general store, elevating them from their status as mill laborers (something he was loth to do in the past, believing that all men possess the equal potential to enrich themselves with enough hard work). The narrative is specific about Langshawe's special support of Nancy. "One of Mr. Langshawe's first cares," the narrator says,

---

[122] *Ibid.*, 2:203.
[123] Dickens, *DS*, 13.
[124] Stone, *WL*, 2:270.

> was to restore Nancy to her parents. She refused at first, with shame and tears, but Mr. Langshawe insisted, and more over, he took her himself, having first prepared her parents by a letter. Not a reproach, spoken or implied, met the repentant wanderer on her return to her father's roof; tears, indeed, there were, but not bitter ones, for they were mingled with heart felt blessing and welcome...her father's kind and judicious remonstrances, and more than that, her mother's and sisters' evident comfort and happiness in having her again, roused her to a better frame of mind. Mr. Langshawe had, with considerate and judicious kindness, left a sum of money sufficient, he said, to prevent the necessity of Nancy's working.[125]

Led by Langshawe's example, the family's loving support of Nancy, who expects to be ostracized because of her unwed pregnancy, offers a vision of a more just society that holds wealthy men accountable for their actions rather than placing all the blame and shame on the women they victimize.

William Langshawe ends by celebrating forms of femininity that stray from the domestic, dutiful, virginal form prescribed by conduct guides, showing that women deserve to be supported in making their own paths through life without the coercion or judgment of society interfering. Nancy, for example, transforms from the naïve, scared, fallen woman she was when Bladow found her to a popular member of her community. After having her baby, she thrives as co-proprietor of her family's general store. Secure and supported as a single mother, Nancy thrives, though the narrator does include a heavy-handed hint of marriage with their family's "respectable" lodger who dotes on her child.[126] Notably, Edith also ends the novel as a single woman. Like Nancy, there is the possibility of a future marriage to her long-time beau Frank (whose wife Bianca – whom he married after Edith's engagement to Balshawe – has recently died). Their life is described as a halcyon-like paradise: "all around, the corn waves wildly in the spring gale, and the lofty trees stretch their free arms to heaven; where the cattle repose in the pleasant pastures, and bees and birds revel in the pure air, and all sights and sounds are those of nature and repose."[127] No signs of commerce, industrialism, or gilded luxuries are anywhere to be found, and the last readers hear of Edith, she is scattering evergreens, myrtle, and bay upon Bianca's grave, "for hope," she says, indicating her feelings toward her own future.[128] That both Edith and Nancy are single at the end of the novel is

---

[125] *Ibid.*, 2:262-3.
[126] *Ibid.*, 2:314.
[127] *Ibid.*, 2:319-20.
[128] *Ibid.*, 2:320.

significant, representing their – and their creators' – resistance to the narrative path that women of both upper and lower classes were expected to follow. The emotional and material support they received from their community, especially Bladow, enabled both women to live contended lives without pressure to conform to certain expectations. For these two women, whatever paths they go down next will be of their own choosing.

Conclusion

These novels by Stone and Dickens expose the complex ways in which social, economic, and familial pressures collude to force even resistant women into unwanted marriages. The heroically disobedient characters featured in *Nicholas Nickleby, Dombey and Son,* and *William Langshawe, the Cotton Lord* face different struggles, but all are rooted in the systemic commodification of women wrought by the period's obsession with wealth accumulation. In *Nicholas Nickleby*, for instance, readers are exposed to the unique ways that post-industrial attitudes toward wealth accumulation impacted masculinity, empowering men like Ralph and Bray to lord over the women in their care with impunity – or so they believe. Capitalism's impacts on the family unit are exacerbated in *Dombey in Son*, not just by men, the traditional figures of patriarchal authority, but also by mothers who lack the means to support themselves and are thus compelled to sell their daughters as sexual commodities. *William Langshawe, the Cotton Lord*, returns to the paradigm of the wealthy, influential father who wants to sell his daughter to augment his standing in the world, and it is a humble – if unlikely – friend who turns the tide against the father's mercenary habits and restores peace to the family unit. Each of these novels confirms Marx's assertion that capitalism necessarily corrupts the family unit but also shows that resistance is possible with the support of friends and chosen family who actively rebel against the capitalist ethos that infects so much of their society, providing women like Nancy, Edith Langshawe, Edith Dombey, Kate Nickleby, and Madeline Bray with the safe spaces they need to live empowered lives.

Chapter Five
"Of course I have to think of myself": Trollope's Non-Conforming Heroines

The previous chapter took the rise of post-industrial capitalism as its topic, focusing specifically on Charles Dickens' *Nicholas Nickleby* and *Dombey and Son* alongside Elizabeth Stone's *William Langshawe, The Cotton Lord* as examples of novels that use forced marriage plots to dramatize the damage done to the family unit by post-industrial capitalist practices in ways that echo the arguments of their contemporaries Karl Marx and Friedrich Engels in *The Manifesto of the Communist Party*. While Marx and Engels are clear that women are among those victimized by capitalists, Dickens and Stone push this notion further, empathetically depicting the specific processes by which women were taught their only value was as sexualized commodities for men's use and – importantly – showing how extra-familial friendships in which women are treated as free, reasoning, self-determining beings provide an escape from the "claptrap," to borrow Marx's word, of capitalist-based oppression.

This final chapter examines this dynamic in the later decades of the nineteenth century, expanding on the impact of speculation raised in connection to Ralph Nickleby in the previous chapter when speculation and corporations gained even more socio-economic power. As is detailed below, several acts of Parliament, such as the Limited Liability Act of 1855 and the Joint Stock Companies Act of 1856, strengthened the power of corporations and expanded access to speculation. The author under consideration here, Anthony Trollope, shows how this economic precarity facilitated the continued abusive commodification of women as a means of wealth transfer between men. The novels considered in this chapter, primarily *The Way We Live Now* (1874-5), with observations on *The Three Clerks* (1857), *Sir Harry Hotspur of Humblethwaite* (1871), *The Prime Minister* (1876), and *The Duke's Children* (1880), dramatize the link between speculation and forced marriages in which women are exchanged as financial commodities. Though these novels were written more than a century after the publication of *Clarissa* (1748), in them, Trollope engages with Richardson's forced marriage plot to highlight the degree to which seemingly archaic eighteenth-century patriarchal ideologies of land, money, and women persisted in late-nineteenth-century Britain. While *Sir Harry* and *The Prime Minister* portray the continued victimization of women, in *The Way We Live Now*, Trollope goes a step further, portraying a heroine, Marie Melmotte, who breaks free from the cycle of financially motivated oppression.

Dueling ideas of modernity and progress

In some ways, this monograph ends right where it begins: with claims that capital "M" Mankind has achieved an enlightened state. Chapter one mentioned philosophers from (and inspired by) the historical Enlightenment, like John Locke, Immanuel Kant, and Adam Smith, whereas this chapter looks at the Enlightenment's Victorian-era sibling: modernization. Late Victorian modernity is often defined by trends pertaining to rising secularism, industrialization, technological innovation, standardized and more widespread education, urbanization, city planning, and a general belief in Britain's teleological progression to an enlightened, improved society. Expanding on Amanda Anderson's work, Frederick Van Dam calls Victorian modernity "the historical emergence of the growth of free will and individual agency. Modernity, in this view, rests on a strong belief in the inevitability of progress; it is an 'ongoing achievement of consciousness with intimate effects on character and on ethical life.'"[1] It is an idea into which many of Trollope's contemporaries bought, such as Thomas Babington Macaulay's claim that "our race has hitherto been almost constantly advancing in knowledge…we are reformers: we are on the side of progress."[2] Macaulay admits "[w]e do not flatter ourselves with the notion that we have attained perfection, and that no more truth remains to be found," but steadfastly believes "we are wiser than our ancestors."[3] Terms like "progress" and "reform" became the watchwords of boosters like Macaulay, who believed that the intellectual, industrial, and legal changes (just to name a few sectors) that took place over time as evidence of a more perfect, improved society. Matthew Arnold echoes this in *Culture and Anarchy* when he proclaims that "the intellectual horizon is opening and widening all round us" and society was moving in a more perfect direction:

> The iron force of adhesion to the old routine,—social, political, religious,— has wonderfully yielded…Now, then, is the moment for culture to be of service, culture which believes in making reason and the will of God

---

[1] Frederick Van Dam, *Anthony Trollope's Late Style: Victorian Liberalism and Literary Form* (Edinburgh University Press, 2016), 2. He is quoting from Anderson's "Victorian Studies and the Two Modernities."

[2] Thomas Babington Macaulay, "Sir James Mackintosh's History of the Revolution," in *The Works of Lord Macaulay*, ed. Lady Trevelyan, vol. 6 (London: Longman's, Green, and Co., 1906), 90.

[3] *Ibid.*, 90.

prevail, believes in perfection, is the study and pursuit of perfection, and is no longer debarred, by a rigid invincible exclusion of whatever is new, from getting acceptance for its ideas, simply because they are new.[4]

Arnold describes a shift in British attitudes toward progress, claiming that society reached a point where blind adherence to traditions was no longer the norm, but where progress – change for the better – was desirable to an increasingly larger group of people. "Not a having and a resting," he argues, but a growing and a becoming, is the character of perfection as culture perceives it"; and he even goes on to claim Britain's "march towards perfection" as God's will.[5] Even popular conduct guide author Samuel Smiles identified his work with the spirit of progress, claiming in his 1859 guide *Self-Help*: "[t]he spirit of self-help is the root of all genuine growth in the individual; and, exhibited in the lives of many, it constitutes the true source of national vigour and strength...National progress is the sum of individual industry, energy, and uprightness, and national decay is of individual idleness, selfishness, and vice."[6] By instructing young Brits how to become industrial, upright men, Smiles believed he was aiding the modernization process.

The financial sector was another area in which progress was widely claimed to have occurred: changes in the ways that British corporations conducted business were often heralded as further examples of modernity. While the 1844 Joint Stock Companies Act, which was discussed in the previous chapter, made incorporation easier, it also laid out "stringent rules for doing so."[7] That is, a parliamentary charter was no longer required, but incorporation was still a lengthy, complex process that maintained a degree of financial risk to the board members. To remedy this, Parliament passed the Limited Liability Act of 1855, which extended limited liability to companies with more than 25 shareholders, so shareholders were only liable for the amount they invested in the company (as opposed to private partnerships, in which personal assets could be seized in the case of the company's failure). The following year the Joint Stock Companies Act of 1856 (which repealed the 1844 Act) streamlined the process by which any group of seven or more persons (previously a group of 25) could create a limited liability corporation while relaxing government oversight of existing corporations. This act also stipulated the only requirement for incorporation was a memorandum of association signed by shareholders – the

---

[4] Matthew Arnold, *Culture and Anarchy*, ed. P. J. Keating (Penguin Classics, 2015), 35.

[5] *Ibid.*, 36.

[6] Smiles, *Self-Help*, 1-2.

[7] Mary Poovey, *Genres of the Credit Economy: Mediating Value in Eighteenth- and Nineteenth-Century Britain* (University of Chicago Press, 2008), 16.

need for Parliamentary approval was eliminated. As Parliament had hoped, these Acts caused a boom in limited liability corporations in the later decades of the nineteenth century. Mary Poovey explains, "between 1844 and 1856, 966 companies had registered with the Registry Office, but, after the repeal of the 1844 Act, applications mushroomed, with nearly twenty-five hundred companies forming between 1856 and 1862 and an additional four thousand companies incorporating between 1862 and 1868" – a huge increase in corporate activity.[8] Incorporation was easier than ever, and hundreds of thousands of Brits across the social spectrum invested in these businesses. In *The History of British Commerce: And of the Economic Progress of the British Nation, 1763-1870* (1872), nineteenth-century British economist Leone Levi calls the politicians who championed for limited liability (and other economic legislation) "noble champions of progress to whose labour, skill, and wisdom the nation is indebted, must prove for ever [sic] valuable."[9] Like other facets of society, Britain's economic system was seen as ever-improving: propelling Britain toward a more perfect version of itself.

This belief in modern progress was also pushed by book publisher Eneas Sweetland Dallas, whose 1868 abridged edition of *Clarissa* includes a Preface in which he singles out society's more equitable treatment of women as a particular achievement. "The sort of oppression to which Clarissa was subject, and which drove her to her doom, is now impossible in English families," Dallas claims:

> The treatment which Clarissa dreaded when she was to be taken to the solitary moated mansion of her tyrannical uncle, where cries for help could not be heard, and whence escape would have been impossible, there to be forcibly married, 'sensible or insensible,' to a suitor whom she loathed, would in the present day be incredible. No parents, however determined, would venture on such a step; and no daughter, in her wits, would fear its fulfilment.[10]

That is, the forced marriage plot of *Clarissa* reflects oppressive eighteenth-century attitudes toward women that Dallas believes are now obsolete since the authoritarian parental authority has been relaxed into a more supportive relationship between parents and daughters. 1868 is, according to Dallas, a much better time to be a woman than 1748 was.

---

[8] *Ibid.*, 17.

[9] Leone Levi, *The History of British Commerce: And of the Economic Progress of the British Nation, 1763-1870* (London: McMillian and Co., 1872), viii.

[10] Richardson, *Clarissa*, 1:xxxv.

Trollope's take on modernity and progress

Many critics use a framework of modernization to analyze Anthony Trollope's novels, looking at the many ways in which they intertwine with notions of progress and modernity. Amanda Anderson, Jenny Bourne Taylor, Deborah Denenholz Morse, Monica C. Lewis, Supritha Rajan, John Sutherland, and Barbara Weiss, just to name a few, distinguish modernity as a looming trope in Trollope's work via socio-historical contexts or the formal elements of the novels, many of which focus on Trollope's criticism of modernity.[11] Supritha Rajan explains that Trollope's fiction depicted modernity – what his peers were calling "progress" – as an "era of cosmopolitan modernity, global exchange, and speculative credit," toward which the author felt "anxiety."[12] Speaking of Trollope's later novels, Lauren Goodlad also pinpoints the economy as an object of critique, explaining: "they portray a disenchanted modernity in which Hobbesian combatants struggle to wrest money and power from the all-but-substanceless flow of capital and commodities."[13]

What most interests me is the degree to which Trollope draws on the similarities between the eighteenth century and his own "modern" time to debunk the progress myth perpetuated by many of his peers. The later decades of the nineteenth century were not, according to Trollope's novels, characterized by progress but by a regression back to archaic ideas about class and gender that resemble those embodied by the Harlowes in *Clarissa* – a novel published 127 years before *The Way We Live Now*. Trollope teases out the far-reaching complexities of economic oppression to show the extreme degree to which late Victorian women, far from being the liberated beings Dallas describes in his Preface to the abridged *Clarissa*, were hedged in on multiple fronts, trapped by archaic obsession with aristocratic endogamy on the one hand and, on the other hand, contemporary glorification of speculation.

In fact, Trollope was so offended by Dallas' claims of social progress in his Preface to the abridged 1868 edition of *Clarissa* that, in a review of Dallas'

---

[11] See: Amanda Anderson, "Trollope's Modernity," *ELH* 74.3, 2007, www.jstor.org/stable/30029570; Supritha Rajan, *A Tale of Two Capitalisms: Sacred Economics in Nineteenth-Century Britain* (University of Michigan Press, 2015); John Sutherland, "Introduction," in *The Way We Live Now*, by Anthony Trollope (Oxford University Press, 1982); and, Barbara Weiss, *The Hell of the English: Bankruptcy and the Victorian Novel* (Bucknell University Press, 1986) respectively, for each scholar's individual arguments.

[12] Rajan, *A Tale of Two Capitalisms*, 200; Rajan also sees a "nostalgia for a premodern social order" in Trollope's work – an idea with which this chapter disagrees.

[13] Lauren M. E. Goodlad, "Trollopian 'Foreign Policy': Rootedness and Cosmopolitanism in the Mid-Victorian Global Imaginary," *PMLA* 124, no. 2 (2009): 448.

Clarissa, Trollope lashes out against the claims Dallas makes in his preface in a way that sets the tone for understanding Trollope's fiction within the framework of this chapter. Most of Trollope's criticisms address Dallas' interpretation of Richardson's female characters and his editorial decision to frame Clarissa Harlowe as a perfect paragon of feminine virtue. For example, in the Preface, Dallas argues, "[i]t is rare for men to succeed in feminine portraiture," but believes Richardson does so effectively in *Clarissa*, going on to praise his depiction of his heroine: "Clarissa is the most resplendent heroine in the whole wide circuit of romance... who walks alone in her saintly majesty, a sinless Margaret, the one perfect image on which the mind can repose amid the grotesque and loathsome demons of the witches' Sabbath."[14] There is a disconnect between Dallas' claims (quoted above) that Victorian women have more individual rights than in Richardson's time and the specific qualities Dallas pinpoints as the basis of Clarissa's perfection. That is, his description of Clarissa as a "perfect," "saintly," "sinless" being serves as a dog whistle for the submissive form of femininity that Dallas claims is no longer in existence in England. As will be described in greater length below, Clarissa Harlowe became something of a mascot for Victorians who wanted to keep women socio-economically disempowered, and Trollope recognizes the mixed messages about ideal femininity and women's rights present in Dallas' new edition of *Clarissa*, arguing in his review that Richardson's female characters are "detestable" due to their creator's "stiff, ungainly, puritanical ideas as to women."[15] While my own understanding of Richardson extends a bit more nuance to Clarissa Harlowe than Trollope's does (in the Introduction to the third edition of *Clarissa*, for example, Richardson explicitly states that Clarissa is not perfect, she has flaws and makes mistakes that are an important part of her), but I suspect Trollope is over-correcting for what he sees as Dallas' misguided praise of her perfection. According to Trollope, "Richardson desired to teach virtue as he saw it; and, in doing so, has repudiated all human nature, as is done by so many who, in these days, endeavour to teach us virtue in godly but false little books, about godly but false little people." [16] In Richardson's time and in Trollope's contemporary moment, there existed an urge to perpetuate an oversimplified – idealized – version of feminine virtue that, by equating femininity with submission, stripped women of autonomy. He claims that Dallas' edition elevates this eighteenth-century submissive femininity in a way that directly contradicts Dallas' other claim (that Victorian women have been

---

[14] Eneas Sweetland Dallas, ed., *Clarissa: A Novel By Samuel Richardson* (London, 1868), xxxiv.
[15] Anthony Trollope, "On E. S. Dallas's 1868 abridgment of Samuel Richardson's *Clarissa*" (1868), in *Writings for St. Paul's Magazine*, ed. John Sutherland (Arno Press, 1981), 168, 167.
[16] *Ibid.*, 167.

emancipated from the more demure, demonstrative aspects of eighteenth-century ideal femininity). Trollope, then, corrects this narrative in his own fiction, showing instead that British socio-economic and legal treatment of women never progressed from the dismal state it was in Richardson's time. Using the forced marriage plot that Richardson made so famous, Trollope exposes the connections between eighteenth-century women as they were imagined by Trollope's contemporaries and the reality women in their own period faced while championing women who refuse to conform to gender norms.

"Fitting company only for the devils": Trollope's flirtations with forced marriage

To combat Dallas' incorrect claims of a more egalitarian society, Trollope's novels are populated with forced (and almost-forced) marriages that represent the precarious, oppressed position of women in the late nineteenth century. In *Sir Harry Hotspur of Humblethwaite*, *The Prime Minister*, and *The Duke's Children*, fathers are directly involved in the marriages of their daughters for economic reasons reminiscent of the struggles dramatized in *Clarissa*. Despite Dallas' claims of a progressed society, Sir Harry, Abel Wharton, and the Duke of Omnium show that, even in the 1870s, patriarchal ideologies of land and femininity persisted, especially among the upper classes, who sought to consolidate power and assets along their own clans; keeping their ranks "impregnable" from outsiders, as the Duchess of Omnium remarks.[17] Though the daughters of these novels are not "taken to...solitary moated mansions," as Dallas describes of eighteenth-century forced marriages, the fathers struggle between respecting their daughters' rights to self-determination and their desires to use their daughters to advance their own socio-economic interests, each eager to close ranks against interfering, lower-class outsiders.

Sir Harry, for example, looks to solidify his family legacy at a time when the landed gentry was on the wane. "It was not his ambition to see his daughter a duchess," the narrator explains, "[t]o have Humblethwaite and Scarrowby lost amidst the vast appanages and domains of some titled family, whose gorgeous glories were new and paltry in comparison with the mellow honours of his own house, would to him have been a ruin to all his hopes."[18] Sir Harry desires a very specific type of husband for Emily: one who will be an effective manager of Emily's fortune and who does not possess a title or estates that will eclipse his

---

[17] Anthony Trollope, *The Prime Minister*, ed. Nicholas Shrimpton (Oxford World Classics, 2011), 585. Hereafter *PM*.
[18] Trollope, *Sir Harry Hotspur*, 48. Hereafter *Harry*.

own. While Sir Harry is not a social climber in the way that Augustus Melmotte (considered below) is, his ideas surrounding his daughter's future husband are rooted in class anxiety that stem from similar sources. That is, both the Sir Harrys and the Melmottes of the world placed immense value in titles and land; the difference between the two resides in the fact that bourgeois Melmotte wants to obtain the status conferred by a title while Sir Harry wants to prevent what he sees as the degradation of his *gens* by men like Melmotte. Sir Harry's ideas of class differ from the bootstrap mentality seen in the earlier part of the century, in which post-industrial capitalism glorified the myth of the self-made man. It is a self-preserving reaction to it – he wants his class of aristocrats and landed gentry to close themselves off against outsiders. Viewing Emily – his only child – as "the transmitter of all the great things that fortune had given him; she, in whose hands were to lie the glories of Humblethwaite and Scarrowby," Sir Harry believes it is her role to transmit Humblethwaite and Scarrowby to the next generation of Hotspurs.[19] Though he will eventually try to force innocuous Lord Alfred on Emily, the novel's conflict derives from his allowing Emily to court her second cousin George, since George, though a profligate gambler, will inherit the Hotspur title. "He knew that Cousin George was no fitting husband for his girl, that he was a man to whom he would not have thought of giving her, had her happiness been his only object," the narrator explains, "yet he vacillated, and allowed Cousin George to come to the house, only because Cousin George must become, on his death, the head of the Hotspurs."[20] Sir Harry's hubristic ideas about the sanctity of the aristocracy – and the Hotspur line in particular – tempt him into considering George's suit, much like William Langshawe overlooks John Balshawe's moral shortcomings (to put it mildly) in *William Langshawe, the Cotton Lord*: the dream of shoring up the Hotspur dynasty by uniting the wealth, land, and title via his daughter's marriage is just too tempting. Once Sir Harry opens the door to George, the latter inserts himself into family life, causing irreparable harm.[21] When the full extent of George's profligacy comes to light, and Sir Harry forbids the marriage, he almost gives in to Emily's protestations: "[h]e almost believed that his girl should be left to herself, as are other girls. But the thing was of such moment that he could not save himself from having it always before his eyes."[22] That is, he "almost" believes in his daughter's right to autonomy over deciding whom

---

[19] *Ibid.*, 50.

[20] *Ibid.*, 51-2.

[21] See Deborah Denenholz Morse, *Reforming Trollope: Race, Gender, and Englishness in the Novels of Anthony Trollope* (Ashgate, 2013), 74: Denenholz Morse argues convincingly that Emily Hotspur dies from a sexually transmitted infection passed to her by George.

[22] Trollope, *Harry*, 47.

she will marry but ultimately decides that his opinion on the matter is more important than Emily's. Despite E. S. Dallas' claim that in the late nineteenth century fathers relinquished control over their daughters' marriages, *Sir Harry* showcases the difficulty with which even loving fathers divest control over their daughters' marriages in the name of estate consolidation.

This dynamic is repeated in *The Prime Minister* and *The Duke's Children*. Abel Wharton, for example, initially discourages Emily's relationship with the speculator Lopez simply because of his profession. "I have the greatest respect in the world for mercantile enterprise, and have had as much to do as most men with mercantile questions. But I ain't sure that I wish to marry my daughter in the City," he tells Lopez, "[o]f course it's all prejudice. I won't deny that on general subjects I can give as much latitude as any man; but when one's own hearth is attacked…" he trails off, configuring Lopez's suit as an attack on his family.[23] Speculators, to Wharton, make up a lower class of businessmen that Wharton associates with dishonesty and gambling, and he worries that Lopez will misappropriate the Wharton money that Emily will bring into the marriage. This, in addition to Lopez's lack of a respectable family and rumored Jewish heritage, causes Wharton to seriously consider forbidding the marriage. Though in the end, he gives in, allowing Emily to marry Lopez, he nevertheless possesses a strong belief that fathers have a deciding vote over their daughter's marriages, especially when it comes to someone like Lopez, who is an outsider. Similarly offended by Mary's infatuation with penniless Frank Tregear in *The Duke's Children*, the Duke of Omnium insists: "'[w]hether I may be wrong or right I think it to be for the good of our country, for the good of our order, for the good of our individual families, that we should support each other by marriage.'"[24] That is, the Duke believes that titled families have a duty – to each other and to England – to marry only amongst themselves to uphold the archaic aristocratic institutions he believes they represent. Though less tyrannical than their prototype, Mr. Harlowe, these men exemplify the extent to which fathers – even kind, loving ones – viewed their daughters as economic tools "to transmit," in Sir Harry's term, their estates properly to the next generation of male caretaker. It is no coincidence that the Duke tells Silverbridge to read *Clarissa* when the two clash over the latter's desire to marry the American Isabel Boncassen instead of titled Lady Mabel Grex; an archaic sense of obedience owed to the *paterfamilias* is strong in the Duke, and the reference to

---

[23] Trollope, *PM*, 28-9.
[24] Trollope, *The Duke's Children*, 449. Hereafter *Duke*.

Richardson's novel suggests that *Clarissa* will help Silverbridge accept this code.25

These novels represent a world in which women face attacks on their autonomy on multiple fronts: not just from rigid fathers who want their daughters to marry within their own caste but also from unscrupulous beaux who also view women as a channel for men to exchange money. Speculation's Victorian heyday encouraged reckless treatment of money, which leads to cavalier, mercenary use of women. The love interests of the female characters in many Trollope novels are wealth-hungry men who, like the suitors in forced-marriage plot novels, select a spouse based on her wealth. For instance, *Prime Minister* Ferdinand Lopez "was not an honest man or a good man."26 Rather, he is "a self-seeking, intriguing adventurer, who did not know honesty from dishonesty when he saw them together... He would not pick a pocket, or turn a false card, or, as he thought, forge a name. That which he did, and desired to do, took with him the name of speculation."27 Lopez's desire for wealth has altered his moral compass, reshaping his definition of morality to facilitate obtaining riches at any cost. As he tells his business partner Sexty Parker, who urges "steady business" over risky speculation, "'[i]t depends upon whether a man wants to make a small income or a large fortune....I own that I am not satisfied with the former,' continued Lopez, 'and that I go in for the fortune.'"28 Lopez resembles Alaric Tudor from Trollope's earlier novel *The Three Clerks* (1857); in both novels, attempts to raise large sums of money quickly lead to serious problems, as "[t]he man who is ever looking after money, is fitting company only for the devils, of whom, indeed, he is already one."29 The same dynamic applies to George Hotspur, who, though already in love with another woman, is in serious debt. When confronted by Sir Harry and asked how he will repay these debts, George boldly asserts: "[w]ell – if I marry Emily, I suppose that – you will pay it."30 These male characters are what Tamara Wagner calls stock market villains: "plotting villain[s] associated with instability, indeterminacy, and a foreignness registers in class or ethnic terms that might perhaps all too easily suggest a desirable expulsion from domestic confines."31 Speculators – gamblers – like Lopez, George, and Alaric so desperately desire wealth that they

---

25 *Ibid.*, 436.
26 Trollope, *PM*, 187.
27 *Ibid.*, 187.
28 *Ibid.*, 105-6.
29 Anthony Trollope, *The Three Clerks* (New York: Harper and Brothers, 1860), 319.
30 Trollope, *Harry*, 113.
31 Wagner, *Financial Speculation*, 15. In this example she is discussing Melmotte, but it is a description that applies to many nineteenth-century villains.

shed any moral scruples regarding the means of obtaining it; each man sinks to deceit, fraud (forgery and embezzlement, to be specific), and – notably for this chapter – (mis)using women as a means of obtaining wealth. Relying on an age-old tradition – marriage as a transaction between men – speculation has enabled and emboldened a whole new class of men to prey on women.

The Way We Live Now: new money, old patriarchy

The issues at the heart of the novels discussed above – class tension, wealth accumulation, and the challenges wrought by speculation – also take center stage in Trollope's 1875 *The Way We Live Now*, particularly in terms of how these issues impact women. *The Way We Live Now* follows the familiar forced marriage plot in which the novel's primary villain, Augustus Melmotte, treats his daughter as an exchangeable commodity. Marie, however, follows in the footsteps of the other heroically disobedient women examined in this project in that, though initially amenable to her father's plans, she experiences a period of self-growth in which she comes to see herself as an autonomous being worthy of making her own choices. Through Marie's heroic rebellion, Trollope offers a critique of British socio-economic systems that can only be overcome by escaping to America.

One of the ways in which Trollope shows the moral vacuity of English values is through the tyrannical father/daughter relationship that exists between Melmotte and his daughter Marie. Often overlooked by critics, Marie has received little sustained attention; those who do analyze Marie often characterize her as an extension of her father. Tamara Wagner, for instance, posits: "[t]he speculator's daughter thus embodies the worst outgrowth of his cosmopolitan identity as well as of his exploitation of various commercial practices," arguing that Marie's emigration to America is "exile."[32] She views Marie's plan to claim her trust fund money and run away with Felix as theft analogous to Melmotte's defrauding his shareholders and casts Marie and Fisker's move to America as a strategy to continue scamming investors in California. Similarly, Robert Tracey writes Marie Melmotte off as a "sullen and rebellious" character who "robs" her father and "denies him money that he placed in her name," an extreme underestimation of her character and a misreading of the financial situation between father and daughter.[33] Linda Hughes and Michael Lund concede Marie "is a character who over the course of the novel's publication developed from reliance on others to a new independence," but argue her independence is overly-conditioned upon

---

[32] Ibid., 167.
[33] Robert Tracey, *Trollope's Later Novels* (University of California Press, 1978), 163-4.

unreliable men: "yet her strength was devoted to alliances first with Felix Carbury, seen by all except his doting mother as without redeeming social value, and later to Hamilton Fisker, a brash and unpredictable American. Thus, Marie moved forward only to regress."[34] These critics only judge Marie based on the men in her life instead of reading her as an individual character.

Marie's father also fails to see her as an independent, rational being, instead utilizing her as a commodity for his own use. "If my daughter marries to please me," Melmotte warns Felix Carbury, "I shall give her money, no doubt. How much is neither here nor there. If she marries to please herself, without considering me, I shan't give her a farthing."[35] Like Mr. Harlowe in *Clarissa*, Melmotte desires to "*rais[e] a family*," as the Harlowes articulate, from mere wealth to social and political prestige and sees his daughter as a mere tool for his own disposal.[36] While Harlowe believes he can catapult his son to a peerage by aligning the Solmes and Harlowe estates via marriage, Melmotte believes his still-precarious social position will be strengthened through the Nidderdale family status. "He did in his heart," the narrator explains,

> believe that could he be known to all the world as the father-in-law of the eldest son of the Marquis of Auld Reekie he would become, not really free of the law, but almost safe from its fangs in regard to such an affair as this. He thought he could so use the family with which he would be connected as to force from it protection which he would need.[37]

Melmotte believes the influential, aristocratic Nidderdale family will provide him with an aura of legitimacy and – most importantly to Melmotte – function as a method of sheltering from any legal backlash he might face because of his unscrupulous business practices.

The Way We Live Now depicts a symbiotic relationship between the landed aristocracy and new money: the bourgeoisie desires status, and those with status desire cash. As Lord Nidderdale puts it, Marie represents the "prospect of endless money."[38] Enticed by the fortune Marie is rumored to inherit, Nidderdale is drawn to her as a mechanism for augmenting his own family's dwindling income. Part of her attraction is that she fits easily into the idea of

---

[34] Linda K. Hughes and Michael Lund, *The Victorian Serial* (University Press of Virginia, 1991),180.

[35] Anthony Trollope, *The Way We Live Now* (1874-5), second edition, ed. Francis O'Gorman (Oxford World Classics, 2016), 179. Hereafter *TWWLN*.

[36] Richardson, *Clarissa*, 1:77. Italics in original.

[37] Trollope, *TWWLN*, 549.

[38] *Ibid.*, 429.

matrimony instilled in him by his class. "It had been an understood thing, since he had commenced life, that he was to marry an heiress. In such families as his when such results had been achieved," the narrator comments, remarking on the Nidderdale's need for cash, "it is generally understood that matters shall be put right by an heiress. It has become an institution, like primogeniture, and is almost as serviceable for maintaining the proper order of things. Rank squanders money; trade makes it; – and then trade purchases rank by re-gilding its splendor."[39] Families like the Whartons, Hotspurs, and the Pallisers, who were among the few old families who were able to maintain their wealth, scorned connections with new money. Desperate families like the Nidderdales, however, relied on them. Marrying wealth as a method of preserving aristocratic lines is, to families like the Nidderdales, an "institution" they rely on for survival, underscoring the close connection between modern forms of financial transactions – capitalism, speculation, gambling – and older forms of wealth such as landed interests. This passage directly echoes the reliance of Robinson's Lord Acreland on the "blessed consolation" in which "we sell what is of little use to us, and obtain for our bargain that which will purchase all the gratifications this world can afford."[40] Much changed in Britain between Robinson's creation of Lord Acreland and *The Way We Live Now*, but the beliefs of the male characters in Trollope's novels represent the degree to which women were still bound by "thinghood," to borrow Marx's terminology: expected to be amenable to the demands of men.[41]

As in earlier novels like *Sir Harry Hotspur of Humblethwaite* and *The Prime Minister*, Trollope depicts rampant moral degradation to question the rhetoric of progress that was so prevalent. Famously citing the "commercial profligacy of the age" as his inspiration for *The Way We Live Now*, Trollope muses:

> Whether the world does or does not become more wicked as years go on, is a question which probably has disturbed the minds of thinkers since the world began to think. That men have become less cruel, less violent, less selfish, less brutal, there can be no doubt; but have they become less honest? If so, can a world, retrograding from day to day in honesty, be considered to be in a state of progress?[42]

While his contemporaries described their society in terms of its progress and advancement, Trollope sees regression, especially in terms of honesty. As Deborah

---

[39] *Ibid.*, 428.
[40] Robinson, *Angelina*, 1:2-3.
[41] Marx and Engels, *Economic and Philosophic Manuscripts*, 153.
[42] Anthony Trollope, *An Autobiography* (New York, 1883), 316.

Denenholz Morse articulates it, *The Way We Live Now* "represents an England in which fraud of all kinds—financial, literary, erotic—is pervasive, a result (at least in part) of the swift changes and ensuing instability of modern life."[43] That is, shifting socio-economic practices impacted not just the ways in which people lived, but how people acted, thought, and interacted with the world around them: their psyche and moral code.

Ultimately, this widespread moral blight is what empowers Melmotte, who is very much a product of his time. While, on the one hand, he is rumored to be the wealthiest man in London: the holder of a "fathomless, bottomless, endless" fortune, on the other hand, there is a serious, if subdued, sense of doubt over the veracity of this rumor.[44] Rumor has it that "[h]e could make or mar any company by buying or selling stock, and could make money dear or cheap as he pleased, – but it was also said that he was regarded in Paris as the most gigantic swindler that had ever lived."[45] Is he the richest, most successful businessman ever to grace British shores? No one really knows, since not all of the stories about him and his business practices are very flattering. One important thing to note about Melmotte, though, is that the British investing public do not care which of the rumors are true since they are so enamored with the possibility of making money by investing in his corporations. As John Reed puts it: "Melmotte is the chief model of the unscrupulous speculator in this novel," but Trollope "loads much of the blame on a gullible and even conspiring public."[46] That is, Melmotte's actions are only possible because they are enabled by others. As a July 1861 *Times* article betrays, Trollope was not just writing about the fictional world he created used life as an inspiration for art: "[s]ome bold and unscrupulous adventurer emerges from utter obscurity, and exhibits a lure to sudden wealth. The whole world flocks around him, and the fools of every class cast themselves at his feet," the article describes, "Yet all these people must know he is but a fraud and a sham...They are all tacitly accomplices in every fraud by which the imposture is kept afloat."[47] Morals, according to Trollope and the *Times*, have changed to justify the public's

---

[43] Deborah Denenholz Morse, "The Way He Thought Then: Modernity and the Retreat of the Public Liberal in Anthony Trollope's *The Way We Live Now*, 1873," *BRANCH: Britain, Representation and Nineteenth-Century History*, edited by Dino Franco Felluga, n.pg.

[44] Trollope, *TWWLN*, 21.

[45] *Ibid.*, 30.

[46] John R. Reed, "A Friend to Mammon: Speculation in Victorian Literature," *Victorian Studies* 27, no. 2 (1984): 188; Van, *Anthony Trollope's Late Style*, 78 and T. Wagner, *Financial Speculation in Victorian Fiction*, 164 also echo this argument.

[47] "The demon of gambling will always have his," *The Times*, 1861, p. 9, The Times Digital Archive 1785-2012, 9.

obsession with wealth. Reflecting on his representation of Melmotte, Trollope wrote: "[i]f dishonesty can live in a gorgeous palace, with pictures on all its walls, and gems in all its cupboards, with marble and ivory in all its corners, and can give Apician dinners, and get into Parliament, and deal in millions, then dishonesty is not disgraceful": an idea that can be found in economic philosophers from Adam Smith to Karl Marx.[48] The widespread acceptance of speculation and legal changes to limited liability laws effectively condone any behavior in which Melmotte cares to indulge – even forcing his daughter into an unwanted marriage.

Trollope's outspoken women

In *The Way We Live Now*, Trollope exposes the numerous ways in which his contemporary socio-economic conditions actively participated in the oppression of women. Because of this, his female characters are justified in their fight for their own best interests despite the forces pushing them down a prescribed path. Like Dickens and Stone, Trollope does not shy away from depicting his disobedient heroines as complex characters who push the boundaries of acceptable gender performance. Confident, brash, and unapologetic, Marie Melmotte and the other disobedient heroines do whatever is necessary to live their lives on their own terms; their struggles and decisions are portrayed with empathy, putting the reader on the side of the heroines.

For instance, when readers first meet Marie Melmotte, she is a reasonably compliant daughter who willingly obeys her father. To the first betrothal her father contracts with Nidderdale, Marie submits easily, childishly willing to follow her father's commands. "She had been almost thrown into Lord Nidderdale's arms," according to the narrator, "and had been prepared to take him at her father's bidding. But she had never had the slightest pleasure in his society, and had only not been wretched because she had not as yet recognised that she had an identity of her own in the disposition of which she herself should have a voice."[49] Like Dickens' Madeline Bray and Elizabeth Stone's Edith Langshawe, Marie initially buys into the dutiful daughter role. This attitude changes over time, however, as Marie's romance with Felix Carbury awakens her to her own desires; she grows increasingly "conscious of a desire to have some hand in her own future destiny...she was picking up a little courage, and was beginning to feel that it might be possible to prevent a disposition of herself which did not suit her own tastes. She was also beginning to think that there

---

[48] Trollope, *Autobiography*, 317-18.
[49] Trollope, *TWWLN*, 36.

might be a disposition of herself which would suit her own tastes."[50] Functioning as a "discovery of female self," to use Rita Felski's language, readers have a front-row seat to Marie's metamorphosis from uncritical obedience to the author of her own life story:

> As days went on she ceased to be a child, and her courage grew within her. She became conscious of an identity of her own, which feeling was produced in great part by the contempt which accompanied her increasing familiarity with grand people and grand names and grand things. She was no longer afraid of saying No to the Nidderdales on account of any awe of them personally.[51]

Following the path of the other heroines examined at length in this study, Marie comes into an awareness that, as a woman, she has a right and ability to stand up for herself. Marie carves out her own identity separate from the submissive one her father – and society – prescript. Marie's awakening is about more than just marriage: it depicts the challenges and triumphs of defining one's own identity despite the significant hurdles placed in their way. As the passage above indicates, Marie can see beyond her immediate situation. She understands that obsessing over rank and wealth only breeds misery. Unlike her father and his many followers, Marie is strong enough to resist such gilding. She is neither an extension of her father nor of the society that enables his mercenary behavior but discovers own identity despite them.

Furthermore, Marie takes action to ensure she will be able to live a life of her own choosing instead of being forced into the economic transaction her father plans for her. In fact, his eventual downfall is precipitated by his underestimating her intellect. Though Melmotte regards Marie "as an absolutely passive instrument" who is ignorant of the economic affairs taking place around her, Marie, in fact, knows that her father has stashed a large emergency fund for himself under her name.[52] "When we were in France papa thought it wise to settle a lot of money on me. I don't know how much, but I suppose it was enough to live on if other things went wrong," she explains in a letter to Felix as she proposes a plan for the two to elope.[53] Marie understands what her father assumed her incapable of grasping: the money in her name is legally hers. "When Marie Melmotte assured Felix Carbury that her father had already endowed her with a large fortune which could not be taken from her without

---

[50] *Ibid.*, 91.
[51] Felski, *Beyond Feminist Aesthetics*, 142; Trollope *TWWLN*, 191.
[52] Trollope, *TWWLN*, 223.
[53] *Ibid.*, 222-3.

her own consent, she spoke no more than the truth," the narrator explains: a fact which Melmotte did not think would matter, since he was so assured of his daughter's submissiveness and ignorance of complex financial laws.[54] Unfortunately for Melmotte, "Marie's memory and also her intelligence had been strong beyond her father's anticipation."[55] Melmotte thinks he hoodwinked Marie, believing "his control over his daughter would be perfect and free from danger," but he underestimates her mental acuity.[56] There is a wonderful irony that the assumption Melmotte makes about Marie's lack of intelligence is exactly what causes his downfall. In Trollope's iteration of the forced marriage plot novel, the submissive femininity on which capitalism depended was also its weak point: an Achille's heel that Marie consciously exploits. Even after Marie's romance with Felix ends, her understanding of finance laws empowers her to hold her fortune, for which Melmotte is desperate, over his head as a bargaining chip. "I know that it did become mine, – legally," she argues with Melmotte, to which he retorts: "[b]y a quibble of the law, – yes; but not so as to give you any right to it. I always draw the income."[57] Her response betrays her unwillingness to oblige his plan: "[b]ut I could stop that, papa, and – if I were ever married, of course, it would be stopped."[58] Deftly maneuvering the situation, Marie positions her father between a rock and a hard place, so to speak. That is, if he forces her to marry Nidderdale, he will obtain the aristocratic alliance he so desperately wants, but he will also lose the money he has settled on Marie. If he releases her from the engagement, he will lose the Nidderdale alliance but retain some sense of control over the emergency fund. Amidst a system that commodifies women as objects exchangeable between men, Marie finds a loophole that flips the power dynamic between her and Melmotte.

Money – wanting it, possessing it, using as one wishes – was a taboo subject when it came to polite women in the Victorian period. For example, in *Daughters of England* (1845), Sarah Stickney Ellis rails against the "self-gratification" and "female selfishness" of girls spending too much of their parents' money.[59] Asserting: "I believe there is nothing in the usages of society more fatal to the interests of mankind, to the spiritual progress of individuals, or to the general well-being of the human soul than laxity of principle as regards

---

[54] *Ibid.*, 547.

[55] *Ibid.*, 547.

[56] *Ibid.*, 578.

[57] *Ibid.*, 579.

[58] *Ibid.*, 579.

[59] Ellis, *Daughters of England*, 190.

our pecuniary dealings with each other," Ellis claims that "no one can act in strict accordance with the principles of integrity, until they have learned to practise economy. By economy, I do not mean simply the art of saving money, but the nobler science of employing it for the best purposes, and in its just proportions."[60] There is an unsavory element to money that women are best to steer clear of; apart from learning household economy, money is not a young woman's domain. Ellis goes on to claim that appropriating a sum for one's self that was intended for another use is the nadir of financial behaviors: "this would be a species of dishonesty, which, if once admitted as a principle of conduct, would be liable to terminate in the most fearful and disastrous consequences."[61] While Ellis does not go into the details of what, precisely, these terrible consequences would be, one gets the distinct sense that taking hold of money in the way that Marie does (against the wishes of her father, through a legal loophole) would certainly be forbidden by the maven of manners.

In *The Way We Live Now*, Marie defies polite society's guidelines regarding women's financial mores and common notions of the obedience that young women owe to their fathers. Rather than condemn Marie for this behavior, Trollope emphasizes Marie's right to assert her will, a steep contrast from Dallas' praise of Richardson's "sinless Margaret," who "walks alone in her saintly majesty."[62] Dallas presents an uncomplicated, unrealistic vision of womanhood that Trollope complicates in *The Way We Live Now* through Marie, who must shirk the sinless, saintly, submissive version of femininity that so enamored Dallas. "Truth let there be – truth of description, truth of character, human truth to men and women," Trollope advocates, indicating that depicting the complexity of life, rather than its idealizations, is the best way to achieve a truthful, empowered representation of femininity.[63]

"I want to pick and choose": women who stand up for themselves

The Way We Live Now presents multiple female characters who, like Marie, make difficult, sometimes taboo, decisions but are portrayed with empathy, rather than judgment. Part of the tragedy of *Clarissa* is the heroine's belief that "[t]o do evil, that good may come of it, is forbidden"; Trollope's women defy the dictates of patriarchal duty by their attempts to overcome the victimhood into which they have been conditioned.[64] One such complex character is Georgiana

---

[60] *Ibid.*, 202-3.
[61] *Ibid.*, 206.
[62] Dallas, "Introduction" to the abridged *Clarissa*, 34.
[63] Trollope, *Autobiography*, 206.
[64] Richardson, *Clarissa*, 2:252.

Longstaffe, whose near engagement to Brehgert, the "fat Jew, old enough to be [her] father," as Georgiana's father describes him, sparks a family controversy.⁶⁵ Needing to take financial austerity measures (thanks, in great part, to the Longstaffe men's penchant for gambling), Longstaffe keeps his family in the country instead of spending the social season in London. Worried that this decision will prevent her from meeting eligible bachelors, Georgiana sees marriage to Brehgert as a chance to avoid spinsterhood. Arguing with her brother Dolly, she explains: "[a] man is so different. You can go just where you please, and do what you like. And if you're short on money, people will give you credit. And you can live by yourself and all that sort of thing."⁶⁶ She points out the stark double-standard of her brother's argument; Dolly believes the Melmottes are unsuitable company for Georgiana, even though he hypocritically serves on Melmotte's board of directors for the railway and her father is in the midst of a business deal with him. Dolly, Georgiana argues, does not understand the struggles that social conventions bring to women's lives nor the desperation inherent in believing that her only options are marriage or spinsterhood. When Dolly claims he "shouldn't mind" being "shut up at Caversham all season," Georgiana retorts:

> 'You have got a property of your own. Your fortune is made for you. What is to become of me?'
> 'You mean about marrying?'
> 'I mean altogether,' said the poor girl... 'Of course I have to think of myself.'⁶⁷

Dolly's flippancy contrasts with Georgiana's desperation: England is a harsh place for a woman who has no money. Georgiana internalizes the "institution," as Nidderdale puts it, of marrying for money: a dynamic that does not apply exclusively to men.⁶⁸ However, for women – such as Georgiana – this "institution" is not simply a method of restoring cash to ancestral estates or settling gambling debts but a necessity for her future maintenance. Her argument with Dolly points out that a man in her situation would have other options: credit, inheritances, family estates, and (though Dolly might not like to consider it) employment. Shelter and food are assured to Dolly, but Georgiana is worried about her future "altogether" given her lack of economic security. As far as Georgiana is concerned, she has no other option for her future maintenance

---

⁶⁵ Trollope, *TWWLN*, 493.
⁶⁶ *Ibid.*, 194.
⁶⁷ *Ibid.*, 194.
⁶⁸ *Ibid.*, 428.

besides marriage, and her fear that Brehgert is her only chance at that is terrifying to her.

This emphasis on the extreme lack of options for women in Victorian Britain is echoed by Lady Mabel Grex in *The Duke's Children*. She tells Silverbridge: "[women] are dreadfully restricted. If you like champagne you can have a bucketful. I am obliged to pretend that I only want very little. You can bet thousands. I must confine myself to gloves. You can flirt with any woman you please. I must wait till somebody comes, -- and put up with it if nobody does...I want to pick and choose."[69] Like Georgiana's argument with Dolly, Lady Gex's monologue addresses more than just the mercenary nature of the marriage market (though that is certainly under fire, as well). The extreme amount of control that keeps women hedged into patriarchal boundaries encompasses their whole existence: who they can dance with, flirt with, marry, and even seemingly benign aspects of their lives, like how they can eat and drink in public. Taken in sum, all these restrictions are meant to force women to ignore any sense of individuality and desire that manages to shine through the prescribed female identity.

That women deserve to fight against these restrictions is of central importance to the heroines in *The Way We Live Now*. "Shall a woman be flayed alive because it is unfeminine in her to fight for her own skin?" Winifred Hurtle asks, "But if a woman finds that men only take advantage of her assumed weakness, shall she not throw it off? If she be treated as prey, shall she not fight as a beast of prey?"[70] Mrs. Hurtle's insight perfectly describes the message behind *The Way We Live Now*'s forced marriage plot. Women, according to Mrs. Hurtle, are conditioned into a position of weakness, which in turn predisposes them to victimization. Like Georgiana, Mrs. Hurtle advocates for women to understand the intentional nature of their victimization and fight back against it. As Margaret Marwick puts it, "Mrs. Hurtle, with no-one to protect her, realised she had to look after herself. When a drunken man tried to rape her, she shot him. When her first husband tried to force her to have sexual intercourse, she threatened to shoot herself. When she was defrauded of her property, she pursued the perpetrators and recovered her fortune."[71] Rather than suffer and be still, Mrs. Hurtle fights back against her aggressors, following Georgiana's philosophy that "of course" she must "think of [her]self," since no one else will.[72] What Mrs. Hurtle, Georgiana, and Maire want is the right to

---

[69] Trollope, *Duke*, 229.

[70] Trollope, *TWWLN*, 388.

[71] Margaret Marwick, *Trollope and Women* (The Hambledon Press, 1997), 73.

[72] Trollope, *TWWLN*, 194.

stand up for themselves in a world where justice for women is severely lacking. "No wonder that female characters, controlled, dispossessed, and disposed of, and faced, in addition, with the threat of harassment and assault," Monika Rydygier Smith notes, "are represented in this novel as anxious, querulous, and resentful. Certainly, they do not passively acquiesce to the intolerable demands of men who believe they have the right to exploit women."[73] The mercenary world in which these characters exist requires women to act in their own best interest if they are to obtain any degree of autonomy.

Marie's rebellion

Of all the female characters in the novel who endure physical and emotional abuse at the hands of the patriarchy, Marie's is given in the greatest detail. In fact, out of all the heroically disobedient female characters discussed at length in this project, Marie is set apart by the constant physical violence she endures. Dombey hit Florence once, Maynard threatened violence against Henrietta, and many of the other characters – like Edith Langshawe, for instance – face emotionally manipulative parents, but in Trollope's telling of the forced marriage plot, the violence against heroically disobedient women is no longer metaphorical: it is literal, profuse, and life-threatening. It is another way in which Trollope shuts down Dallas' claim that modern Victorian society was more advanced and genteel than earlier eras, especially where women were concerned. Additionally, Marie's belief that her life is of more value than just as a financial pawn between undeserving men is tested to an extreme degree, thanks to Melmotte's beatings; holding steadfast even in the face of these makes her heroic disobedience even more remarkable.

On numerous occasions, Marie declares her resolve to stand up to her father, even if he "were to beat me into a mummy."[74] Such language is not hyperbolic: Melmotte meets Marie's resistance with extreme violence. On one such occasion, when Marie refuses to sign her fortune over to him outright, Melmotte "He did not know whether to approach her with threats, with entreaties, or with blows. Before the interview was over he had tried all three...And at last he took her by both arms and shook her violently. But Marie was quite firm."[75] On another occasion, the "cutting her up into pieces was commenced after a most savage fashion" to the point that Madame Melmotte thinks her husband has killed Marie, who once again refuses to let her father's

---

[73] Monika Rydygier Smith, "Trollope's Dark Vision: Domestic Violence in The Way We Live Now," *Victorian Review* 22, no. 1 (1996): 23.

[74] Trollope, *TWWLN*, 216.

[75] *Ibid.*, 550.

physical abuse sway her determination.⁷⁶ Melmotte's resorting to violence betrays his sense of desperation, but Marie is stronger – emotionally and physically – than he imagined. Furthermore, Melmotte's violence against Marie is not just an impulsive outgrowth of his anger but something he "longed" to perpetrate, yoking male violence against women to a desire for power that has deeper, more sinister roots than reactive anger. "*The Way We Live Now* can be used to demonstrate how masculinist structures, which rely on the oppression of women, are facilitated not only by epistemic violence as feminists have cogently argued, but also by means of battery and assault," Rydygier Smith explains in her influential essay on domestic violence in *The Way We Live Now*.⁷⁷ Melmotte's villainy knows no bounds, but it is clear that Marie is not, as so many twenty-first-century critics have argued, his accomplice: she is his victim. "He had taught her to regard him as her natural enemy, making her aware that it was his purpose to use her as a chattel for his own advantage," the narrator explains, instructing readers to view them in opposition to each other.⁷⁸ Yet, amidst all his risky financial speculations, his most ill-advised gamble is assuming Marie's ignorance and compliance. Any credit, so to speak, that he has with Marie is gone; fully aware of his mercenary usage of her as an object of sale, Marie prioritizes her right to create her own sense of self – her own future – over her father's selfish plan for her.

The land of the free: Trollope's America

"On the 3rd of September," the narrator of *The Way We Live Now* declares, "Madame Melmotte, Marie, Mrs. Hurtle, Hamilton K. Fisker, and Herr Croll left Liverpool for New York; and the three ladies were determined that they never would revisit a country of which their reminiscences certainly were not happy."⁷⁹ After Melmotte's many frauds are exposed, and he dies by suicide, those previously tethered to him are free to cast out on their own. Herr Croll and Madame Melmotte settle in New York City, while the futures of Marie, Fisker, and Mrs. Hurtle lie in the American West. Some critics liken Marie and Fisker's emigration to Melmotte's suicide or Felix's being sent to the continent: banishment or exile mired in shame. Tamara Wanger concludes: "Miss Melmotte eventually returns to America, importing money made out of European scams," while John Sutherland likens Marie's economic decisions to

---

⁷⁶ *Ibid.*, 582.
⁷⁷ Rydygier Smith, "Trollope's Dark Vision," 16-17.
⁷⁸ Trollope, *TWWLN*, 581.
⁷⁹ *Ibid.*, 740.

Dolly Longstaffe's and Felix Carbury's wanton profligacy.[80] However, when analyzed alongside contemporary American property laws, Trollope's decision to send Marie to America informs a much more empathetic reading of her that supports her role as a heroine. In the novel, England is aligned with oppression, whereas "America is certainly the country for women, – and especially California," according to the narrator.[81] Axiomatic differences between the two locations represent different attitudes toward business, progress, and – importantly – women's rights.

In contrast to T. Wagner and Sutherland's analysis of Marie's future in America, Annette Van considers Trollope's portrayal of America and speculation in a more nuanced manner, arguing that Trollope viewed the ubiquity of British speculation as "a cultural crisis about value," which he solves by "imagin[ing] a spatial and temporal relocation of the speculative to the frontier. This move allows him to preserve the integrity of English culture while instantiating a logic of transatlantic relations wherein England can play both innocent victim and power player in a world experiencing the rapid emergence of global capitalism."[82] That is, the greed and dishonesty that underpin speculation are at odds with traditional British values and thus risk contaminating them. However, speculation done in America is different, according to Van's reading of *The Way We Live Now*, since white Americans and Europeans saw the American frontier as *terra incognita*, and thus there is nothing there to ruin. Van goes on to argue that the characters who go to the "frontier" to speculate (Fisker, Mrs. Hurtle, and Marie) retain their "self-worth, and dignity" and are, unlike many of the novel's characters, actually likeable.[83] However, what Van overestimates is "Trollope's longing for an England uncorrupted, an old-fashioned England."[04] In fact, as Rajan has argued, Trollope shows little reverence for antiquated traditions like titles and ancestral manors: "Trollope inserts Melmotte's desire for the legitimacy of land and 'real property' into his narrative not simply to gesture nostalgically to a firmer basis for wealth and the values of civic humanism associated with the landowning gentleman," she argues, "but also to make vivid to the reader the hypocrisy of maintaining these values in an age of modernity. Melmotte exemplifies this hypocritical shuttling between the old and new

---

[80] See Wagner, *Financial Speculation in Victorian Fiction*, 167 and Sutherland, "Introduction" to the 1982 Oxford UP edition of *The Way We Live Now*, ix, respectively.

[81] Trollope, *TWWLN*, 739.

[82] Annette Van, "Ambivalent Speculations: America as England's Future in 'The Way We Live Now,'" *NOVEL: A Forum on Fiction* 39, no. 1 (2005): 94-5.

[83] *Ibid.*, 93.

[84] *Ibid.*, 92.

values systems that is pervasive among the novel's English characters."⁸⁵ Trollope is not looking back nostalgically at the way the English lived then but condemning the degree to which the English clung to outdated notions of land, titles, and (I argue) gender norms. In *The Way We Live Now*, America is portrayed as an escape from the confines of such archaic ideologies; rather than characterizing it as the frontier, as Van does, it is helpful to think of Trollope's America as the future.

Throughout his 1862 *North America*, Trollope categorizes America, especially the American West, as a land of prosperity and success. "The most successful child that ever yet has gone off from a successful parent and taken its own path into the world, is without doubt the nation of the United States," he lauds.⁸⁶ While, on the one hand, the parent/child analogy emphasizes the connections between the two countries, it also, on the other hand, signifies generational differences. A young child is dependent on parents, but a child who has "gone off" is independent. This child's independence is characterized by an ethos of success:

> [t]here is very much in the mode of life adopted by the settlers in these [Western] regions which creates admiration. The people are all intelligent. They are energetic and speculative, conceiving grand ideas, and carrying them out almost with the rapidity of magic. A suspension bridge half a mile long is erected, while in England we should be fastening together a few planks for a foot passage. Progress, mental as well as material, is the demand of the people generally.⁸⁷

In America, according to Trollope, people are motivated by what he characterizes as a genuine sense of progress and innovation – "mental" and "material" progress – that is constantly looking ahead. This contrasts with the British speculators in *The Way We Live Now*, who sing the praises of modernity while also clinging to antiquated socio-economic institutions. Additionally, his point about the bridges suggests that, in America, grand schemes are carried out efficiently and tied to physical structures that represent American innovation. The humble wooden footbridge for which the British settled suggests a quaint but outdated method of problem-solving that is not up to the standards needed for actual progress. It mirrors Mrs. Hurtle's feelings for Paul Montague; despite the fact that "[s]he loved Paul Montague with all her heart...she despised herself for loving him. How weak he was; – how inefficient; how unable to seize

---

⁸⁵ Rajan, *A Tale of Two Capitalisms*, 294.
⁸⁶ Anthony Trollope, *North America* (Leipzig, 1862), 127.
⁸⁷ *Ibid.*, 224.

glorious opportunities; how swathed and swaddled by scruples and prejudices; – how unlike her own [American] countrymen in quickness of apprehension and readiness of action."[88] Paul wants to advance himself in the world but, like his fellow Brits, lacks the intelligence and boldness of American men. American men like Fisker have a sense of ingenuity that helps them take calculated risks, follow through on their plans, and enact real progress that British men, who are stuck between archaic and modern mindsets, simply cannot.

In an oft-quoted passage from *North America*, Trollope writes of American speculation:

> It seems to be the recognized rule of commerce in the Far West that men shall go into the world's markets prepared to cheat and to be cheated…When I was a child there used to be certain games at which it was agreed in beginning either that there should be cheating or that there should not. It may be said that out there in the western States, men agree to play the cheating game; and that the cheating game has more of interest in it than the other…this selling of things which do not exist, and buying of goods for which no price is ever to be given, is an institution which is much honoured in the West. We call it swindling; – and so do they. But it seemed to me that in the western States the word hardly seemed to leave the same impress on the mind that it does elsewhere.[89]

The code of ethics present in the American West differs from that in 1870s England. Though there is cheating, it is of a different nature than the fraud in British speculation, since in America the cheating is openly acknowledged: there is a dog-eat-dog air of the Wild West to Trollope's description that suggests a code of honor among thieves. This openness, then, changes the nature of American speculation as compared to British speculation, which attempts to retain the façade of honor. For instance, cheating is rampant among Beargarden members who pretend they will eventually settle their IOUs: an impossibility, as the reader knows, because they are all chronically skint. There remains a desperate attempt to maintain the gilt of aristocrats, though all are penniless scoundrels. One might also recall the smoke and mirrors with which Melmotte conducts the board of the South Central Pacific and Mexican Railway Company, keeping his board members in the dark while pocketing their investments.

There is another difference between British and American speculation: America's priority, Trollope makes clear throughout *North America*, is national

---

[88] Trollope, *TWWLN*, 726.
[89] Trollope, *North America*, 224-5.

progress – not just personal enrichment. That is, in America, speculation is a legitimate method of raising capital, advancing civilization, and building magnificent structures, whereas, in Britain, speculation is a means of advancing one's own interests. America has a different code of ethics, but it is a code of ethics nonetheless, unlike the self-serving fraud seen in British speculation. In his *Autobiography*, Trollope wrote: "the novelist, if he have a conscience, must preach his sermons with the same purpose as the clergy man, and must have his own system of ethics. If he, can do this efficiently, if he can make virtue alluring and vice ugly, while he charms his readers instead of wearying them" then the novelist is successful.[90] Trollope calls on authors to curate their own code of ethics rather than adopting a universal, moralizing code. The author, then, should strive to share these ethics with his readers by making "vice ugly" and "virtue alluring"; applying this logic to *The Way We Live Now*, it is easy to see that the ugly, vice-ridden characters are those who attempt to use modern methods of money-making to uphold or yoke themselves to an outdated model of society, while the characters who embody virtue are those who carve out their own code of ethics, removing themselves from the oppressive, stagnant forces of England for the modern, progressive, future-oriented space of America.

Interestingly, Trollope refers to his mother Fanny's failed foray into American commerce as a "speculation," writing: "she built a bazaar, and I fancy lost all the money which may have been embarked in that speculation. It could not have been much, and I think that others also must have suffered. But she looked about her, at her American cousins, and resolved to write a book about them."[91] In Trollope's novels, failed speculations often set off a disastrous chain of events, but Fanny's "speculation," conducted in America, is simply shrugged off as she moves on to her next (successful) endeavor.

Additionally, Fanny Trollope's own writings about America also highlight the "equality" indicative of the American business ethic. In her 1832 *Domestic Manners of the Americans*, which is highly disdainful of American culture, she describes a laborer she meets: "I have no doubt that every sun that sets sees him a richer man than when it rose. He hopes to make his son a lawyer; and I have little doubt that he will live to see him sit in Congress."[92] To some extent, this upward mobility has echoes of the self-made man ethos that was so popular throughout much of the Victorian period, but this man, a lumberjack,

---

[90] Trollope, *Autobiography*, 200.

[91] *Ibid.*, 200.

[92] Frances Milton Trollope, *Domestic Manners of the Americans* (London: Richard Bentley, 1839), 93.

is employed in hard – but honest – manual labor, not the scheming sort of wealth accumulation attempted by so many of the fathers in forced marriage plot novels. Additionally, Fanny notes that when the laborer's son makes it into Congress, "the idea that his origin is a disadvantage, will never occur to the imagination of the most exalted of his fellow-citizens...Any man's son may become the equal of any other man's son."[93] Written in 1832, of course, it is worth mentioning the caveat that, of course, this equitable dynamic only applied to white men, but in her representation of America, Fanny Trollope differentiates between American and British methods of business, characterizing the former by vigorous motivation, action, and equality.[94]

While useful in distinguishing American speculation from British, the American spirit of progress is also useful in coming to terms with Marie's role as a rebellious heroine since the role of women in the American economy differed from that in Britain. America, for instance, provided more protections for women as property owners, expanding women's access to their own financial security instead of forcing them to look to men for financial security. In his examination of British and American investment practices in the nineteenth century, George Robb explains that women had more economic freedom, which "might be attributable to less rigid gender roles in the States, though it could also be due to a more libertarian and freebooting American economic system."[95] White women were treated as individuals capable of managing their own assets rather than simply as conduits for wealth exchanged between men. For instance, states began passing laws as early as 1839 (continuing through the 1850s) that allowed all non-enslaved women – single and married – to own, retain, and manage their own property. In fact, historians define the Western United States as particularly liberal in the treatment of women's property, ensuring progress took precedence over maintaining patriarchal control of assets. Article XI, section 14 of The Constitution of California of 1849 (the document drawn in preparation for California's 1850 statehood) states: "[a]ll property, both real and personal, of the wife, owned or claimed by her before marriage, and that acquired afterward by gift, devise, or descent, shall be her separate property; and laws shall be passed more clearly

---

[93] *Ibid.*, 94.

[94] Fanny wrote negatively of the "familiarity [between classes], untempered [*sic*] by any shadow of respect, which is assumed by the grossest and the lowest in their intercourse with the highest and most refined. This is a positive evil, and, I think, more than balances its advantages" (see *Domestic Manners*, 94).

[95] George Robb, "Ladies of the Ticker: Women, Investment, and Fraud in England and America, 1850-1930," in *Victorian Investments: New Perspectives on Finance and Culture*, edited by Cannon Schmitt and Nancy Henry (Indiana University Press, 2008), 122.

defining the rights of the wife in relation as well to her separate property, as to that held in common with her husband."[96] Zorina Khan notes that in 1872 – following Great Britain's failure to protect married women's property rights – California passed additional measures to protect women's rights to inherit and maintain property, earnings, and the right to conduct business independently.[97]

These protections for woman-owned property contrast sharply with women's slim property rights in England. Though the Married Woman's Property Act of 1870 did pass (expanding working women's rights to the wages they earned), many of its supporters – such as Trollope, who campaigned for its passage – saw the 1870 bill as a disappointment in that it was "wholly inadequate in protecting women's rights to retain the property they brought to a marriage… The law continued to be based on the notion that women were irresponsible beings" who required their husbands to manage their assets, as Deborah Wynne puts it. [98] Furthermore, "[t]here was a belief that middle-class and upper-class women did not need the law to be changed because their husbands were 'gentlemen' and thus unlikely to be violent and abusive," a notion shown to be false in *The Way We Live Now*, given the systemic abuse of women.[99] The Act retained coverture, the institution through which nearly all of a married woman's property transferred to her husband upon marriage, and she lost her legal status as an individual: men's perceived right to all of his wife's possessions was legally reinforced.

Unlike England, California supported a women's right not just to own and inherit property but to make her own decisions in financial matters, and it is for these very reasons that Marie decides to make it her future home. She aspires to a life like that of American Isabel Boncassen, who: "hardly seemed to be under the control of the father. She went alone where she liked; talked to those she liked; and did what she liked. Some of the young ladies of the day thought there was a good deal to be said in favor of the freedom which she enjoyed."[100] When it comes to marriage, Isabel tells Dolly Longstaffe, "[m]y father has nothing to do with it, and I don't know what settlements mean. We never think anything of settlements in our country. If two young people love

---

[96] "Married Women's Property Laws," Library of Congress, accessed 15 November 2018, https://memory.loc.gov/ammem/awhhtml/awlaw3/property_law.html. n.pg.

[97] Zorina Khan, *The Democratization of Invention: Patents and Copyrights in American Economic Development, 1790-1920* (Cambridge University Press, 2005), 168.

[98] Deborah Wynne, *Women and Personal Property in the Victorian Novel* (Ashgate, 2010), 24.

[99] *Ibid.*

[100] Trollope, *Duke*, 200.

each other they go and get married."[101] Strikingly different from British attitudes toward feminine propriety and marriage as depicted in *The Way We Live Now*, America is configured as much more equitable in its treatment of women.[102]

Furthermore, though some scholars have tethered Marie's future to the speculations of Fisker (as T. Wagner does), the narrative is clear that Marie will make her own way in California, highlighting the extent to which she values her newfound independence. The American West is the ideal place for Marie to create her own future, obsessed as it is with progress, but she is careful to make informed decisions toward safeguarding her independence within that future. "Marie had now been wooed so often that she felt the importance of the step which was suggested to her," the narrator explains in reference to her prospective marriage with Fisker, "the romance of the thing was a good deal worn, and the material view of matrimony had also been damaged in her sight."[103] Furthermore:

> She had over a hundred thousand pounds of her own, and, feeling conscious of her own power in regard to her own money, knowing that she could do as she pleased with her wealth, she began to look out into life seriously…She had opinions of women's rights, – especially in regard to money…She had contrived to learn that, in the United States, a married women has greater power over her own money than in England, and this information acted strongly in Fisker's favour. On consideration of the whole subject she was inclined to think that she would do better in the world as Mrs. Fisker than as Marie Melmotte, – if she could see her way clearly in the matter of her own money.[104]

---

[101] *Ibid.*, 303.

[102] See: Amanda Claybaugh, "Trollope in America," in The Cambridge Companion to Anthony Trollope, ed. Carolyn Dever and Lisa Niles, 210-223 (Cambridge: Cambridge University Press, 2011), 211. Claybaugh offers a different perspective on American/British relations, focusing on the connections Trollope draws rather than the fissures. She argues Trollope: "offers an unusually rich account of the relations between the two nations, emphasizing that the former colony stood poised to become a partner in imperialism. In the process, he describes an Anglo-American alliance held together by the ties of business, politics, and love." However, a reading of *The Way We Live Now* centered on the female characters, specifically Marie, suggests the distinctions between American and British property laws are crucial to Trollope's portrayal of America.

[103] Trollope, *TWWLN*, 452.

[104] *Ibid.*, 738.

Trollope codes Marie's empowered financial savvy as wise, especially when read alongside his other writings on America. Fighting against becoming Melmotte's "chattel" sparks a new chapter for Marie; America provides the perfect backdrop to escape her unhappy past in a place that affords women economic security.[105] What Marie wants is a new identity, divorced from the oppression she faced as Melmotte's daughter ("she would do better in the world as Mrs. Fisker than as Marie Melmotte"), yet she ensures that she will remain economically independent in her new life as Mrs. Fisker. "You may consider yourself engaged to me," she tells Fisker, "[b]ut if I find when I get to San Francisco anything to induce me to change my mind, I shall change it. I like you very well, but I'm not going to take a leap in the dark, and I'm not going to marry a pig in a poke."[106] This phrase, "pig in a poke," refers, as the *Oxford English Dictionary* explains, to not buying something without properly inspecting it, similar, one might say, to speculating.[107] That is, Marie will not marry Fisker without investigating all the ramifications of that union – she will not treat her marriage like a gamble. Before, it was up to the patriarch to do the inspecting, deliberating, and deciding on his daughter's future: now, she will do that herself. Furthermore, her firm tone indicates her resolve to advocate for herself; she holds the bargaining chips and is no longer shy of making her own demands.

Peter Conrad argues that in Victorian novels, America functions as a locus of rebirth for British ex-pats: "Europe equips you with a hereditary, natal self. America allows you to invent a self better adjusted to the individual you have become since outgrowing the imposition of birth."[108] Furthermore, he argues that to Trollope, "America has altered time. Instead of incorporating the present into a retentive, protective past, it cancels the past (by seceding from the ancestral corruption of European history) and hustles the unworthy present into the promised future."[109] Shirking obsession with ancestral lands and titles, America is future-oriented rather than stuck in the past, which allows for greater expression of individuality. That is, America enables characters like Marie to fully realize Frederick Van Dam's markers of modernity, "free will and individual agency," to the extent that is impossible for her in England, a land

---

[105] *Ibid.*, 581.
[106] *Ibid.*, 740.
[107] "Pig, n.1," *OED Online*, Oxford University Press, March 2017, Web.
[108] Peter Conrad, *Imagining America* (Oxford University Press, 1980), 5.
[109] *Ibid.*, 44.

that, despite its emerging modernity, was still mired in archaic patriarchal mindsets about women and money.[110]

Conclusion

In many of his novels, Trollope portrays the extent to which outdated patriarchal ideologies collude with modern financial practices, such as speculation, to turn young women into exchangeable objects between men. Six years after criticizing Dallas' claims of Victorian gender equality, Trollope wrote his own version of a forced marriage plot that shows how adherence to social and financial manifestations of eighteenth-century patriarchalism persists. Importantly, *The Way We Live Now* depicts women who are awakened to their subordinate positions and feel empowered to fight back against these mercenary practices. Marie Melmotte transforms from an obedient girl to a woman insistent upon making her own future, reclaiming her position as the subject – rather than object – of her own life even though doing so required great risk on her part. Like Georgiana and Mrs. Hurtle, some of these decisions were risky, controversial decisions (such as disobeying her father and claiming the money he put in her name), but they underscore Trollope's dedication to writing complex, empowered female characters.

---

[110] Van Dam, *Anthony Trollope's Late Style*, 2.

Coda:
"I do not repent":
Heroic Disobedience Beyond 1880

As the preceding pages have explored, the forced marriage plot was a popular plot line in eighteenth- and nineteenth-century British novels. These centuries saw significant changes, particularly the rise of industrial capitalism, that had significant impacts on personal relationships and freedoms. To Samuel Richardson, Charlotte Lennox, Charlotte Smith, Mary Robinson, Jane Austen, Charles Dickens, Elizabeth Stone, and Anthony Trollope, using the forced marriage plot in their novels provided a method of exploring the devastating ways in which the capitalist ethos impacted women's fight for autonomy. Drawing on the exchange of one's daughter in ancient plays like Euripides' *Iphigenia in Aulis* and contemporary plays like Aphra Behn's *The Forc'd Marriage*, Samuel Richardson utilizes the forced marriage plot to dramatize the mercenary attitudes toward wealth and status that drove fathers to see their own daughters as exchangeable commodities. There is a clear cause-and-effect relationship between Harlowe's capitalist-fueled greed and the dehumanizing, commodifying way they treat Clarissa. Richardson's forced marriage plot prototype humanizes his young female protagonist in a way that was new, focusing on her painful internal struggle to decide between obeying her father and listening to her own sense of morality in a world in which obeying one's father was typically equated with morality. Though the sum of oppressive forces working against Clarissa Harlowe leads to her death, readers are led to empathize with her struggle against good and evil and, furthermore, see her transition from blindly obedient to rebelliously defending her own opinion as inherently moral. As the Parliamentary debates surrounding the Clandestine Marriages Act (and its subsequent approval in 1753) show, England's hegemonic power structure was predicated on the subordination of women.

Richardson's forced marriage prototype was taken up and emended by later writers who also saw the effectiveness with which it represented the specific barriers that capitalist practices introduced to the fight for women's rights. Charlotte Lennox, Mary Robinson, Charlotte Smith, Jane Austen, Charles Dickens, Elizabeth Stone, and Anthony Trollope transported Richardson's plot into their respective contemporary moments, dramatizing the many ways in which capitalist markets encouraged the continued subjugation of women. Characters like Arabella Glanville, Henrietta Maynard, and Edith Langshawe, just to name a few, all come to understand the ways in which they been conditioned to function as exchangeable commodities within the patriarchal economic systems of their respective periods; a realization that leads them to act on their own desires and moral codes.

As I have argued throughout this project, the repeated use of the forced marriage plot in England is linked to this specific historical period in which capitalism became the driving economic ethos. The waning of royally chartered trading companies throughout the eighteenth century to the expansion of limited liability and joint-stock companies toward the end of the nineteenth century coincided with a barrage of legislation and social norms that restricted the freedoms of women. Between the Clandestine Marriages Act of 1753 and the Married Woman's Property Act of 1883 were 130 years of stifling women's rights. Some of these measures were active – like the Clandestine Marriage Act, which codified a father's authority to dictate the marriage of his son or daughter, allowing employers to pay women less than men, or the Married Woman's Property Act of 1870, which most women's rights advocates (including Anthony Trollope) saw as a limited, placating measure that still left society's most vulnerable women without any significant financial protections. Other measures were more passive, such as the inadequate education that women received or the large body of conduct literature that taught women to value everyone else's needs above their own. Such laws and customs intentionally colluded to leave women without any options besides dependence on men: whether their father, husband or – in the case of the working poor or sex workers that are discussed in chapter four – a boss or trafficker.

That's not to say that the forced marriage plot disappeared from British novels after 1880. For instance, Mona Caird's 1889 *The Wing of Azrael* combines the forced marriage plot with an exploration of New Women. In a familiar potline, the tragic heroine, Viola Sedley, is sacrificed to a cruel, unloving man to pay her father's significant gambling debts. Caird's narrator minces no words when it comes to the sacrificial nature of femininity at the end of the nineteenth century:

> [T]he girl, beloved as she was, must always be prepared to make sacrifices for her brothers. In order that they should have a college education and every social advantage, Viola had to go almost without education at all; to afford them means to amuse themselves stylishly, their sister must be stinted of every opportunity and every pleasure. The child of course accepted this without question; her whole training dictated subordination of self.[1]

---

[1] Mona Caird, *The Wing of Azrael* (London, 1889), 6. Hereafter "*Azrael.*"

Raised by a mother who teaches her to "[e]ndure bravely, and in silence; that is the woman's part, my daughter," Viola believes in the ideology of submissive femininity as espoused by the conduct-guide authors discussed throughout this book.[2] Allestree and Stickney Ellis, for instance, glorified women who were submissive, dutiful, silent, and merciful with the aim of creating women who would obey their patriarchs rather than question their own powerlessness. Though those conduct guides were written much earlier than Carid's novel – some of them centuries earlier – Carid's novel shows the deep grip their oppressive ideologies maintained over late-nineteenth-century England and the active role parents took in shaping subservient daughters. Harry, the young man whom Viola loves, explains:

> 'You and they are not on equal terms; they can coerce you. Their power over you is despotic; and to resist such power all methods are justifiable.'
> 'Oh! you cannot mean what you say! I have always been taught that the will of parents is sacred, and that no blessing can come to a child who acts in opposition to their wishes.'
> 'Taught by whom?' Harry inquired; 'by your parents.'[3]

This exchange encapsulates the ease with which Viola's parents have indoctrinated her into the cult of feminine submissiveness. Until she has Harry's help, she does not realize the insidious nature of her upbringing. Her awakening to this injustice reveals the psychological damage she endures. "What was she? What did she know? What had she seen? What could she do? To all this there was only one answer: Nothing. Books had been forbidden her; human society had been cut off from her; scarcely had she been beyond the gates of her home."[4] Mocking her offer to work for a living rather than marry wealthy Philip Dendraith, her father taunts: "[e]verything is open to you; you have only to choose. And you know so much, don't you? You are so learned and capable, so well able to force your way in the world. Oh pray! don't think of marrying; a far more brilliant and congenial career lies before you."[5] He bluntly (and cruelly) lays out the whole machinery he, like so many other men, has used to shape her into an object of exchange between himself and whoever will pay the highest price.

Unlike the other forced marriage plots discussed at length in this project, Viola marries her father's choice in a husband: there is no last-minute maroon rebellion to kill off her cruel father or caring friend to call off the wedding with

---

[2] *Ibid.*, 75.
[3] *Ibid.*, 153.
[4] *Ibid.*, 79.
[5] *Ibid.*, 79.

proof of her intended's sexual profligacy. Viola's rebellion against the marriage comes later, and its results are disastrous for her. Her marriage is both verbally and emotionally abusive, and the threat of marital rape constantly hangs over Violet's head. Though she tries to leave him, Phillip thwarts her attempt and finally makes good on his attempts to rape her. Pushed to the brink of despair, Viola stabs and murders Phillip; though she insists: "'I knew it would kill him. I would do it again, I would do it again!' she cried in wild excitement. 'I leave a life behind me so loathsome, so intolerable- Yes,' she broke off fiercely, 'I would do it again,'" she ultimately does not believe she can exist after his murder.[6] "For her whose every breath had been cursed, who was stained and tainted through and through with shame and crime – for her was only a bottomless grave where she would fall and fall, weighted with her crime and her curse, through the darkness for ever and ever!"[7] Her plot arc, like Clarissa Harlowe's, ends in her death; however, whereas Clarissa faces her impending death with peace and conviction – it is presented as a sweet release from the earthly suffering inflicted by her father's actions – Violet's death by suicide (jumping over the edge of a rocky cliff) is seen by her as a punishment for murdering her husband. It is irrelevant to her that she was driven to that point by her father's forcing her into an unwanted marriage and her husband's relentless abuse to the point of marital rape. Viola never fully emerges from her indoctrinated state. Her story, then, is presented as a tragedy bearing witness to the deeply miserable existence of women who are taught to ignore their own subjectivities.

In a way, Viola Sedley's death mirrors the metaphorical death of the forced marriage plot as a literary mechanism for exposing the oppressive nature of capitalist practices. The end of the nineteenth century saw women – New Women, as Sarah Grand coined them – who consciously shirked society's expectation that they would live their adult lives as obedient, ministering wives and mothers. As Barbara Gerrish defines the "New Woman" in Emma Wolf's 1896 novel *The Joy of Life*, new women are "women who believe in and ask for the right to advance in education, the arts, and professions with their fellow-men, you are speaking of a phase in civilisation which has come gradually and naturally, and is here to stay. There is nothing new or abnormal in such a woman."[8] Many reactions to these desires were negative, especially, as Sally Ledger points out, when it came to the fear of British women shirking motherly, domestic duties. But, as Ledger also points out, the reaction against new women ran deeper. New Women were often "regarded as a threat to the economic supremacy of bourgeois men in Britain, and this was certainly another

---

[6] *Ibid.*, 377.

[7] *Ibid.*, 378.

[8] Emma Wolf, *The Joy of Life* (New York: A.C. McClurg, 1896), 121.

factor which contributed to the spite with which she was condemned."[9] A financially independent woman was a threat to white patriarchal hegemony on many levels. For a century and a half, forced marriage plot novels reflected the ways in which controlling money meant being able to control women, but as fewer women married and more women worked, the figure of the tyrannical father was no longer an accurate representative of the socio-economic injustices against women.

All of this is not to say that familial, economic, and social pressures to marry ceased to exist for women in Britain in the late nineteenth century. In fact, many of what are now considered classic New Woman novels depict female characters who feel compelled to marry despite not really wanting to. Sue Bridehead in Thomas Hardy's *Jude the Obscure*, for instance, has progressive views on the necessity of formal marriage – she even at one point compares bridal flowers to "the garland which decked the heifers of sacrifice in old times!" – but ends the novel unhappily married to Phillotson.[10] In *The Odd Woman*, George Gissing's Monica says of Widdowson: "[h]e loves me so much that he has made me think I *must* marry him. And I am glad of it. I'm not like you, Milly; I can't be contented with this life."[11] She is, of course, referring to the life of a single woman working for her own room and board; Monica does not protest when Mildred states: [y]ou will marry him for a comfortable home—that's what it amounts to." For Monica, that is the point.

It is, I think, fair to say that many of the heroically disobedient heroines discussed throughout this project are the prototypes for, or perhaps harbingers of, the New Woman. That is, rather than following the servile path that their society dictated, heroically disobedient characters actively fight to carve out their own paths through life that is grounded in their newly awakened sense of self. Later in the nineteenth century, some of these heroic characters (like Edith Dombey, Edith Langshawe, and Marie Melmotte) even end their respective storylines unmarried: a nod to their self-sufficiency and, especially in Edith Dombey's case, a total rejection of typical domestic life. These are all characters created by writers who saw the ways in which the growth of capitalism impeded women's fight for more autonomy – more choices – within their own lives and believed that, despite the uptick in oppression, it was still possible for women to fight for their freedoms.

---

[9] Sally Ledger, *The New Woman: Fiction and Feminism at the Fin de Siècle* (Indiana University Press, 1997), 121.

[10] Thomas Hardy, *Jude the Obscure*, ed. Patricia Ingham (Oxford: Oxford University Press, 1985), 301.

[11] George Gissing, *The Odd Women*, ed. Patricia Ingham (Oxford: Oxford University Press, 2000), 125.

Bibliography

Primary Texts

Allestree, Richard. *The Ladies Calling*. 8th ed. Oxford, 1705. *EEBO*.
Arnold, Matthew. *Culture and Anarchy*. Edited by P. J. Keating. Penguin Classics, 2015.
Austen, Jane. *Mansfield Park*. Edited by Kathryn Sutherland. London: Penguin Classics, 2014.
---. *Pride and Prejudice*. Edited by Donald Gray and Mary A. Favret. New York: Norton, 2016.
---. "Sanditon." In *Northanger Abbey, The Watsons, and Sanditon*, edited by James Kinsley, 347-451. Oxford: Oxford University Press, 2003.
---. *Selected Letters*. Edited by Vivien Jones. Oxford: Oxford University Press, 2009.
Blackstone, William. "Introduction." In *Commentaries on the Laws of England*. Accessed May 26, 2023. Yale Law Library: The Avalon Project. https://avalon.law.yale.edu/18th_century/blackstone_intro.asp.
Caird, Mona. *The Wing of Azrael*. London, 1889. *Google Books*.
Carroll, John, ed. *The Selected Letters of Samuel Richardson*. Clarendon Press, 1964.
Cobbett, William. *Cobbett's Parliamentary History of England: From the Norman Conquest in 1066 to the Year 1803*, Vol. 15. London, 1813. *Google Books*.
Collins, Philip, ed. *The Critical Heritage of Charles Dickens*. Routledge, 1995.
Cugoano, Ottobah. *Thoughts and Sentiments on the Evil of Slavery*. Penguin Classics, 1999.
Dallas, Eneas Sweetland, ed. *Clarissa: A Novel By Samuel Richardson*. London, 1868. *Google Books*.
Dallas, Robert Charles. *The History of the Maroons, Vols. 1-2*. London, 1803. *Google Books*.
Defoe, Daniel. *The Family Instructor*. 16th ed. London, 1766. *Google Books*.
---. "A Plan of the English Commerce: Being a Compleat Prospect of the Trade of this Nation, as Well the Home Trade as the Foreign; in Three Parts [...]." In *The Novels and Selected Writings of Daniel Defoe*, edited by William K. Wimsatt Jr. and Ronald S. Crane, vol. 7, 349-480. Shakespeare Head Press, 1927.
"The demon of gambling will always have his." *The Times*, 1861, p. 9. The *Times Digital Archive 1785-2012*.
Dickens, Charles. *Dombey and Son*. Edited by Andrew Sanders, Penguin Classics, 2002.
---. "Home for Homeless Women." In *The Works of Charles Dickens, Miscellaneous Papers*. Chapman and Hall, 1908. *Google Books*.
---. *The Letters of Charles Dickens*. Edited by Mary "Mamie" Dickens and Georgina Hogarth. 2 vols. New York, 1879. *Google Books*.
---. *Little Dorrit*. Edited by Helen Small, Penguin Classics, 2004.

---. *Nicholas Nickleby*. 1838-9. Edited by Mark Ford, Penguin Classics, 2003.

Edwards, Bryan. *The History, Civil and Commercial, of the British Colonies in the West Indies*. London, 1793. *Google Books*.

Ellis, Sarah Stickney. *The Daughters of England: The Position in Society, Character and Responsibilities*. 1842. New York, 1843. *Google Books*.

---. *The women of England, their social duties, and domestic habits*. London, 1838. *Google Books*.

Engels, Friedrich. *The Origin of the Family, Private Property and the State*. 1884. Chicago, 1902. *Google Books*.

Filmer, Robert. *Patriarcha: or, The Natural Power of Kings*. London: 1680. *Liberty Fund Online*.

Fordyce, James. *Sermons for Young Women*. 14th ed. London: Printed by T. Bensley for T. Cadell and W. Davies, 1814. *Google Books*.

Gissing, George. *The Odd Women*. Edited by Patricia Ingham. Oxford: Oxford University Press, 2000.

Hardy, Thomas. *Jude the Obscure*. Edited by Patricia Ingham. Oxford: Oxford University Press, 1985.

Hays, Mary. *An Appeal to the Men of Great Britain in Behalf of Women*. London, 1798. *Eighteenth Century Collections Online*.

Kant, Immanuel. *Toward a Perpetual Peace and Other Writings on Politics, Peace, and History*. Edited by Pauline Kleingeld, translated by David Colclasure. Yale University Press, 2006.

Lennox, Charlotte. *The Female Quixote*. 1752. Edited by Margaret Anne Doody, Oxford World Classics, 2008.

Levi, Leone. *The History of British Commerce: And of the Economic Progress of the British Nation, 1763-1870*. London: McMillian and Co., 1872. Google Books.

Lewis, Matthew Gregory. *Journal of a West India proprietor: kept during a residence in the Island of Jamaica*. London: John Murray, 1834. *Internet Archive*.

Locke, John. *Second Treatise of Government, 1689*. Early Modern Texts Online. Edited by Jonathan Bennett, 2008. Accessed from https://www.earlymodern texts.com/assets/pdfs/locke1689a.pdf.

Long, Edward. *The History of Jamaica or, General Survey of the Antient and Modern State of that Island*. London: T. Lowndes, 1774. Vols. 1-3. *Google Books*.

Macaulay, Thomas Babington. "Sir James Mackintosh's History of the Revolution." In *The Works of Lord Macaulay*, edited by Lady Trevelyan, vol. 6, 45-107. London: Longman's, Green, and Co., 1906. *Google Books*.

"Married Women's Property Laws." Library of Congress. Accessed 15 November 2018. https://memory.loc.gov/ammem/awhhtml/awlaw3/property_law.html.

"The Maroon War." *Times* (London), 8 July, 1796. *The Times Digital Archive*. Accessed 24 Jan., 2018.

Marx, Karl. *Capital: A Critical Analysis of Capitalist Production*. Edited by Frederick Engels. 1887. Translated by Samuel Moore and Edward Aveling. London, 1889. *Google Books*.

---. *The Poverty of Philosophy: Being a Translation of the Misère de la Philosophie (a Reply to "La Philosophie de la Misère" of M. Proudhon)*. Edited by Harry Quelch, et al., United States, 1910. *Google Books*.

Marx, Karl, and Frederick Engels. *Economic and Philosophic Manuscripts of 1844 and the Communist Manifesto*. Translated by Martin Milligan. Prometheus Books, 1988.

Mitford, John. "Dr. Johnson's Literary Intercourse with Mrs. Lennox." *The Gentleman's Magazine*, vol. XX, 1843, pp. 132. *Google Books*.

Nelson, James. *An Essay on the government of Children, under three general heads: viz. Health, Manners and Education*. London, 1763. *Google Books*.

Richardson, Samuel. *Clarissa. Or, the History of a Young Lady: Comprehending the most Important Concerns of Private Life*. Third edition. London, 1751. *English Short Title Catalogue*.

---. *Pamela: Or, Virtue Rewarded, In a Series of Familiar Letters from a Beautiful Young Damsel to Her Parents: and Afterwards, in Her Exalted Condition, Between Her, and Persons of Figure and Quality, Upon the Most Important and Entertaining Subjects, in Genteel Life. Publish'd in Order to Cultivate the Principles of Virtue and Religion in the Minds of the Youth of Both Sexes*. Fourth Edition. London: 1742. *Google Books*.

---. "Rambler No. 97." *The Rambler*. Edited by Samuel Johnson. London, 1751. *Google Books*.

Robinson, Mary. *Angelina; A Novel*, Dublin, 1796. Vols. 1-2. *Eighteenth-Century Collections Online*.

---. *A Letter to the Women of England and The Natural Daughter*, edited by Sharon Setzer, Broadview Press, 2002.

---. *Mary Robinson: Selected Poems*, edited by Judith Pascoe, Broadview Press, 2000.

Schurer, Norbert, editor. *Charlotte Lennox: Correspondence and Miscellaneous Documents*. Bucknell UP, 2012.

Smiles, Samuel. *Self-help: With Illustrations of Character, Conduct and Perseverance*. 1859. London, 1878. *Google Books*.

Smith, Adam. *An Inquiry into the Nature and Causes of the Wealth of Nations*. 1776. Dublin, 1801. 2 vols. *Google Books*.

Smith, Charlotte. *The Collected Letters of Charlotte Smith*, edited by Judith Phillips Stanton. Indiana UP, 2003. *ProQuest Ebook*.

---. "The Emigrants." *Major Poetical Works*. Edited by Knowles and Horrocks, Broadview Press, 2017.

---. *The Story of Henrietta*. Edited by Janina Nordius. Richmond: Valencourt Books, 2021

Steele, Richard. *The Tatler and the Guardian, complete in one volume*. Edinburgh, 1880. *Google Books*.

"Stock Exchange No. 1," *Fraser's Magazine For Town and Country*. London, vol. 4, no. 20, September 1831. *Google Books*.

Stone, Elizabeth. *William Langshawe, the Cotton Lord*. London, 1842. 2 vols. *Google Books*.

Thackeray, William Makepeace. *The Newcomes: Memoirs of a Most Respectable Family*. 1854. London, 1904. *Google Books*.

Thelwall, John. *The Daughter of Adoption: A Tale of Modern Times*. Edited by Michael Scrivener, Yasmin Solomonescu, and Judith Thompson. Broadview Press, 2021.

Trollope, Anthony. *An Autobiography*. New York, 1883. Google Books.

---. *North America*. Leipzig, 1862. Google Books.

---. "On E. S. Dallas's 1868 abridgment of Samuel Richardson's Clarissa." 1868. *Writings for St. Paul's Magazine*, edited by John Sutherland, Arno Press, 1981, pp. 163-172.

---. *The Prime Minister*. Edited by Nicholas Shrimpton. Oxford World Classics, 2011.

---. *Sir Harry Hotspur of Humblethwaite*. 1870. London, 1882. Archive.org.

---. *The Three Clerks*. New York: Harper and Brothers, 1860. Google Books.

---. *The Way We Live Now*. 1874-5. Second Edition. Edited by Francis O'Gorman, Oxford World Classics, 2016.

Trollope, Frances Milton. *Domestic Manners of the Americans*. United Kingdom: Richard Bentley, 1839. Google Books.

Wilberforce, William. *An Appeal to the Religion, Justice, and Humanity of the Inhabitants of the British Empire, in Behalf of the Negro Slaves in the West Indies*. London, 1823. Google Books.

Williams, Cynric. *Hamel the Obeah Man*. London, 1827. Google Books.

Wolf, Emma. *The Joy of Life*. New York: A.C. McClurg, 1896. Google Books.

Wollstonecraft, Mary. *Historical and Moral View of the Origin and Progress of the French Revolution and the Effect it Has Produced in Europe*. London, 1794. Eighteenth-Century Collections Online.

---. *Mary and The Wrongs of Women*. 1798. Edited by Gary Kelley, Oxford World Classics, 2007.

---. *Thoughts on the Education of Daughters: With Reflections on Female Conduct, in the More Important Duties of Life*. London: J. Johnson, 1787. Google Books.

---. *A Vindication of the Rights on Women*. 1792. Edited by Janet Todd, Oxford World Classics, 2008.

Secondary Texts

Airey, Jennifer L. "'Abused, Neglected,—Unhonoured,—Unrewarded': The Economics of Authorial Labor in the Writings of Mary Robinson." *ABO: Interactive Journal for Women in the Arts, 1640-1830* 6 (1), 2016. https://doi.org/10.5038/2157-7129.6.1.1.

Anderson, Amanda. "Trollope's Modernity." *ELH* 74.3, 2007. www.jstor.org/stable/30029570.

Andrews, Kerri. "'Herself... Fills The Foreground': Negotiating Autobiography in the Elegiac Sonnets and the Emigrants." In *Charlotte Smith in British Romanticism*, edited by Jacqueline M. Labbe and Mark Parker, 97-113. Routledge, 2008.

Armstrong, Nancy. *Desire and Domestic Fiction: A Political History of the Novel*. Oxford University Press, 1987.

Bailey, Martha. "The Marriage Law of Jane Austen's World." *Persuasions* 36, no. 1 (Winter 2015): n. pg.

Ballaster, Ros. *Seductive Forms: Women's Amatory Fiction from 1684 to 1740*. Oxford University Press, 1998.

Baptist, Edward E. *The Half Has Never Been Told: Slavery and the Making of American Capitalism*. Hachette Book Group, 2016.

Besley, Catherine. "A Future for Materialist Feminist Criticism?." In *The Color of Equality: Race and Common Humanity in Enlightenment Thought*, edited by Devin J. Vartija, 194-214. Philadelphia, University of Pennsylvania Press, 2021.

Binhammer, Katherine. *The Seduction Narrative in Britain, 1747-1800*. Cambridge UP, 2009.

Gunn, Daniel P. "Is Clarissa Bourgeois Art?" In *Passion and Virtue: Essays on the Novels of Samuel Richardson*, edited by David Blewett. University of Toronto Press, 2001. http://www.jstor.org/stable/10.3138/9781442678293.13.

Bodenheimer, Rosemarie. *Knowing Dickens*. Cornell University Press, 2007.

---. *The Politics of Story in Victorian Social Fiction*. Cornell UP, 1988.

Boulukos, George E. "The Horror of Hybridity: Enlightenment, Anti-slavery and Racial Disgust in Charlotte Smith's *Story of Henrietta* (1800)." In *Slavery and the Cultures of Abolition: Essays Marking the Bicentennial of the British Abolition Act of 1807*, edited by Brycchan Carey and Peter J. Kitson, 87-109. Woodbridge, Boydell & Brewer Ltd, 2007.

---. "The Politics of Silence: Mansfield Park and the Amelioration of Slavery." *Novel*, vol. 39, no. 3, 1 November 2006, pp. 361–383, https://doi-org.proxygw.wrlc.org/10.1215/ddnov.039030361.

Bourdieu, Pierre. "The Forms of Capital." *Handbook of Theory and Research for the Sociology of Education*. Edited by J. Richardson. Greenwood Press, 1986, pp. 241-258.

Bowen, John. "Performing Business, Training Ghosts: Transcoding Nickleby." *ELH*, vol. 63, no. 1, 1996, pp. 153–175. *JSTOR*, www.jstor.org/stable/30030277.

Bowers, Toni. "Family." In *Samuel Richardson in Context*, edited by Peter Sabor and Betty Schellenberg, 273-280. Cambridge University Press, 2017.

Brack, O. M., and Susan Carlile. "Samuel Johnson's Contributions to Charlotte Lennox's 'The Female Quixote.'" *The Yale University Library Gazette*, vol. 77, no. 3/4, 2003, pp. 166–173. *JSTOR*, www.jstor.org/stable/40859294.

Brantlinger, Patrick. *Fictions of State: Culture and Credit in Britain, 1694-1994*. Cornell University Press, 1996.

---. *Taming Cannibals: Race and the Victorians*. Cornell UP, 2011. ProQuest Ebook.

Brodie, Laura Fairchild. "Society and the Superfluous Female: Jane Austen's Treatment of Widowhood." *Studies in English Literature, 1500-1900* 34, no. 4 (1994): 697-718. www.jstor.org/stable/450866.

Brooks, Peter. *Reading for the Plot: Design and Intention in Narrative*. Harvard UP, 1992.

Bueler, Lois. *The Tested Woman Plot: Women's Choices, Men's Judgments, and the Shaping of Stories*. Ohio State UP, 2001.

Burgan, Mary A. "Mr. Bennet and the Failures of Fatherhood in Jane Austen's Novels." *The Journal of English and Germanic Philology* 74, no. 4 (October, 1975): 536-552.

Carlile, Susan. *Charlotte Lennox: An Independent Mind.* University of Toronto Press, 2018.

Claybaugh, Amanda. "Trollope in America." In *The Cambridge Companion to Anthony Trollope*, edited by Carolyn Dever and Lisa Niles, 210-223. Cambridge: Cambridge University Press, 2011.

Conrad, Peter. *Imagining America.* Oxford University Press, 1980.

Copeland, Edward. "Money." In *The Cambridge Companion to Jane Austen*, edited by Edward Copeland and Juliet McMaster, 127-138. Cambridge: Cambridge University Press, 1997.

Craciun, Adriana. "'Empire without end': Charlotte Smith at the Limits of Cosmopolitanism." *Women's Writing* 16:1, 2009, pp. 39-59, T&F Online, DOI: 10.1080/09699080902768265.

Crayton, Bernard. "Strangers within the Realm: The Pomeroon People and the Atlantic World." In *Strangers within the Realm: Cultural Margins of the First British Empire*, edited by B. Bailyn & P. D. Morgan, 241-270. University of North Carolina Press, 1991.

Dalley, Lana A., and Jill Rappoport, editors. *Economic Women: Essays on Desire and Dispossession in Nineteenth-Century British Culture.* Ohio State UP, 2013.

Davidoff, Leonore, and Catherine Hall. *Family Fortunes: Men and Women of the English Middle Class, 1780-1850.* 2nd edition. Routledge, 2003.

Denenholz Morse, Deborah. *Reforming Trollope: Race, Gender, and Englishness in the Novels of Anthony Trollope.* Ashgate, 2013.

Denenholz Morse, Deborah. "The Way He Thought Then: Modernity and the Retreat of the Public Liberal in Anthony Trollope's The Way We Live Now, 1873." *BRANCH: Britain, Representation and Nineteenth-Century History*, edited by Dino Franco Felluga. Web. 15 November 2018.

Deresiewicz, William. "Thomas Hardy and the History of Friendship Between the Sexes." *The Wordsworth Circle*, vol. 38, nos. 1-2, 2007, pp. 56-63.

Doody, Margaret Anne. "Shakespeare's Novels: Charlotte Lennox Illustrated." *Studies in the Novel*, vol. 19, no. 3, 1987, pp. 296–310. JSTOR, www.jstor.org/stable/29532509.

Downie, J. A. "Who Says She's A Bourgeois Writer? Reconsidering the Social and Political Contexts of Jane Austen's Novels." *Eighteenth-Century Studies*, vol. 40, no. 1, 2006, pp. 69-84. www.jstor.org/stable/30053492.

Duckworth, Alistair M. *The Improvement of the Estate: A Study of Jane Austen's Novels.* Johns Hopkins University Press, 1971.

Eagleton, Terry. *The Rape of Clarissa: Writing, Sexuality, and Class Struggle in Samuel Richardson.* University of Minnesota Press, 1982.

Eddleman, Stephanie M. "Mad as the Devil but Smiling Sweetly: Repressed Female Anger in Mansfield Park." *Persuasions*, vol. 28, 2006, n.p.

Elliot, Geoffrey. *The Mystery of Overend and Gurney: A Financial Scandal in Victorian London.* Methuen, 2006.

Ellis, Kate Ferguson. *The Contested Castle: Gothic Novels and the Subversion of Domestic Ideology.* University of Illinois Press, 1989.

Fay, Elizabeth. "Mary Robinson: On Trial in the Public Court." *Studies in Romanticism*, vol. 45, no. 3, 2006, pp. 397-423. JSTOR, www.jstor.org/stable/25602059.

Felski, Rita. *Beyond Feminist Aesthetics: Feminist Literature and Social Change*. Harvard University Press, 1989.

Ferguson, Moira. *Colonialism and Gender Relations from Mary Wollstonecraft to Jamaica Kincaid: East Caribbean Connections*. Columbia University Press, 1993.

Fraiman, Susan. "Jane Austen and Edward Said: Gender, Culture, and Imperialism." *Critical Inquiry*, vol. 21, no. 4, 1995, pp. 805-821. JSTOR, www.jstor.org/stable/1344068.

Francis, Keith A. "Canon Law Meets Unintended Consequences: The Church of England and the Clandestine Marriage Act of 1753." *Anglican and Episcopal History* 72, no. 4 (2003): 451-87. http://www.jstor.org/stable/42612360.

Froide, Amy M. *Silent Partners: Women as Public Investors during Britain's Financial Revolution, 1690-1750*. Oxford University Press, 2016. Oxford Scholarship Online.

Fry, Carol. "'Misery is...the Certain Concomitant of Slavery': The British Anti-Slavery Movement in Charlotte Smith's Novels." *PMPA*, 2002-2003, no. 27, pp. 45-53.

Furneaux, Holly. *Queer Dickens: Erotics, Families, Masculinities*. Oxford University Press, 2009.

Gikandi, Simon. *Slavery and the Culture of Taste*. Princeton University Press, 2011. JSTOR, www.jstor.org/stable/j.ctt7svr8.

Gilbert, Deirdre. "'Willy-Nilly' and Other Tales of Male-Tails: Rightful and Wrongful Laws of Inheritance in Northanger Abbey and Beyond." *Persuasions On-Line*, vol. 20, no. 1, 1999, https://jasna.org/persuasions/on-line/vol20no1/gilbert.html.

Goodlad, Lauren M. E. "Trollopian 'Foreign Policy': Rootedness and Cosmopolitanism in the Mid-Victorian Global Imaginary." *PMLA*, vol. 124, no. 2, 2009, pp. 437-454. *JSTOR*, www.jstor.org/stable/25614285.

Hager, Kelley. *Dickens and the Rise of Divorce: The Failed-Marriage Plot and the Novel Tradition*. Ashgate, 2010.

Hall, Lynda A. "Addressing Readerly Unease: Discovering the Gothic in Mansfield Park." *Persuasions* 28 (2006): 208-216.

Hobsbawm, Eric. *The Age of Capital: 1848-1875*. Abacus Books, 1975.

Hopkins, Lisa. "Jane Austen and Money." *The Wordsworth Circle* 25 (1994): 172-177. doi:10.1086/TWC328756.

Howard, Susan K. "Identifying the Criminal in Charlotte Lennox's The Life of Harriot Stuart." *Eighteenth-Century Fiction*, vol. 5, no. 2, 1993, pp. 137-152. *Project Muse*, https://doi.org/10.1353/ecf.1993.0027.

Hudson, Nicholas. "Literature and Social Class in the Eighteenth Century." *Oxford Handbooks Online*. Oxford: Oxford UP, 2015. doi:10.1093/oxfordhb/9780199935338.013.007.

Hughes, Linda K., and Michael Lund. *The Victorian Serial*. University Press of Virginia, 1991.

Hume, Robert D. "Money in Jane Austen." *The Review of English Studies* 64, no. 264 (April 2013): 289-310. doi:10.1093/res/hgs121.

Jones, Vivien, ed. *Women and Literature in Britain* 1700-1800. Cambridge UP, 2000.

Kaplan, Deborah. *Jane Austen Among Women.* Baltimore: Johns Hopkins University Press, 1992.

Kenney, Theresa. "Why Tom Bertram Cannot Die: 'The Plans and Decisions of Mortals.'" *Persuasions Online* 35, no. 1 (Winter 2014): n. pg.

Kestner, Joseph. *Protest and Reform: The British Social Narrative by Women, 1827-1867.* University of Wisconsin Press, 1985.

Keymer, Thomas. *Richardson's Clarissa and the Eighteenth-Century Reader.* Cambridge University Press, 1992.

Khan, Zorina. *The Democratization of Invention: Patents and Copyrights in American Economic Development, 1790-1920.* Cambridge University Press, 2005.

Kowaleski-Wallace, Elizabeth. *The Father's Daughters: Hannah More, Maria Edgeworth, and Patriarchal Complacency.* Oxford University Press, 1991.

Latimer, Bonnie. *Making Gender, Culture, and the Self in the Fiction of Samuel Richardson: The Novel Individual.* Ashgate, 2013. ProQuest Ebook.

Ledger, Sally. *Dickens and the Popular Radical Imagination.* Cambridge University Press, 2007.

Ledger, Sally. *The New Woman: Fiction and Feminism at the Fin de Siècle.* Indiana University Press, 1997.

Le Faye, Deirdre. "Sanditon: Jane Austen's Manuscript and Her Niece's Continuation." *The Review of English Studies* 38, no. 149 (Feb. 1987): 56-61.

Lévi-Strauss, Claude. *The Elementary Structures of Kinship.* Beacon Press, 1969.

Libin, Katheryn L. Shanks. "Lifting the Heart to Rapture: Harmony, Nature, and the Unmusical Fanny Price." *Persuasions* 28 (2006): 137-149.

Lubitz, Rita. *Marital Power in Dickens' Fiction.* Peter Lang Press, 1996.

McAleavey, Maia. *The Bigamy Plot: Sensation and Convention in the Victorian Novel.* Cambridge University Press, 2015.

Malchow, Howard. *Gothic Images of Race in Nineteenth-Century Britain.* Stanford University Press, 1996.

Marwick, Margaret. *Trollope and Women.* The Hambledon Press, 1997.

Meyer, Susan. *Imperialism at Home: Race and Victorian Women's Fiction.* Cornell University Press, 1996.

Michie, Elsie B. "Austen's Powers: Engaging with Adam Smith in Debates about Wealth and Virtue." *NOVEL: A Forum on Fiction* 34, no. 1 (Autumn, 2000): 5-27. JSTOR 1346145.

---. *The Vulgar Question of Money: Heiresses, Materialism, and the Novel of Manners From Jane Austen to Henry James.* Johns Hopkins University Press, 2011.

Midgley, Clare. "British Women, Women's Rights and Empire, 1790-1850." In *Women's Rights and Human Rights: International Perspectives*, edited by Grimshaw, Holmes, and Lake, Palgrave, 2001.

Miller, Andrew H. *The Burdens of Perfection: On Ethics and Reading in Nineteenth-Century British Literature.* Cornell University Press, 2008. JSTOR, www.jstor.org/stable/10.7591/j.ctt7z5m3.

Mintz, Sidney W. *Sweetness and Power: The Place of Sugar in Modern History.* Penguin Books, 1985.

Bibliography

Mitchell, Sally. "Elizabeth Stone [née Wheeler], (1803–1881), novelist and historian." *Oxford Dictionary of National Biography*. 2004-09-23. Oxford University Press. Date of access 28 Jun. 2018, http://www.oxforddnb.com/view/10.1093/ref:odnb/9780198614128.001.0001/odnb-9780198614128-e-46563.

Moretti, Franco. *The Bourgeois: Between History and Literature*. Verso, 2013.

Morse, Deborah Denenholz. "The Way He Thought Then: Modernity and the Retreat of the Public Liberal in Anthony Trollope's The Way We Live Now, 1873." In *BRANCH: Britain, Representation and Nineteenth-Century History*, edited by Dino Franco Felluga. Web.

Ogborn, Miles. "A war of words: speech, print, and script in the Maroon War of 1795-6." *Journal of Historical Geography* 37 (2011): 203-215.

O'Gorman, Francis. "Introduction." *The Way We Live Now*. Oxford World Classics, pp. xiii-xxxii.

Paravisini-Gerbert, Lisbeth. "Colonial and Post-Colonial Gothic: The Caribbean." In *The Cambridge Companion to Gothic Fiction*, edited by Jerrold E. Hogle, Cambridge University Press, 2002, pp. 229-257.

Perry, Ruth. "Austen and Empire: A Thinking Woman's Guide to British Imperialism." *Persuasions* 16 (1994): 21-29.

"pig, n.1." *OED Online*, Oxford University Press, March 2017. Web. Accessed 16 November 2018.

"politic, adj. and n." *OED Online*, Oxford University Press, December 2019. Accessed 31 January 2020.

Poovey, Mary. *Genres of the Credit Economy: Mediating Value in Eighteenth- and Nineteenth-Century Britain*. University of Chicago Press, 2008. ProQuest.

Probert, Rebecca. *Marriage Law and Practice in the Long Eighteenth Century: A Reassessment*. Cambridge University Press, 2009.

Rajan, Supritha. *A Tale of Two Capitalisms: Sacred Economics in Nineteenth-Century Britain*. University of Michigan Press, 2015. JSTOR, www.jstor.org/stable/10.3998/mpub.7664610.10.

Reed, John R. "A Friend to Mammon: Speculation in Victorian Literature." *Victorian Studies* 27, no. 2 (1984): 179–202. www.jstor.org/stable/3827131.

Richardson, Leslie. "Leaving Her Father's House: Astell, Locke, and Clarissa's Body Politic." *Studies in Eighteenth-Century Culture*, vol. 34, 2005, pp. 151-171. JSTOR.

Robb, George. "Ladies of the Ticker: Women, Investment, and Fraud in England and America, 1850-1930." In *Victorian Investments: New Perspectives on Finance and Culture*, edited by Cannon Schmitt and Nancy Henry. Indiana University Press, 2008.

Rose, Jonathan. "Was Capitalism Good for Victorian Literature?" *Victorian Studies*, vol. 46, no. 3, 2004, pp. 489-501. Project MUSE.

Ross, Deborah. "Betsy Thoughtless & Harriot Stuart: Unacknowledged Sisters." In *The Excellence of Falsehood: Romance, Realism, and Women's Contribution to the Novel*, edited by Deborah Kaplan, University Press of Kentucky, 1991, pp. 66–93. www.jstor.org/stable/j.ctt130jsjz.8.

Rubin, Gayle. "The Traffic in Women: Notes on the Political Economy of Sex." In *Toward an Anthropology of Women*, edited by Rayna R. Reiter, Monthly Review Press, 1975, pp. 157-210.

Rydygier Smith, Monika. "Trollope's Dark Vision: Domestic Violence in The Way We Live Now." *Victorian Review*, vol. 22, no. 1, 1996, pp. 13–31. JSTOR, www.jstor.org/stable/27794820.

Said, Edward W. *Culture and Imperialism*. Vintage Books, 1994.

Schellenberg, Betsy. *The Professionalization of Women Writers in Eighteenth-Century Britain*. Cambridge University Press, 2005.

Scheuermann, Mona. *Her Bread to Earn: Women, Money, and Society from Defoe to Austen*. University Press of Kentucky, 1993.

Schor, Hilary M. *Dickens and the Daughter of the House*. Cambridge University Press, 2000. ProQuest.

Setzer, Sharon M. "The Marriage Market, the Slave Trade and the 'Cruel Business' of War in Mary Robinson's Angelina." In *Didactic Novels and British Women's Writing, 1790-1820*, edited by Hilary Havens, Routledge, 2017.

Shea, Allison. "'I am a wild beast': Patricia Rozema's Forward Fanny." *Persuasions* 28, (2006): 52-58.

Stone, Lawrence, and Jeanne C. Fawtier Stone. *An Open Elite? England, 1540-1880*. Clarendon Press, 1984.

Sturrock, June. "Money, Morals, and Mansfield Park: The West Indies Revisited." *Persuasions* 28 (2006).

Surridge, Lisa. *Bleak Houses: Marital Violence in Victorian Fiction*. Athens: Ohio University Press, 2005.

Sutherland, John. "Introduction." In *The Way We Live Now*, by Anthony Trollope, Oxford University Press, 1982.

Taylor, James. *Creating Capitalism: Joint-Stock Enterprise in British Politics and Culture 1800-1870*. The Boydell Press, 2006.

Todd, Janet. *The Sign of Angellica: Women, Writing and Fiction, 1660-1800*. Columbia University Press, 1989.

Tosh, John. "Masculinities in an Industrializing Society: Britain, 1800–1914." *Journal of British Studies*, vol. 44, no. 2, 2005, pp. 330–342. www.jstor.org/stable/10.1086/427129.

Tracey, Robert. *Trollope's Later Novels*. University of California Press, 1978.

Turley, David. "Complicating the Story: Religion and Gender in Historical Writing on British and American Anti-Slavery." In *Women, Dissent, and Anti-Slavery in Britain and America, 1790-1865*, edited by Elizabeth J. Clapp and Julie Roy Jeffrey, 19-37. Oxford University Press, 2011.

Van, Annette. "Ambivalent Speculations: America as England's Future in 'The Way We Live Now.'" *NOVEL: A Forum on Fiction*, vol. 39, no. 1, 2005, pp. 75–96. www.jstor.org/stable/40267639.

Van Dam, Frederick. *Anthony Trollope's Late Style: Victorian Liberalism and Literary Form*. Edinburgh University Press, 2016.

Wagner, Tamara. *Financial Speculation in Victorian Fiction: Plotting Money and the Novel Genre, 1815-1901*. Ohio State University Press, 2010.

Wallerstein, Immanuel. *Historical Capitalism*. Verso Books, 2014.

Watt, Ian. *The Rise of the Novel: Studies in Defoe, Richardson, and Fielding*. University of California Press, 1957.

Weiss, Barbara. *The Hell of the English: Bankruptcy and the Victorian Novel.* Bucknell University Press, 1986.

Williams, Eric. *Capitalism and Slavery.* 3rd edition. University of North Carolina Press, 1994.

Wynne, Deborah. *Women and Personal Property in the Victorian Novel.* Ashgate, 2010.

Index

A

Allestree, Richard
   The Ladies Calling, 9
Austen, Jane
   Mansfield Park, xxv, 70, 71, 79, 80, 81, 82, 85, 89, 90, 91, 92, 93, 97, 105, 124
   Pride and Prejudice, xxv, 69, 70, 71, 72, 74, 75, 77, 79, 95, 97, 100
   Sanditon, xxv, 70, 94, 97, 100
   Sense and Sensibility, 71, 84

B

Behn, Aphra, 64
   The Forc'd Marriage, xxiv, 2, 169
Blackstone, William, 73
British abolition, 51
British West Indies, 37, 38, 39, 43, 44, 49, 50, 58, 59, 63, 82
Bubble Act of 1720, 102
Burdett-Coutts, Angela, 114

C

Caird, Mona
   The Wing of Azrael, 170
California, 147, 159, 163, 164, 165
Cannibalism, 57, 58, 59
Caribbean gothic, 58
Clandestine Marriages Act, 18, 20, 169
Cugoano, Ottobah
   Thoughts and Sentiments on the Evil of Slavery, 44

Culture and Anarchy, 138

D

Dallas, E. S.
   Abridged Clarissa, 140, 142
Dallas, Robert Charles
   The History of the Maroons, 43
Defoe, Daniel
   A Plan of the English Commerce, 54
   The Family Instructor, 6
Dickens, Charles
   "A Home for Homeless Women", 114
   A Christmas Carol, 123
   Bleak House, 100
   Dombey and Son, xxvi, 99, 111, 112, 114, 116, 117, 121, 123, 124, 134
   Little Dorrit, 100
   Our Mutual Friend, 100
   Urania Cottage, 114, 115

E

Edward, Bryan
   A History, Civil and Commercial, of the British West Indies, 58
Edwards, Bryan
   The History, Civil and Commercial, of the British Colonies in the West Indies, 43
Engels, Friedrich, xx, xxiii, 94
Entails, 73, 74

F

Felski, Rita
   Beyond Feminist Aesthetics, xiv, 2, 152
Filmer, Sir Robert
   Patriarcha, 6
Fordyce, James, 10
Fraser's Magazine, 107

G

Gissing, George
   The Odd Woman, 173

H

Haitian Revolution, 43, 63
Hardy, Thomas
   Jude the Obscure, 173

I

Industrial Revolution, 3
Iphigenia, xiii, xxiv, 2, 169

J

Johnson, Samuel, 16, 24, 25
Joint Stock Companies Act of 1844, 102, 139, 140
Joint Stock Companies Act of 1856, 137, 139

K

Kant, Emmanuel, 7, 29, 138

L

Lennox, Charlotte
   Harriot Stuart, 28
   The Female Quixote, xxv, 1, 15, 16, 17, 20, 29
Levi-Strauss, Claude, xix
Lewis, Matthew Gregory
   Journal of a West India Proprietor, 58
   The Monk, 37
Limited Liability Act of 1855, 137, 139
Locke, John, 138
   Second Treatise, xviii, 6, 7, 42
Long, Edward
   History of Jamaica, 59
   The History of Jamaica, 49, 64

M

Macaulay, Thomas Babington, 138
Married Woman's Property Act of 1870, 164, 170
Married Woman's Property Act of 1883, 170
Marx, Karl
   Capital, 109
   Economic and Philosophic Manuscripts, 117, 120, 149
   Hegelian dialectic, xiv
   The Communist Manifesto, 116
   The Poverty of Philosophy, 34
Mitford, John, 24
Modernity, 138

N

New Women, 122, 170, 172, 173
Nicholas Nickleby, xxvi, 99, 101, 104, 105, 106, 109, 110, 118

Q

Quarterly Review, 107

Index

R

Radcliffe, Ann, 37
Richardson, Samuel
  Clarissa, xvi, xxiv, 1, 2, 4, 5, 7, 8,
    11, 13, 14, 15, 40
  Pamela, 14, 27
  Rambler no. 97, 26
Robinson, Mary
  "The African", 65
  "The Negro Girl", 65
  *A Letter to the Women of
    England*, 62
  Angelina, xxv, 53, 55, 56, 58, 59,
    60, 61, 63, 64, 66

S

Second Maroon War, 43, 63
Smiles, Samuel
  Self-Help, 101, 139
Smith, Adam, 138
  *The Theory of Moral
    Sentiments*, 61, 127
  The Wealth of Nations, 4, 103
Smith, Charlotte
  "The Story of Henrietta", xxv, 36,
    38, 41, 42, 43, 44, 45, 46, 49,
    51, 52
  and the slave trade, 50
  Letters of a Solitary Wanderer,
    35
  The Emigrants, 47
Steele, Richard, xx
Stickney Ellis, Sarah
  Daughters of England, 153
  The Daughters of England, 131
  The Women of England, 130
Stone, Elizabeth
  *William Langshawe, the
    Cotton Lord*, xxvi, 99, 125,
    126, 127, 128, 129, 131, 132,
    133, 134, 135, 144

T

Thackeray, William
  The Newcomes, xiii, xxi
  The History of British Commerce,
    140
The Industrial Revolution, 102
Thelwall, Thomas
  The Daughter of Adoption, 38,
    45, 47
Trollope, Anthony
  Autobiography, 149, 151, 162
  North America, 160, 161
  *Sir Harry Hotspur of
    Humblethwaite*, xxiii, xxvi,
    137, 143, 149
  The Duke's Children, xxvi, 137,
    143, 145, 156
  The Prime Minister, xxvi, 137,
    145, 146, 149
  The Three Clerks, xxvi, 137,
    146
  The Way We Live Now, xxvi,
    137, 141, 147, 148, 149, 151,
    154, 156, 158, 159, 160, 162,
    164, 165
Trollope, Frances
  *Domestic Manners of the
    Americans*, 162

W

Walpole, Horace, 37
Wilberforce, William
  *An Appeal...in Behalf of the
    Negro Slaves*, 51
Williams, Cynric R.
  Hamel, the Obeah Man, 58
Wolf, Emma

The Joy of Life, 172
Wollstonecraft, Mary
   A Vindication of the Rights of
      Woman, 55, 61, 62, 92
   Mary

A Fiction, xxvii
Progress of the French
   Revolution, 48
Thoughts on the Education of
   Daughters, 55

www.ingramcontent.com/pod-product-compliance
Lightning Source LLC
Chambersburg PA
CBHW071355290426
44108CB00014B/1556